Achieving Success through Academic Assertiveness

Academic assertiveness is an essential capability that is required of students who wish to achieve academic and professional success. Written for students who are aiming to achieve college success, *Achieving Success through Academic Assertiveness: Real Life Strategies for Today's Higher Education Students* focuses on the challenges that learners face, and encourages positive actions that support triumphs in learning situations. Jennifer Moon creatively explores the importance of this emerging topic and how assertiveness is linked to the process of learning and overall student development, critical thinking, and academic achievement. This book offers a substantial section of resources, practical advice, and features:

- Techniques for implementing academic assertiveness into student development
- "Real life" scenarios and quotations from students about their experiences
- Questions and exercises about topics in the chapters to raise self-awareness
- Dialog exercises that encourage best practice techniques and learner reflection
- Fictional journals threaded throughout the book that creatively engage readers
- Loads of examples of everyday challenges that students experience
- Guidance on how to cope and manage difficult learning situations in a successful manner

The book will be an essential resource for students involved with undergraduate College Success courses, First Year Seminar courses in the U.S., and Personal Development Planning courses in the UK. *Achieving Success through Academic Assertiveness: Real Life Strategies for Today's Higher Education Students* is a valuable resource full of insight into the challenges that students face today. The scenario-based approach is designed to bring student issues alive, it further demonstrates best practice examples to advise students to become academically assertive.

The Author

Jennifer Moon BSc MPhil, MEd, MSc, PhD

Jennifer Moon has worked in education, health and professional development in higher education. In recent years, her focus has been on pedagogy, with an interest in how humans learn (reflective learning, critical thinking, the learning of non-traditional students, etc.). She worked for five years on educational development at the University of Exeter and now has a part-time post as a senior lecturer (research) at Bournemouth University in the Centre for Excellence in Media Practice. Jennifer also runs workshops at universities in the UK, Ireland, and abroad. She is a Consultant for Oxford Centre for Staff and Learning Development. She covers a range of topics that are related to learning, teaching, and assessment processes. These include reflective learning, the use of learning journals to support learning and professional development, programme and module structure and the effective running of short courses and workshops, critical thinking, the learning of students with non-traditional backgrounds, and issues in cheating and plagiarism, academic assertiveness, and the role of story in higher education. In 2006, she gained a National Teaching Fellowship. Jennifer has published eight books, and many papers, reports, and articles.

Achieving Success through Academic Assertiveness

Real Life Strategies for
Today's Higher Education Students

Jennifer Moon

Routledge
Taylor & Francis Group

NEW YORK AND LONDON

First published 2009
by Routledge
270 Madison Ave, New York, NY 10016

Simultaneously published in the UK
by Routledge
2 Park Square, Milton Park, Abingdon, Oxon OX14 4RN

Routledge is an imprint of the Taylor & Francis Group, an informa business

© 2009 Taylor & Francis

Typeset in Minion by
Keystroke, 28 High Street, Tettenhall, Wolverhampton
Printed and bound in the United States of America on acid-free paper by
Edward Brothers, Inc.

Library of Congress Cataloging in Publication Data
Moon, Jennifer A.
  Achieving success through academic assertiveness : real life strategies for
today's higher education students / Jennifer Moon.
    p. cm.
  Includes bibliographical references and index.
  ISBN 978-0-415-99142-1 (alk. paper) — ISBN 978-0-415-99143-8 (alk. paper) —
ISBN 978-0-203-88720-2 1. College student orientation. 2. Teacher-student relationships.
3. Academic achievement. 4. Assertiveness (Psychology) I. Title.
  LB2343.3.M645 2008
  378.1'98—dc22   2008047303

ISBN 10: 0–415–99142–0 (hbk)
ISBN 10: 0–415–99143–9 (pbk)
ISBN 10: 0–203–88720–4 (ebk)

ISBN 13: 978–0–415–99142–1 (hbk)
ISBN 13: 978–0–415–99143–8 (pbk)
ISBN 13: 978–0–203–88720–2 (ebk)

Contents

Preface

Assertiveness is about becoming more effective in personal and social terms. It involves behavior, language, and personal confidence and self-esteem. Assertiveness is clearly distinguished from aggression or aggressive tactics and it is about effective achievement of needs and rights, taking into account the needs and rights of others. This is a book for male and female, younger and mature students, under and postgraduates.

The book is about "academic assertiveness" because it is addressed primarily to those who are engaging in advanced education courses. By "advanced education," I largely refer to post-16 courses in further education, college, university, adult education, professional development, or other forms of formal education at these levels. It is likely, however, that it will be useful for some students at earlier stages in education. The context, however, is the experience of being a student, both in academic terms and in terms of the social and living experiences. This is the source of the content of the scenarios that are used as a means of illustrating the points made in the text, that relate it to education. The principles in the text, and the points that are made, are relevant to the whole population, though I should say that some may clash with accepted norms of behavior in other cultures.

The book is written, in the first place, directly for students and it is designed to be readable and entertaining as well as informative. At the end of many of the chapters, for example, are the contents of fictitious learning journals of two fictitious students who experience an academic assertiveness course based on the book. However, the book is relevant to many situations directly within the educational context and reviews have indicated that it is likely to have a place within formal courses as well as as an informal read. I have therefore added a chapter (Chapter 11) for those who might lead courses on academic assertiveness. Within Chapter 11 I have written a detailed list of formal situations for which the book or its content may be useful (pages 185–9). I summarize them here.

- Personal development planning (PDP).
- Student success courses.
- Professional development.
- Professional education (e.g. for courses in which students need to learn to deal with people).

- Work with groups of students who have specific needs.
- Work in the context of counselling and student support services.
- New teachers and others who need to understand the challenges that students face.
- Careers contexts.
- Single gender groups (gays and other single sex groups).
- Student development programs in student unions.
- Postgraduate students and postgraduate researchers.
- As part of a general induction for all students; student mentors.
- Students who are going into service learning or work experiences.
- Academic assertiveness as a basis for the development of critical thinkers.
- Staff development.

Another group who may need to do some work on academic assertiveness are those who are going to lead such courses with others. This could be staff, students, student union staff, librarians, and the many mentioned above.

The book is not meant to be a passive read. It is designed to engage identification with situations, thought and reflection, active working and change in the reader. There are "stop and think" text boxes, activities and exercises that prompt action or observation, and illustrations that entertain, as well as the fictitious journals and a quick reference guide to definitions and techniques at the back of the book. What is not to be found in the pages of this book is theory and a mass of references. The book is, however, backed up by broad and informed reading of literature in education, psychology, counselling, health education, mental health and therapy, and the experiences of being a counselor, health educator, a parent of students in higher education and a teacher of students. Since this book has been completed, I have developed material, based on the concept of academic assertiveness for the purpose of enhacing students' work in groups (Moon, J. 2009. Make Groups Work – Bristol Escalate, www. ESCalate.ac.uk)

I thank those who have made possible the writing of this book, for example my colleagues at the Centre for Excellence in Media Practice in the Media School at Bournemouth University, United Kingdom, particularly Lizzie Nixon for her translation of the fictitious journals into "student speak." I thank those who have worked with me on the development and elaboration of the initial idea (such as the members of the META project at University of Gloucestershire), and others who participated in workshops on academic assertiveness—and all those "further" others who have tolerated my enthusiastic explorations of the idea at various times. I thank also the publishers, who have supported the development of this somewhat "different" project into a viable and publishable format.

Part I

About Using This Book

1
Introduction

This Book . . .

This short chapter is designed to indicate the structure of this book and briefly to introduce how to use it. The important thing to say is that the content of the book is about academic assertiveness for students and the description of what I mean by that term and the concepts that lie behind it are presented in Part II, Chapter 2. This is an introduction to the use of the book.

The book is arranged in three parts. "**Part I: About Using This Book**" introduces the whole of the book. The largest part by far—"**Part 2: Learning How to Live More Assertively: Academic Assertiveness for Students**"—is written directly for students and is presented in a manner that relies on illustrations and examples that are likely to be in the experiences of students (though I acknowledge that there are very many different identities of students these days). The third part of the book—"**Part 3: Leading Courses in Academic Assertiveness**" is written directly for those who might lead courses in academic assertiveness. This might be lecturers, or staff in student support organizations, or other outside trainers—or it might be students themselves who take a lead or who decide to run a self-help course.

So you can read whichever parts of the book are useful to you. If you are to lead a course, it will be the whole book. If you are a student, you may only be interested in the second part of the book and will be able to ignore the last chapter, though you might find the synopsis of the contents of the book in Chapter 11 useful as a quick reminder (pages 195–8).

The Content of the Chapters

Because the content of the chapters is laid out in Chapter 11, I won't go into substantial detail here—but will provide a paragraph or two of orientation to the book.

Academic assertiveness is an application of the principles and practices of assertiveness in an academic (higher education) environment. The way I have chosen to write the book is to rely a great deal on scenarios to illustrate the points that I want to make. The fact that the book relates to academic settings does not detract from its relevance to other situations—the principles, tools and techniques will all be the same. So this book of is relevance to being a student, and to life beyond being a student. It is about learning to cope better generally, as well as specifically in the academic environment.

Learning to be more assertive in an academic environment is about learning to manage better in the various relevant interactions, situations, and activities in higher education. There is a general introduction to academic assertiveness in Chapter 2. It helps to understand what assertiveness is when it is contrasted with other behaviors that are not assertive—nonassertion, aggression, and manipulative behaviors. This contrast is made in Chapter 3, along with a discussion of some of the ways in which "assertiveness" is misconceived. Chapter 4 is about the ways in which assertiveness is displayed—verbally, nonverbally, and in things about the whole person—even down to the furniture that you choose! Chapter 5 takes a look at how the way in which we are assertive, or not, develops, and the manner in which individuals differ from each other in their reactions to particular situations. One of the traditional components of books about assertiveness is to say that, as human beings, we have rights. I have selected and worded the rights in Chapter 6 to be those that are most relevant to academic situations and those associated with being a student. The notion of rights is important for academic situations in which there is the possibility of failure or making an error. Chapters 7, 8, and 9 really focus on how to manage better in a range of situations using the tools and techniques of assertive behavior. Chapter 7 mainly deals with the techniques themselves. Chapter 8 considers particular situations and how to manage them, making use of the techniques (e.g. giving and receiving criticism, giving and receiving compliments, and so on). Chapter 9 is about ways of managing the mental side of assertiveness—of, for example, preparing for situations that are going to be difficult. As I say in the introduction to these three chapters, it may be necessary to shuffle backwards and forwards through the pages, linking anticipation with techniques and the details of actual situations. There seems to be no logical order in which to present the material. Chapter 10 is a bit different because it takes a broader look at failure and achievement in academic life, and the fears that are common among students. It is mostly directed towards the assertive behaviors of recovery—and of recognizing failure and error as part of growth and development.

Chapter 11 is for those who want to lead a course in academic assertiveness. It provides suggestions on the areas of academic life to which academic assertiveness is relevant, and discusses the range of situations in which courses may fit. It also considers the ways in which the material of academic assertiveness may be presented—and provides some hints and tips about, for example, managing role play (where that is a possibility). Towards the end of Chapter 11 there is, as I have said, a fairly detailed synopsis of the book that may be of value for any reader.

At the end of the book, I have included a list of definitions and, in particular, some techniques of assertiveness for quick reference and memory-jogging.

On many occasions the reader will be asked to consider or to do something. There are activities and exercises at the end of most of the chapters and I will suggest you use a journal. There are also, in the later chapters, "stop and think" spots—text boxes that ask the reader to think about some issue—or to do something that is directly related to that subject. There are also the fictitious journal entries of two fictitious students—Christina and Tom—who are on a course that coincides with the content of the chapters. In their journals they talk of their reactions to things in the course and how it relates to their lives.

How to Use This Book

I have tried to write this book so that it can be as flexible in use as possible. Here are some of the ways in which it might be used.

- As a guide for students working individually.
- As a guide for students working in small groups.
- As a background text for personal development planning (PDP) or student success programs. It provides longer-term reference after the course has finished.
- As a formal text for a course—in which the content is matched directly to the classes.
- As a guide for teachers who would like, informally, to support their students in learning to cope better with academic life.
- As an aid to new teachers who need to understand the challenges of being a student.
- As a manual for a short course on academic assertiveness.

(I have expanded on these in Chapter 11).

A Note About How This Book is Written

Unless the gender of a person is obvious, I have usually used the feminine gender for the examples. This is the case with all my books. I dislike the incorrect use of "they" to avoid gendered language (she and he; his and hers, etc.). Addressing both genders in this way is cumbersome—so instead of the more usual adoption of masculine gender, I use the feminine. We are, after all, half the population, and mostly, if we have not been written out of history entirely, we have been addressed as part of the universal male.

Some Other Books on Assertiveness

Books on assertiveness tend, as I have said, to cover the same general topics, though this book is more comprehensive than most. Sometimes it is useful to read about the same ideas in different sources because sometimes there is a different slant given. In addition, several books are focused towards specific situations. Some general books on assertiveness are Smith, 1975; Alberti and Emmons, 1983, Lindenfield, 1987, Rees and Graham, 1991. Books on assertiveness for women include: Dickson, 1982; assertiveness at work: Back and Back, 1982, Stubbs, 1985; assertiveness for managers: Gillen, 1992; and assertiveness for young children: Lenett and Crane (1985).

Part II

Learning How to Live More Assertively

Academic Assertiveness for Students

2
Coping with Challenges in Higher Education

Introduction

Going into anywhere new is scary for most of us, but education is, by its very nature, challenging. It seeks to change you for ever. Hopefully you will find it comfortable to go along with the changes and hopefully a tide of enthusiasm will carry you along, making the difficult bits worthwhile. . . .

Here is someone who is facing a typical challenge on the first days on his higher education course.

> It is early October. Jamie has just started at Sallymae College. He arrived last week and this is the period for induction. Jamie is following a list of things to go to and things he must do. He is missing home, does not know anyone, and does not always know where things are. Nor does he always understand what he is meant to be doing. He does not, for example, fully understand what "induction" means but he is trying to go along with it. A fellow new student, Jules, has told him that he should have been signing on for module choices yesterday but he missed it. He is hoping that someone will notice and find him, or that it will not matter. He is pretty miserable. . . .

And here is another example:

> Chen is from mainland China. He has come to the UK to do a degree in Engineering. While he has been studying English for a long time in China, it seems different here and he is finding day-to-day life very difficult. He has gone into a supermarket to buy some rice and he cannot find it on the shelves. There is a girl stacking shelves. He knows that at home he would ask her where the rice is (though he would be embarrassed not to know . . .) but here she might not understand him and then he would feel foolish. He imagines her screwing up her face at him. Then again, he might not understand her and he imagines pretending to understand and promptly walking in the wrong direction. He would feel even more foolish. He goes on looking and not asking and feeling more bewildered about how he will ever fit in.

The aim of this section of the book is to open up the issues that are involved in being effective in facing challenges, whether they are in your academic life or more generally in the life of being a student—which can include the difficulties of living in college accommodation, in shared accommodation, of coping away from home, taking part-time work, and so on. I use the term "academic assertiveness" to cover all of this. What you learn from this book will not stop being relevant when you leave your studies and take a career job, because assertiveness is a capacity for life in all its future forms. The principles that are covered in the book will be relevant to everything. The principles should help Jamie to go and ask for help and not to hope that someone will notice that he has missed out a stage in his induction processes, and it should help Chen to face the challenge of asking the supermarket girl to show him where the rice is, and to cope with the probably that he will not initially understand what she says. Learning about academic assertiveness should help you to feel more confident generally. It will not make challenges go away, but you should be able to cope with them more effectively.

At the end of this chapter, there is a suggestion that you set up a learning journal alongside reading this book. As with most of the other chapters in Part II of the book, there are activities and journal exercises for you to do that relate to the content of the chapter. There is also the start of the fictitious journals of Christina and Tom. These are students who are attending a course based on the chapters of this book. Their journals relate to their experiences.

A Thumbnail Sketch of Assertiveness

I use the term "thumbnail" here because we will return to the topic of assertiveness in more detail in the next chapter.

Academic assertiveness is related to a range of training initiatives that are generally called "assertiveness training." They were developed in the United States in the 1970s, largely emerging from the women's liberation movement, which has more recently become known as feminism. The idea then was that women needed to assert themselves more in society and in their relationships in order to attain equality with men. In the last two decades it has become recognized that all men and women need to develop a reasonable level of assertiveness, though sometimes the issues for the genders are different. There are people who still believe that assertiveness is only needed by women.

In addition, assertiveness training has been used in work with disadvantaged and disabled people, older adults and those with mental health problems, and in the context of business and management training. Books on assertiveness have been written for people in their workplaces, for managers, for women, for children, and directly for some particular work roles (for example, nurses). In general the principles in these books are fairly similar and broadly match this one. Some examples of them are listed in the bibliography at the end of the book.

Assertiveness training has sometimes been conducted in higher education situations. In particular, it is provided for students who are going to be course or program representatives and usually then the course is offered in the student union. This book will cover broadly the same issues as most of the courses, with the focus on both learning situations and the social situations that are related to being a student.

So what is this thing called assertiveness when it is applied to academic situations? It is the capacity to cope better with challenges that are associated with the learning in, and experiences of, advanced education. Academic assertiveness is a mix of self-awareness, the development of capacities, some new ideas and specific techniques, and a willingness to apply this to yourself, to learn from it and change. More explicitly, the areas of learning in the course are from:

- A recognition and review of some aspects of how you behave.
- You recognizing that you can change—and having the will to change!
- Learning some new ideas.
- Developing some new capacities.
- Learning some useful techniques.
- Developing an increased awareness of how people interact.

I tend to use the word "capacities" to cover the general combination of skill, knowledge, and ability. "Skills" is too narrow, as is "knowledge," and neither incorporates the idea of raising awareness.

It is important for all students in advanced education to become reasonably assertive, whether they are school leavers, mature students, international students, undergraduate, or postgraduate, in vocational or nonvocational courses, student representatives, and those who would never take on such roles. However, there are different issues that affect them and part of learning to be assertive is to recognize issues that are related to your particular context and actively apply those ideas to your situation. The scenarios in this book are designed to bring out issues that affect particular identities of students as well as those that affect the majority.

The next section features some scenarios that demonstrate this.

Some Good Things About Learning About Academic Assertiveness

If you are not convinced by what I have said about the value of being assertive in academic and social situations, here are a few more reasons why it is a good thing:

- When you are assertive you are more likely to get what you need to be successful. For example, if you need help you are more likely to find it.
- You will avoid some frustrations.
- You will feel less stuck in some situations.

- You will be more aware of your rights as a human being and your responsibilities to others who also have rights.
- In academic situations such as seminars, you are likely to be able to function better and can feel better about yourself because you can be more involved.
- You may be able to become better at critical thinking because you are more willing to engage in it and to express yourself. Critical thinking is central to achievement in higher education.
- In situations of disagreement or confrontation you are likely to be seeking solutions in which both or all parties feel comfortable—such as compromises.
- If you are part of a minority group, you will be better equipped to think about how things should be for you in your education, and better equipped to ensure that your experiences are good.
- You are likely to stop waiting for things to happen, and will start to make them happen!

The development of your capacity to be assertive can help you in the context of your studies, but it will also help you in your career and in your home and social lives. While the scenarios in this book are related to academic or academic-related situations, as I have said, the principles are general and can be applied to all other areas of your life now and in the future. Sometimes, too, I will be encouraging you to look back to the past and think about how things could have been different in situations that you have experienced previously.

Some Buts . . .

There are some "buts" to learning about academic assertiveness, too. For example, you will not avoid all frustrating situations because, despite your increased capacity to be assertive, others will still be aggressive and bent on getting what they want regardless of anyone else. Some people who are aggressive will go on being aggressive. Nor will you find all your rights achievable, or all of your needs met. If you fail in an assignment, it will still hurt, and if someone insists on dominating a seminar you cannot make that person change through your different behavior.

It is also the case that people in some areas of society do not want people to be more assertive. They will suppress assertive behavior if they can (Alberti and Emmons, 1983: 3). This applies to some male-dominated situations such as religious orders, and it is not unusual for staff in educational situations actually to say that they do not want more assertive students. On the other hand, many staff would argue that they want students to be more assertive and proactive. They cannot have it both ways!

There is no "perfect" assertive state. Few of us are consistently assertive. I, as writer of this book, often feel that I have not handled a situation as well as I could have handled it—I could have stood up for myself better in particular situations, for example. Being aware that I could have done better enables me, though, to think about how I could improve on another similar occasion, and a quick re-reading of books on assertiveness is helpful too. I often think of assertiveness as a language—and having the language enables me more effectively to consider how to cope with situations or to reflect on them when they have not gone well. It is a language that enables me to think about what has gone wrong in some interactions with which others are having difficulties too. I can put words to it.

I want to make it clear that being assertive does not solve every difficult situation. Here is a scenario that illustrates this:

> Gill is in a seminar and, though she does not normally say much, she has thought of an important comment that she wants to make on the subject matter of the seminar. There are, at the seminar, several articulate and vocal students whom the tutor does not seem to be able or willing to control. Gill waits for one of these students, Simon, to make his last comment and then she comes in with her comment. Before she has finished, Emma, another participant in the seminar, launches loudly into a further comment, seeming deliberately to obliterate Gill's voice. Gill tries to catch the tutor's eye in order to make her comment, but the tutor seems to be satisfied with getting the comments from Simon and Emma, looks at them and encourages them further. It is, of course, easier for her to have a small number of willing speakers. Very soon it is the end of the class.

Gill's first attempt to be assertive has failed. However assertively one person behaves, another might be bent on getting her own way in a situation. However, there is more that Gill could do if she is willing to pursue the situation. We will return to this scenario.

Where This Book Came From . . .

It is sometimes helpful to understand where a book comes from—why the writer has come to write a particular book. Such information helps you to assess the credibility of the writer and the value of what is written. This is a section that I put into the books that I have written for teaching staff, and it is just as relevant to other readers who may be students.

The idea for writing this book came from quite a few sources. First, I knew about the idea of assertiveness and assertiveness training from my engagement in such activities in the past. I ran adult education courses on assertiveness and I became convinced of its value because of what I saw it do for people and because I found it helpful for myself. The very act of writing this book is helpful in reminding me of the techniques and the ideas behind it. The last work I did on the development of assertiveness was in the context of a Masters degree in Health Education, in which my dissertation was on assertiveness courses for older adults. Elderly people are often in situations where they lose their sense of personal power and self-esteem, or this can occur because their health changes. In becoming less able bodied, they may be less able to stand up for themselves. Some elderly adults cope by becoming more aggressive and this causes their social relationships to suffer. Some of the group with which I worked—which was largely female—also came from a generation in which women were not expected to have a "say" or their own "voice." It seemed useful to them to think about these issues and to learn a few ideas.

The idea of academic assertiveness came into my life when I was writing a book on critical thinking. Critical thinking is a term widely used in education, but it is nebulous, and teachers have different views of what it is. I was trying to clarify the idea of critical thinking and how to manage it better in teaching and learning. I began to realize that I was reading a lot about the essence of critical thinking being the facing of intellectual challenge. I thought about the challenge, but I also began to think more of the person who is the critical thinker—what does it take to think critically? I began to realize that you need to be reasonably assertive to be able to put forward your views on something. You need to feel strong enough to admit that perhaps your first thoughts were wrong. You need to be able to say sometimes that you have changed your mind. You need "voice" and the willingness to express yourself. From this thinking, the notion of academic assertiveness arose—and the term floated into my mind and, as ideas sometimes do, it grew and picked up other thoughts and grew more, snowball-like!

In writing about critical thinking, I also began to think critically about the subject matter of a number of other books that I have written on reflective learning. Reflective learning has become something of a buzz word in recent times, and many students groan when they are set yet another assignment that involves reflection. I am sceptical about the value of some of the uses to which I see this term applied. Reflection is too often a process of looking back at personal strengths and weaknesses. There may be some notion that you apply what you have learnt to future activity, but often academic reflection is narrow, retrospective, and mechanical, and does not really then contribute properly to the active, lively, and proactive people that students are meant to be. There was something missing. What is the gap between any awareness gained from reflection, and actively doing something differently or better? Again, it seemed to me that the development of some awareness and practical knowledge of assertiveness could help with this gap.

Then there were other reasons why it seemed important to think about academic assertiveness. I have a daughter who had fairly recently started an undergraduate program. I was aware of the challenges that faced her—in coping with the induction process, in finding her way around, in facing the first assignments, and also in coping with the issues in college residences, and later in coping with the responsibilities of sharing a house with a group of other students.

The final reason why I developed the idea of academic assertiveness relates to the situation of those who are in a minority in advanced education, who need some special strengths to "make it" in a mass educational system. I am talking of disabled students, dyslexic students, those students who come to university from a background in which no other members of their family have experienced higher education, those who are much older or much younger than their group of fellow students. In particular, too, I want to mention the international students who are in a new country, often working in a language that is foreign to them, trying to settle into a new culture that may be based on very different values to those to which they are accustomed. All of these people need to be assertive in order to look after themselves, their self-esteem, and their rights—and to look after each other. This issue is compounded by the fact that some overseas students come from cultures in which assertiveness is not valued in the way it is in western society, particularly for women.

I should add that any of us can suddenly be in a situation where we feel different from those around us, and become a "minority." For example, you break your leg and are on crutches, and cannot keep up with the others. You are depressed and feel unheard; you fail an assignment and feel that you as a person have failed. In these situations having well-developed assertiveness skills can help us to keep going.

How You Can Learn From This Book

This book is designed to help you to become aware of what being assertive is like, how assertiveness differs from aggression and nonassertion and to recognize those behaviors in others. You may be reading the book on your own or it may be associated with a course on academic assertiveness. You may even be running such a course. Since the idea of the book is that you learn *to do things differently* (by which I mean that you do not just learn *about* them), the best way to learn is to practice. If you are on a course it may be that some of the practice is done by role play or exercises within the course. By role play I mean that a simple scenario is given and learners act out the roles, and then there is discussion of what happened in the role play among those with roles and those who are watching. This discussion is likely to refer to how it felt as well as to overt behavior. It might, for example, be a scenario like the following:

A book has been recommended in a geography class. Megan wants it for her essay but there are very few copies available. Jo got to the library early and took out one of the few copies. Megan asks Jo if she can borrow it and Jo gives it to her on the proviso that the book is brought back tonight by five o'clock because then Jo will be wanting to use it. Five o'clock comes and goes and there is no book. Jo goes round to the house in which Megan lives and quietly asks for the book. Megan says that she had to go and see her tutor this afternoon and could not do the essay. She will be finished with the book soon and is sure that a well-organized person like Jo is not desperate for it immediately. There is actually no evidence that Megan has even started to read the book (she has just washed her hair). Megan offers to bring the book to Jo at seven o'clock and she adds that she is sure "that you will not mind, Jo because you're such a nice person." Jo had planned to get on with her essay tonight. At seven o'clock there is no sign of the book.

What does Jo say when she goes round to Megan's house? This would be the role play. When you act out a role, you really feel how the behavior is working. It is nothing to do with good acting—because, ironically, when the role play goes wrong there is often more to be learnt than when it goes smoothly! However, role play is not going to be possible if you are reading this book on your own. Instead, this can be substituded by the scenarios in the text—as above—that exemplify situations that are likely to arise on a common basis for you as a student. Many of these scenarios are based on the actual experiences of the students with whom I spoke as I wrote the book. The scenarios are designed to illustrate the ideas that are being proposed and to trigger your thinking.

However, there is also another source of learning for you. As you learn the ideas that are presented in the chapters of this book, you can begin to observe them being played out in the big laboratory of life that is happening all around you—of which you are a part. Every day, all the time, people are behaving assertively, or aggressively, or nonassertively, or are manipulating others near where you are standing. Listen and learn from them. Here is one example. I stayed in a hotel last night because I am running a course today in Oxford. The hotel advertised that it had wireless connections in every room, and I had work that urgently needed to be done. In my room, wireless would not work. The hotel staff simply said, "Oh no, you are too high up in the building." I pointed out their advertising and asked for another room. They moaned, and said how difficult it would be. I quietly repeated my request (using the broken record technique—see page 100). They found a different room for me. I was pleased to have so recently thought through these ideas on assertiveness!

Things To Do—An Introductory Overview

At the end of each chapter of this book there are going to be a number of items to help you to think about academic assertiveness in different ways. First I will be suggesting that you start a journal for yourself in order to reflect on what you learn. I will make some suggestions about things you can do with the journal beyond just writing the usual kinds of entries. There will also be some self-awareness exercises, which you may want to copy and put into the journal, or just use them as material that can stimulate your reflection. In Chapter 4, I add some text boxes that make suggestions about considerations or activities based directly on the material in that chapter.

There will also be a section that contains the journals of two fictitious students who are, like you, doing the exercises in the book and watching the world around—and trying to be more assertive. Tom and Christina are on a course on academic assertiveness that involves reading this book.

Things To Do—Starting Your Journal

You can call your journal whatever you like—a diary, logbook, notebook, thinkplace, Julie's journey, Allan's antics, the diary of an aspiring somebody—whatever you like. It is good to make it yours. In terms of making it yours, use whatever format you like. I prefer to use loose-leaf journals because I can add material to them. For example, you can add copies of the exercises from this book if you wish. But you can use anything for a journal—even the backs of old envelopes collected in a shoebox. . . . Portability can sometimes be an important issue, and shoeboxes have limitations in this respect. If you have a big journal, it is also less likely to be with you all the time—but that is up to you. I like to be able to write wherever I am—on a bus, when there are a few moments in a workshop, and so on.

Make the journal yours, for example, with a favourite picture on the cover—or a picture that inspires you to be strong. You might want to use unlined paper so that you can draw . . .—you can decide. Alternatively, create a journal electronically.

I suggest that you do not try to write in your diary every day—but write every couple of days and try to keep it up over the time you are reading the book, or for three weeks—whichever is the best for you. You might just use it as a repository for the activities and exercises (and possibly the text box ideas) and/or you might use it as a place to record your developing capacity for being assertive. It will help you to remember ideas, and you will gain a sense of how your academic assertiveness is growing. You will have something to look back on—or to go back to later if your self-confidence takes a dip.

Keeping an academic assertiveness journal may be helpful to you in other contexts. You may be on a program that involves reflective writing or the keeping of a journal—or you may be a postgraduate student doing a research project and using a research journal. You may decide at the start to make this journal more general than just academic assertiveness. Do what feels right to you. You may start with one system and then realize that you want to do it in a different way. Keeping a journal and learning some techniques to develop it may have uses beyond the obvious.

An initial task is to sort yourself out with a journal and make a first entry—which could, of course, be from the exercises below.

Activities and Journal Exercises

You may wish to copy these activities and exercises and include them in your journal. What you have written will be interesting to you when you look back at a later stage. Hopefully it will show you how you have become more assertive.

Think of Someone More Assertive

Think of someone who you feel is more assertive than you—who seems to be better able to stand up for her/himself. List three ways in which this person would behave differently from you in a situation that you would find difficult. If you cannot think of a situation, consider how you and this person would react in the situation that Megan found herself (page 15).

Think About Your Own Experience

Think of a time when you feel you could have done with being more assertive. Note down what happened, what seemed to go wrong, and how you felt. Have you any ideas for how you could have helped the situation to turn out better?

Some Academic Situations That May Be Challenging

Here are some situations that you may have encountered in your student life. Using the list to jog your memory, see if you can list ten situations in which you may have felt that you needed a bit more assertiveness. These may have been one-off situations or they may be things that happen on a regular basis. Some of these situations are to do with managing your own feelings and thoughts—which is all part of being more academically assertive:

- Seminars or tutorials.
- Situations around the development and handing in of assignments.
- When your thinking has been challenged in an academic situation.
- Situations in which you feel you needed to seek support or more information about something (e.g. help with IT, study skills, library searches, what an assignment brief means and so on).
- Supervision sessions.
- Laboratory or fieldwork situations.
- When you have had to do something in a group.
- Times when competitiveness has been an issue (your competitive feelings or those of others).
- Times when you are disappointed with yourself or have failed.
- Situations when you are given feedback on work that you have done.
- Giving presentations in class.

- When you have been asked to think critically or to give a critique of something.
- Situations associated with the feeling that you are a small fish in a big pond.
- Situations that have involved criticism or feedback.

The Journals of Christina and Tom

Christina, Tom and their Journals—An Introduction

Christina and Tom have started to attend sessions in their student union on academic assertiveness. They do not know each other at first. The eight-session course happens to coincide in content with chapters 2–9 of this book. It is run by Phil and Dee, who work in the union on student affairs. As part of the course, participants have been asked to keep a journal about what they have learnt and how they are using the ideas in their lives, and as a place in which to keep observations of the behaviors of others, which they can learn from. It is also suggested that they may want to comment on their responses to the exercises in their journals. They have been told that no one will expect to look at their journals, though it is up to them whether or not they share the content with others.

Christina has kept a diary before and finds the idea of keeping one on academic assertiveness quite appealing. However, several people on the course do not find the idea of a journal so comfortable and Tom is one of these. He says to one of his friends that journals are "girly," but he manages to keep it up.

In this chapter, we assume that they have attended the first session of the course. Here is a bit more background on Christina and Tom themselves:

Christina is 19. She is in the first year of a degree in biology at Somanton University. She is living in university accommodation, sharing a flat with several others. She is not doing all that well on her program, somehow not having properly engaged with higher education study. She is not very sure of herself, and at times can come over as prickly. She is often short of money and works in a bar two evenings a week. Christina got her friend, Steph, to come along with her to the course—mainly because she did not want to come on her own. Steph is quite assertive.

Tom, aged 22, has a tendency to be stand-offish and sometimes aggressive. His girlfriend, Gemma, is going to this academic assertiveness course and she has suggested that he should come with her. He did not want to come at first but changed his mind when they found themselves in the Union bar the night on which the course started. He is in the second year of a degree in geography at Somanton. He lives in a rented flat in the town. He is fairly studious and is keen on his subject. He wants to be a meteorologist eventually.

Christina's journal

Tues Feb 1st

Hello diary—I am told I have to write you for the academic assertiveness course, so here we go.

The session of the course today was the introduction. We learned what academic assertiveness is and how it is important to learn to be assertive in order to get though uni. Have to go to bed now . . . too tired to write this.

Wed Feb 2nd

We were asked to write something down in the course about where we thought we could have been more assertive. Well—we had to work as a group in the microbiology seminar today. Jan (tutor—a postgraduate student) gave us a problem and we had to discuss it, do a bit of research and bring back the result an hour later. We had no choice about the groups and I was with Pete, Abdul, and Calum, and they would not have been my choice. Pete just started it off—typical—by saying "I think I know the answer" in that quiet and sneaky voice of his and he then proceeded to tell us. He's clever. He might have been right but the other three of us wanted to talk about the problem properly—not just come up with the answer. Pete just kept on about the solution. So that wasted time and then we spent quite a time arguing about how to do it. It was like nobody took charge. Then the time was up and we had to go with Pete's idea and I think that none of us felt good about it apart from Pete, even though Jan said our response (I mean—his response) was good. I was a bit snappy with him when we all went for lunch. I knew I was unhappy about how the group had gone, and when he tripped over my chair in the refectory I really went for him. I think I was not being assertive at all there—not in the group and also not when he went flying over my chair. So there are things for me to learn. And he has things to learn too, I think.

There was another example yesterday at work. I had to ask Dave (the bar manager at work) again for my last week's pay. I felt frightened—he's always drunk and he treats me like a child. I guess I felt very nonassertive then. I am always very unassertive with him. I knew I was going to feel like that.

"What can I do for you, my beautiful?" he said at first—smarmy as usual. It really gets to me when he speaks like that—sort of disarms me. I'm not his beautiful and nor would I ever want to be. I am sure that he knows what he is doing when he calls me that. It was like my voice shrivelled up and I felt as if the rest of me was shrivelling as well. I told him about the pay being late again. There was quite a pause (I think he does that deliberately too) and he said quite aggressively, "I told you

before that I am seeing to that—you don't need to go on asking." I just said, "OK Dave," and hated myself for not having anything better to say to him. I went away feeling I really want to leave that place—but I need the money and I still don't know when I am going to get it. I've got Steph's birthday pressy to buy next week.

Oh yes, I sort of got Steph to come to the session because I didn't want to go alone. I don't think Steph needs it—she says what she thinks and gets on with people. She really liked it though.

Tom's journal

Tues Feb 1st

God knows why I am doing this. Gemma got me into it. She schemed for me to be at the bar and then said "Oh, it is time for the course. I'm going—are you coming?" I thought I'd see what was going on so I went. I told her that I may not go again though.

They asked for some examples in this diary thing—OK (still asking myself why I am doing this). It helped that Pete and Sam were there, and Loui. I sometimes feel as if I follow Gem around. If I'm honest, I am scared that she'll go off with someone else if I don't go with her—that's being really honest. She knew what she was doing all along when she got me to the course. Reminds me of when I was a kid and it felt like this with Tone—always dragging me to things even when I didn't want to go— telling me little stories to get me there. I went to football training for years because I didn't know how to say I wasn't interested in football. Maybe I should tell him sometime—maybe not. The parents were so pleased with him making me play. They didn't know what he said he'd do to me if I didn't go.

I didn't mean to write about that—odd how it came out. When do I think I could do with being more assertive (apart from with Gemma and Tone)? I could do with being more assertive with Jon. He keeps coming round to borrow the books that I bought for the course and then I have to go and ask for them back. He should get them for himself. I even told him the website for most of the secondhand books I get—not sure that was wise—but he still turns up. Says he can't be bothered to buy books. . . . I guess if I can find out how to deal with Jon this course would be OK.

Sun Feb 6th

Whoops—sort of forgot this . . . not so good week. Only average for test results in Dr Carnwell's unit. Did well in human geog module though. No more time. . . .

3
Learning to Cope
Fight, Flight or Be Assertive!

Introduction

In this chapter I start with a bit of thought about change. Most people who are reading this book will be interested in change and presumably they believe that they can change. However, there are others who think that the way they are now is the way they are going to be for ever. This is not a helpful way of thinking if one is wanting to become more assertive because becoming more assertive involves change. I then go into more detail about what academic assertiveness is. One of the ways of learning about assertiveness is to learn also what it is not. It is not aggression, nonassertion, or manipulation. I will explore those ideas and their outcomes because it is important to be able to recognize them as behaviors. It is a part of increasing your awareness. Then there are, in common with other chapters, the sections with exercises and the journals that are written by Christina and Tom.

Changing . . .

The first message of this chapter, then, is that you can change and become more assertive if you want to. An area of well-documented research that is currently widely referenced is that of Carol Dweck. Based on her research, Dweck (2000) suggests that when it comes to the notion of personal change, there seems to be two groups in the population. People in one group think that the way one is as a human is the way one will always be. Much of Dweck's work is in the context of education, and those with this mindset feel that their level of intelligence is fixed and they cannot change it. They are likely to think, "Why should we try harder? We are the way we are." However, the other group has a view that humans are adaptive and can change and nothing is fixed. Even if they experience low grades in a course in comparison with their friends, they recognize that they can still achieve and change. The important point from this research is that it is what you think about this issue of change that makes the difference. If your "self theory" (as these thoughts are called) is "I can change," then you can change. People who have decided that they cannot change would probably not read this book, and they will have a hard time swimming against their self-generated tide. I subscribe totally to the view that one can change.

What Academic Assertiveness Is—Some More Detail

It is now time for a formal definition of academic assertiveness, so that we can pull the general idea together:

> Academic assertiveness is a set of emotional and psychological orientations and behaviors that enables a learner appropriately to manage the challenges to the self in the course of learning and their experiences in formal education.

Academic assertiveness includes the following areas of behavior in the contexts of academic work and in the general experience of being a learner. The list is in no particular order and there are overlaps:

- Finding an appropriate "voice" or form of expression through which to engage in critical thinking or debate.
- A willingness to challenge, to disagree, and to seek or accept a challenge.
- The ability to cope with the reality or the likelihood of not being "right" sometimes, making an error or failing, and make an effective recovery from these situations.
- A willingness to change one's mind if necessary; an openness to feedback on one's performance (academic or otherwise).
- A willingness to listen to and take account of the viewpoint of others, an awareness that others can make mistakes and a reasonable tolerance of their failings.
- Autonomy—a willingness to be proactive; to make and justify independent judgments and to act on them.
- An appropriate level of academic self-esteem.

In more everyday language, when you are being assertive, the following tend to apply. You:

- Can ask for what you want or need; can ask for favors.
- Are open and honest.
- Are able to stand up for yourself without undue anxiety.
- Can express feelings reasonably openly.
- Face up to matters in your life.
- Have a sense of self-confidence.
- Are able to say "no" without undue guilt.
- Are aware of your rights as a human and the responsibilities that these entail.
- Can express negative feelings appropriately.
- Are aware when others are putting you down, or when you are putting them down.
- Can give and receive constructive criticism.

- Can deal with unjustified criticism.
- Can gracefully give and receive compliments.
- Can see that it can be all right to express anger sometimes.
- Tend to be socially responsible.
- Can think rationally about issues such as guilt and blame with regard to self and others.
- Would normally aim to negotiate and discuss as a first course of action if there is confrontation.

These are the "perfections" of assertive behavior—and no one would be able to claim that they could match up with a list such as this at all times; but if you have an idea of how you can be more effective in your behavior, you have a chance to change it. Consider the following examples:

> Hannah and Marie are working in the chemistry laboratory with three other students who also are friends with each other. Hannah and Marie are fairly quiet and they tend to discuss the work that they are doing with each other because they feel somewhat daunted by the other three, who are more boisterous. One of the others, for example, has decided what they should be doing in this experiment—without much consultation—but his friends clearly look up to him as the leader. Under his leadership they are, as a group, not making much progress. Hannah has been learning about assertiveness, while Marie said it was not for her. The situation in the lab bothers Hannah because she can see what is going on, and she decides that she should do something about it. In the next lab session, instead of sitting quietly while the "leader" dictates what they will be doing in the set work for the afternoon, she takes a step forward and says, "Look, I realize that I have not been saying much up to now—just following along with your decisions—but we are not being all that successful in this work, are we? Perhaps we need to think again about how we are making decisions about the experiments". The others are surprised, but actually she has echoed their own thoughts. Marie is astonished at her friend. She is horrified at her daring at first, but as the group re-forms and begins to function in a more effective way, she starts to admire Hannah's action.

And so we go on. We have said these things before in more general terms in the first chapter—but here they are again in a more defined form. As an assertive person, you need to recognize that:

- Being assertive may lead to feelings of guilt because you will be going against behaviors that you learnt were "correct" as a child. You will need to learn to recognize the guilt and to let it go. It is of no use to you!

Jem has finished an essay that needs to be handed in tomorrow. Tod has not done his yet. He comes round to see Jem, chats for a while over a coffee and then asks Jem if he can have a look at his completed essay "Just so I can get some ideas," he says. Jem is not naive. He knows that Jem wants to use his references and probably to copy some of the ideas or structure. He says "No."

Tod says, "I thought you were a friend. I've left this a bit late and am in trouble with it, and you won't help. Thanks, mate!" He picks up his coat and walks out. Jem feels pangs of guilt and sadness for not helping, but thinks that he has made the right decision.

- You do not need to win every battle and you will not "win" every argument. Some situations can be defined as "no win"—and you need to gracefully withdraw from these. Withdrawal may also be a form of assertion.

You have to write an essay on the formation of cirrus cloud in your meteorology module. You have discussed the topic in class and you continue to discuss it with your friend (Jenna) on the way home. There were things in the lecture that are important for the essay and your friend makes a statement about the formation of cirrus cloud with which you disagree. It is not what you recall being said. You make your point, and she comes back strongly again. You quietly change the subject. You know what you think was said and there is no gain in pursuing this issue. Later she tries to open the issue again and you quietly say, "We disagree on that point, Jenna. Let's leave it." Jenna starts again. You say "Jenna, I don't want to talk about that any more."

- To be assertive is to recognize that others have the right to ask for what they want too!

Pedro agrees to meet with his group in the library to discuss a project that they are doing together. He forgets to come to the meeting. It is particularly annoying for the group because they needed to allocate the areas of work to everyone. They forgive his mistake. A little while later in the course of the work, Sam forgets a meeting with Pedro. Pedro is inclined to be irritated, but recalls that he was forgiven.

- You can only change your own behavior—not that of others.

Emma is in a relationship with Neil. She feels frustrated by his vagueness and his inability to make a decision. He is studying zoology and, at the end of his second year, he has to choose modules that lead towards ecology or modules that focus on physiology. His choice has implications for the kind of career he might aim for but he cannot make up his mind, swinging from one thing to the other. Emma keeps reasoning with him, and is getting frustrated with his indecision, but it seems that the more she says, the more he swings between the two.

- While you can only change your behavior and not that of others, if you act assertively you give others the chance to change their behavior in ways that may be helpful to them.

Charlie is doing postgraduate research. He and another student—Sara—use the same desk but Sara seems to be having it for more than her fair share of the time and she tends to leave her things all over the place, as if it is her own desk. Charlie's supervisor has noticed this and says to Charlie that he should assert his right to his share of time at the desk. Charlie is not very assertive and makes an excuse that Sara has been using the desk for longer and he would not like to upset her routine. One week, however, Sara is at the desk all the time. Charlie points out to her that he needs to use the desk sometimes. He is nervous—but surprised also when Sara turns to him and says, "I am pleased that you have said that. Of course you need it sometimes—it is just that you had not said anything before. I assumed that you did not need to be here."

A Warning: There are Sometimes Misinterpretations of What it is to Be "Assertive"

Sometimes the word "assertive" is used to describe someone who is bent on getting her own way. You might recognize this, which could come out of a novel, for example:

He had asked her to move. She did not see why she should move, but now he went right up to her and assertively demanded that she should get out of his way.

The use of the word "assertively" here sounds like it is actually describing aggression and I would consider it a misuse of the word assertive. "Assertiveness" is not to be confused with learning to be aggressive and expecting to get one's own way, regardless of others. It is to do with recognizing rights and responsibilities and asking for, or saying, what we want in a reasonable manner—or it may be a matter of saying "no" in a reasonable manner. Assertiveness is not just for weaker people who cannot act decisively or say what they want; it is for everybody, whether they want to behave less aggressively or to become more assertive.

You may find that others accuse you of being aggressive when you are intending to be assertive, because they do not understand that you are rightly and simply making a point or stating a need (for example). If this happens, you should do a quick check and ensure that you are behaving assertively. This might involve thinking of how your voice sounds, what it is that you are saying, and also your nonverbal behavior (see pages 38–49). If you are happy that you are being assertive and not aggressive, carry on with the interaction. You might need to take care not to get sidetracked into discussion about your behavior rather than the issue that you wanted to address. Distracting others from making the point that they have set out to make is one of the games of the aggressive other! The broken record technique (see page 100) may be helpful here.

Here is another one to think about too. It is another situation that could lead to misinterpretation:

> Selema is a mature student on a fine arts degree. She has a good first degree and a career background in local government. She had a senior post in an arts organization, and is now, in following this program, fulfilling a lifetime ambition. She knows that she can speak more fluently and in a more sophisticated manner than other students, many of whom have fairly recently left school. In seminars, though she longs to dive into the depths of discussions, she recognizes that she needs to hold back in order not to dominate the situation and, in effect, to make others feel inadequate.

Selema's assertiveness is expressed here in recognizing the situation and holding back her opinions.

Thinking About What Assertiveness is by Recognizing What it is Not (Nonassertion, Aggression, and Manipulation)

In order to understand better what assertiveness is, it is helpful to think about what it is not. We can do this by looking at states of nonassertion, aggression, and manipulation. You will notice that aggression and nonassertion relate to the notions of fight and flight as responses to threat in animals. In effect, we are saying that by virtue of our humanity, the truly human response to threat and challenge can be different. In these descriptions of behavior, it is important to describe the behavior of a person, rather than the (assertive or nonassertive) person, because everyone displays the whole range of behaviors at some time. However, most people tend toward styles of behavior that are typified by one or other of these stances. (I will sometimes be contradicting myself below, and talking of people and not just behaviors in order to make the points I need to make).

Being Nonassertive—or Being Passive

States of nonassertion are exemplified by the person who does not have a strong "voice," who is tentative and indecisive when there is no justification for indecision. You can sometimes be indecisive because you need time or more information to make an appropriate judgment. In this situation, if you are assertive and if the request does not infringe the rights of others, you simply ask for more time or information. Nonassertive behavior may be termed "people-pleasing behavior." The person behaving in this way is overtly, and often repetitively, apologetic and may seem to feel the need to apologise before she says anything at all. There is a sense in which, in being nonassertive, people may feel that they do not have any particular right to have their point of view heard. Dickson (1982: 5) says that the nonassertive person often has a "victim" mentality, clinging on to her stories of how life is hard on her, and she seems to "stagnate in her passivity."

Do you recognize these ways of starting a conversation?

- I do hope you don't mind if I say this . . .
- Forgive me for saying this but . . .
- I am sorry to say this but . . .

I have to be a little careful about generalizing here, because aggressive people sometimes use an apology in order to hide or tone down an aggressive or potentially hurtful statement—it depends on the intonation of the speech and other nonverbals (e.g. "Sorry to say this, but . . ." or, "If you don't mind me saying . . .").

In addition, the person displaying nonassertive behavior is not likely to complain appropriately when her rights have been disrespected, but might whine about it or "dump" the issues on friends by constantly moaning and sometimes abusing their rights too! Nonassertive friends will just "take it" and then probably feel unhappy about being "used" later. More assertive friends are likely to listen at first then suggest that there are more appropriate things to do than whine! Nonassertive behavior also involves not liking to ask for help from appropriate sources when it is needed. In a seminar, it is unlikely that a nonassertive person will volunteer an opinion unless spoken to—and then the responding voice is likely to be tentative. We should not, of course, equate shyness directly with nonassertive states. Very assertive and efficient people may experience shyness as a crippling feeling, while they manage to behave outwardly in a manner that seems assertive and effective. It can also happen that shy people overcompensate and take on an inappropriately aggressive style. Shyness may make assertive behavior more difficult, but it is not a lifelong excuse for being nonassertive or aggressive.

To summarize, if you are behaving in a nonassertive or people-pleasing manner, you:

- Hope that you will get what you want.
- Hope that others will guess what you want.
- Try to please people.
- Suppress your feelings when you do not succeed.

You do not:

- Ask for what you want.
- Express your feelings openly.

- Upset anyone if you can possibly help it—and if you do, you probably blame yourself.

You may not get what you want—indeed, your needs are probably not even noticed.

Being Aggressive

In assertiveness training, aggression is usually described as "going for what one wants without taking account of the needs or rights of others"—a fairly broad definition. It might be illustrated in the academic context by the person who pursues her point with a loud voice, who takes an aggressive stance, or does not listen to other points of view. It is an act of aggression to take over a situation regardless of the rights or feelings of others. In this respect, one could say that some teachers are aggressive when they do not listen to the viewpoints of their students, or who put students down with constant sarcasm. Some aggression is not expressed in a loud manner, though. There are quiet people who do not say much, but, when they speak, there is an uncomfortable edge. More generally, you could say that if a person with aggressive tendencies feels threatened, she will tend to go rapidly for attack rather than negotiation—and she may overreact to situations.

Forms of sarcasm or ridicule can also be aggressive when they intentionally put another down in order that the speaker may get what she wants. When you hear someone ridiculing another or being sarcastic, think about what is really going on. Is it a way of putting that person down in a manner that seems to be socially unacceptable? Is the teaser reducing another so that she—the teaser, the deliver of sarcasm—can feel better about herself? I remember a family in which an older brother constantly teased his (only slightly younger) siblings. It often ended with tears. I felt that he was needing constantly to bolster his position in the family by enlarging his own fragile self-esteem at the cost of others.

Aggressive people may seem to be those who have got their act together, who may seem to feel confident and "sorted." That is what they want you to see. Often they are not sure of themselves, and the more they act aggressively, the more difficult it is for them to do what they need to do, such as ask for help, or find a shoulder to cry on when difficult situations arise. They may tend to isolate themselves because nonassertive people will not want to confront them and assertive people, having tried once or twice to have a conversation, may have decided that there is no gain for them in pursuing communication. It is worth reiterating what we have said of nonassertive people above though. Some nonassertive people are not skilled as communicators, and in their state of anxiety about communication can be brittle and edgy and may seem to be aggressive.

Aggression is not, therefore, characterized just by threats or acts of violence and, like non-assertion, it is expressed through much more than words alone.

We summarize—in aggressive behavior, you are likely to:

- Try to get what you want in any way that works.
- Act regardless of the feelings of others.

You may threaten, cajole, be sarcastic or fight or ridicule. You do not:

- See that others have a right to have their needs met.
- Seek situations in which you could both get your needs met.

Manipulative Behavior

Manipulative behavior is an effort to achieve goals in a covert manner that does not take account of the rights of others. It is often described as a kind of aggressive behavior on the grounds that it is a matter of going for what the person wants, regardless of the needs or rights of others. However, some of the characteristics of a manipulative person are those of non-assertion, such as not being direct, not expressing herself, and not being open. It is as if the manipulator cannot manage the direct approach (often because she has low self-esteem), and therefore "goes behind someone's back" or is indirect in her armoury of methods. The words deceit and dishonesty can often be applicable— they might apply, for example, when someone appears to be praising another, but it is evident that there is a reason behind the praise. Something is wanted— we might say it is a form of flattery.

Manipulative behavior has some characteristics that are aggressive and some that are nonassertive. As with aggressive states, a manipulator goes for what she wants, regardless of the rights of others. For example, manipulative behavior may involve leading others into showing weaknesses in order that they can be put down. Equally, manipulative behavior may involve "sucking-up" to someone so that the manipulator is favored, or achieves advantages. I often think that people who are excessively patronizing are manipulators, because they want to maintain an air of dominance and superiority without being open and honest and involved in an interaction of equals. I would, then, include here those irritating people who always have the answer to everything and will never say "I don't know." In my experience as a female, there are often gender issues here! Men more often seem to take on this role of the all-knowing person.

To summarize, in manipulative behavior you:

- Do not state directly and openly what you want.
- Try to get you want in any way that works, without considering the rights or feelings of others.
- Use communication as a means of achieving what you want. It is not an honest interaction. You will work to achieve this behind people's backs because you do not want to face them openly. They cannot therefore have their needs met because you are not being straight with them.

In contrast to aggressive and nonassertive behavior, assertive behavior is confident, open, direct, honest, and appropriate. The assertive person does not violate the rights of others, but recognizes that she has responsibilities to them. She does not expect others to know magically what she wants and she does not freeze with anxiety. If her communication is affected by anxiety, she may well say that this is how she feels. That is fine.

Activities and Journal Exercises

You and Your Theories of Change

You might like to look up Carol Dweck's work on self theories (e.g. Dweck, 1999). The idea behind the self theories is very simple. Think about whether you consider yourself a person who can change, or a fixed entity—"I am as I am." It can be interesting to think about what messages about change you gained from parents and those around you as you grew up. Do a bit of exploring of the idea in terms of personal habits and behaviors. What do you think others who are close to you feel about change?

Furnish the Idea of Academic Assertiveness With Some Examples

I have listed below the areas of behavior that make up the definition of academic assertiveness. Using the list, think of at least one instance in your life as a student (the academic and social aspects) that illustrates each of the points. The more explicitly you write about the example, the better.

If you are new to being a student, or cannot find examples associated with the student part of your life, look at other parts of your life too.

1. The style or form of expression through which to engage in critical thinking or debate.
2. The willingness to challenge, to disagree, and to seek or accept a challenge.
3. The ability to cope with the reality or the likelihood of not being "right" sometimes, making an error or failing, and making an effective recovery from these situations.
4. The willingness to change one's mind if necessary; the openness to accept feedback on one's performance (academic or otherwise).
5. The willingness to listen to and take account of the viewpoint of others; an awareness that others can make mistakes, and a reasonable tolerance of their failings.
6. Autonomy—a willingness to be proactive; to make and justify independent judgments and to act on them.
7. An appropriate level of academic self-esteem.

The Recognition of Assertiveness, Nonassertiveness, Aggression, and Manipulation

I have listed a number of different situations in Table 3.1. Based on the verbal cues alone, and covering up the right hand column as you do this exercise, judge what kind of behavior is occurring. You cannot, of course, always judge the nature of the communication from the words used by a person—sometimes it is the intonation or other nonverbal communication that indicates this most clearly. There are lots of different ways of saying "no" and "yes," for example!

Table 3.1 What kind of behaviour is being used?

Context	What is said	Nature of comment
A friend wanders up and admires your new jeans without looking at them, and then says . . .	'and . . . you've got that book that we need from the library haven't you . . . you wouldn't mind letting me have a little time at it, would you?"	Manipulative
You are just coming out of a seminar. You have taken part in the discussion in a reasonable manner. One of your colleagues says to you facetiously . . .	"You don't say much in seminars, do you?"	Aggressive
You have just been given an essay title for the current module. A friend says . . .	"You're lucky, you've got notes for all of the lectures. I missed the important one when I was ill and I really do need to see what was said, don't I . . . you write so clearly. . . ."	Manipulative
Sam has run out of milk for the third time this week and he comes knocking on your door asking to "borrow" some. You say . . .	"Sam, this has happened before, very recently. I do not want to give you any this time."	Assertive
Sophie asks you if you will be in college for the lecture tomorrow. You say . . .	"Stop asking where I'm going to be all the time. If you see me there, I am there. If not, I am not."	Aggressive
Jason is finishing an essay. He comes into the kitchen moaning . . .	"I can't do essays. I am slow and useless at writing. I can never sort out how to end them . . . I was never taught how to do these things."	Nonassertive
You are in the café and have just bought a latte. You wait a moment, go to drink it, and it is cold. You take it back to the counter and say loudly . . .	"This place is seriously run down. The coffee is cold—are you going to get me a hot one or not? By the way, I am not coming here again."	Aggressive

You are in the refectory at lunchtime and have jacket potatoes with cheese. Unfortunately melted cheese has obscured a large section of the potato that is black and inedible. You push the whole potato onto the side of the plate and then push the plate away, dejectedly saying . . .	"They use the cheapest of ingredients here. After all, we're only students—they do what they like. . . . There's no point in complaining to them, they will just do it again and again."	Nonassertive
Your tutor is commenting on a draft for an essay. He says that you have made a good start. You are not used to compliments and you just look down and mumble . . .	"I suppose it was all right."	Nonassertive
You are in the kitchen of the flat on the phone to your mother. A flatmate comes in and starts talking to you about the payment of rent that is overdue. You indicate the phone and mouth that you will speak soon with her. She says . . .	"OK, so you don't care that we're all just about to be chucked out on our ears— see if I care. . . ."	Aggressive
You are a second year student and you have been asked to think critically about an academic paper in an assignment. You say to your tutor, "How am I expected to know enough at this stage to be able to do this?" Your tutor says . . .	"You were given guidance as to how to go about the task. I can tell you no more than that—you need to sit down and think it through."	Assertive
Jane has come to borrow your art materials. She has asked and you say . . .	"No, Jane. I don't lend them to other people. They are rather personal things."	Assertive

You as a Behavior-Collector

This is a similar exercise to the last one, but it is one in which you will be providing the examples. Draw a table as in the previous exercise, and start to collect snippets of behavior. Write them in the same format as above—with a bit of context and the words said, and then add at the end of the column whether they are examples of assertive, nonassertive, aggressive, or manipulative behavior. Remember that sometimes nonverbal communication can be more indicative of the form of communication than what is verbalized.

Try to collect two examples of each (assertive, nonassertive, aggressive, and manipulative behaviors). You may find it quite interesting going about this people-watching. If you are short of a few examples, make them up.

You and Your Behavior

So you now know a bit more about these different forms of behavior that are not assertive. At different times, we are probably all aggressive, manipulative and nonassertive. This is time for a bit of thinking about your own behaviors. See if you can put down two examples of when you behaved in each of these ways (and you can add two that were of you being assertive too). Since I am asking you to think about yourself, you will know about the internal feelings and you can note those down as well. Were you wanting to be seen to be aggressive—or did it just come out that way in the situations that you chose as examples?

The Journals of Christina and Tom

Christina's Journal

Tues Feb 8th

Academic assertiveness this evening. Phil and Dee again.

We were asked to think about how we feel about changing—whether we think that we simply are made the way we are made, or whether we might be able to be different. I guess I had not thought about this before. Well, I have actually changed quite a bit. I wasn't good in primary school at all and I was always in trouble. I feel bad about the way it upset Mum. I think I didn't want to learn at all. Then there was some sort of field trip and I got interested, and I came to like nature and then I suppose I liked biology at St Marks secondary school and it went on from there. I suppose you could say I changed a lot. Did I think about changing, though? I guess not—I just changed. It is good to know that I can change.

I have always found it difficult with new people and situations but I managed pretty well when I first came to uni—somehow it felt kind of right. There were loads of new people then. I did change in order to manage that. Now I could do with changing again in order to cope better with everything—like with Dave at the pub— he still makes me feel like a child with his silly comments. I really would like to leave.

Dee also asked us about situations in which we had noticed others behaving assertively, nonassertively, aggressively, and manipulatively. I saw someone being really aggressive today. I was in the lab. We were in small groups and were making some slides for examination under the microscope. Jayne threw a book across the lab bench and it knocked our carefully made slides all over the place and completely messed them up. She came round immediately and was very apologetic. Chris, who had been messing around, and had told her to "sling the book across,"—well he went absolutely crazy. It was as if she had done something really dreadful and damaged something that was not replaceable. I had never seen him like that and it made me wonder if there was something else going on. He said Jayne never cared about anyone else, just herself, and all sorts of things that weren't really relevant. Shel and me just got on and remade the slide. I ended up feeling sorry for Jayne. She obviously felt really bad. Chris did not let it go either, even after the lab. He really wanted her to suffer. Yes, that was aggression.

Wed Feb 9th

I have been thinking about examples of manipulative behavior . . . well there was a good example in the academic assertiveness session itself. There was this guy, Tom—a second year and quite quiet—and he was there with his girlfriend, Gemma. I got talking to Gemma in the bar after the course when Tom had gone home. Well, she is obviously a bit fed up with Tom's wimpyness—well that is what she called it, anyway. She said that she had deliberately manipulated Tom into coming on the course—she knew he wouldn't have come otherwise. She got him into the bar just next door to where the course was to be held that evening and then when the time came for the course, she said "OK, I'm off to the course. Coming?" She knew he'd come. It was funny because she sort of wanted Tom to be—well I suppose it is "assertive"—but she used the fact that he is not assertive in order to get him to do what she wanted. I didn't think he was terribly happy about it—but he didn't have to come. He was really nonassertive.

Me being assertive—yes well I did say some things in front of all the group in the biology seminar yesterday—and I actually disagreed with what Chris was saying. It was quite cool really. It was a module on population and he was talking loudly as usual, sounding very knowledgeable. Anyway, I was able to contradict him because I had been reading about the H5N1 bird flu virus and he said something I knew was wrong. I felt really pleased with myself when Mo, our tutor, said it was a good point. What was hard was finding a moment to make my point— I usually just listen. I felt good about speaking out, though.

And Steph was assertive I think when she went up to Dee and Phil after the assertiveness session and said "Thank you," and said that it was good. That was really cool. I must try to remember to do that next time.

Sun Feb 13th

Thinking of sending a valentine card to Charlie, but being in the flat might make it difficult—like I see him every day but I do like him. . . . If I am to be assertive, I have to do this sort of thing and not hold back. OK—I will but I won't sign it . . . well might just give a hint . . . otherwise what's the point?

Tom's journal

Tues Feb 8th

Went to this assertiveness course again a couple of days ago. I wasn't going to go, but Gem persuaded me again—and I guess it did get me thinking a bit. For a start it made me think a bit about Gem's and my relationship. It's not so good really. She keeps on at me and I can't say it makes me feel too great. I'd pack it in but I think I find it easier to have someone to go around with, and there's no one else who I fancy who's, like, available. Donna's all right but she's with Seb at the moment.

I guess it may not last with them—and then maybe I will make use of some of these assertiveness things we're learning.

One thing we had to do was to think about some examples of things that had happened to us that were relevant to assertiveness. Well one was that occasion at home a few weeks ago. I was at home for Mum's birthday, and we went out for a meal, and the parents asked what I was doing other than work. I said I was out with Gemma and usually did something with her a few times a week, like the bar or clubbing. Dad started to get tetchy. I could see it coming.

"Using up all my money on drink, I suppose. Thought you were meant to be there to work," he said. As usual I did not know what to say. It is his money but I am meant to have a life too. I know I went quiet after that. Dad goes like that sometimes and I suppose I always go silent when that happens. The atmosphere went awkward. Then I thought about this course and decided I was being a bit nonassertive. I thought I would try to relax and be more open—to be a bit more assertive and improve the atmosphere by saying something to Mum. I made an effort and told her about this course. I knew it was a risk, telling her, and I made sure Dad did not hear. Straight away she told Dad. He said, "I remember those kind of courses when I was a teenager. They were for women who wanted to be aggressive and domineering. God knows what for. I can't think why you want to do that." Then he said, "Oh, I see, it's the influence of that girlfriend of yours." Everything went seriously pear shaped for the rest of the meal. I wonder if I can get to be more assertive with Dad or at least cope better with him.

I was thinking about that list of things that academic assertiveness covers. It covers failure. I suppose it is relevant to that essay I did so badly in my first assignment at uni last year. I got 36%. I felt as if I should pack up my things and leave—a total failure. For a while I believed that my good grades were a sham and I should go and work in a bar somewhere, and that was all I was worth. When I saw Leon, my tutor, he said not to worry. He said I had got a bad mark because I did not answer the question and that and it was a good lesson for me. He showed me how the stuff I had written was not relevant. I just got quite interested in the subject and wrote that down. Seems silly to think I nearly left. That was a seriously bad time, though.

Sat Feb 12th

Quite interesting thinking about all this stuff. I am noticing more about how other people behave towards each other. Still fed up with the way Gem is. I don't know whether to get her a valentine card—a first for me (sending—well I did get one at school from Jenna . . . but then I think she sent them to all the boys in my class— she was hopeful that someone might take notice of her). The question is—or the QUESTION is—will Gem be into that sort of thing and—if I sent one, would she think it silly? Or would she like it? And well I don't really know how I feel about her. Don't know, don't know—may just have a look at some . . . there might be a sort of middle line one that works for my sort of mid-line state of mind—a sort of neutral one.

4

The Display of Assertive Behavior

Introduction

Three elements make up the assertive behavior of an individual—what is said, what is done (behavior), and the inside components—the thought, emotion and self-confidence that underlie behavior. I touched on the issue of what is said in the last chapter—but there is much more to come on that. Then there is the display of behavior—how a person speaks, how she stands, how her face looks, gestures, and so on. There is also the inside component that is the driving force of behavior—feelings, thoughts, emotions, and the longer-term orientations such as self-esteem, where a person feels she fits in her academic, social, family, and personal worlds. In this chapter, I am mainly going to focus on the overt display of behavior and I will begin to deal with thought, emotion and self-confidence, and in particular its relationship to the display of behavior. Sometimes these mental activities (thought, emotion, and self-confidence) and display of behavior are at odds, and you need to be aware of this in yourself and in others. Though you can often only guess what is going on in the mind of another, your guessing is likely to affect the manner in which you choose to behave with her.

As in the last chapter, I will describe displays of behavior broadly in relation to assertive, nonassertive, aggressive, and sometimes manipulative behaviors. This is partly because it makes the demonstration easier for me as the writer, partly because we, as humans, learn better from comparisons and also because, as an assertive person, it is important that you recognize these other forms of behavior in order that you can deal with them appropriately.

So that you know where you are in covering these three important aspects of assertiveness, I will summarize how they appear in the chapters of this book. It is obviously not straightforward because they relate and interrelate with each other.

- What is said—this is covered in brief in the first chapters and in more detail in later chapters (in particular, in the practical sense in Chapters 7 and 8). It is not a focus in this chapter.
- What is done—the display of behavior—how things are said and the display of nonverbal behavior. This is a focus more generally of

later chapters. The relationship between the display of behavior and thoughts, emotions, and self-confidence is covered in this chapter.

- Thoughts, emotions, and self-confidence—the mental aspects of assertiveness are introduced in the current chapter, and there is a particular practical focus on this in Chapter 9.

I have included in this chapter a number of short exercises for you to do as you read the text, as well as some at the end of the chapter, as usual. I will use the term "boxed tasks" in order to distinguish these from the exercises at the end of the chapter. This is because you can learn a great deal more effectively if you do more than just read, but actually feel yourself *doing* the actions that are described. The first box (page 39) is about the quality of speech. Feeling yourself talking in different ways will help you to remember the difference much better than just reading the text, even if the words you say are not audible to anyone else. You could do any writing that is involved in the boxed tasks in your journal, of course.

The Display of Behavior

I have divided this section into three further parts. All of them can be described as nonverbal behavior, though I slide a little beyond what is usually called "behavior" in the third part. The first part is about the qualities of speech and voice. The second part is about body language. The third part is about some whole-person matters, including personal space and relative height. I have included this here because it is broadly to do with choices that you make about how you display behavior in relation to physical space.

The Qualities of Speech and Voice

I have said that being assertive goes far beyond words. I could almost say that it is a quality that oozes from every cell in the body . . . but our starting point will be the words. Jane has asked Markus if he will come with her to see a new film that is on. Markus says:

"No, I won't come with you. I have other things to do today."

Is Markus being assertive or not? Well he might be being assertive, simply saying that he does not want to come. In this case, his voice would be friendly and relaxed and he might add suggestions as to others whom Jane might ask. On the other hand, supposing he says (with italicized emphases) in an altogether harder manner:

"No I *won't* come with you. I have other things to do today."

Then you could probably interpret his response as aggressive. He might be using aggressive intonation to counter persistent nagging by Jane. He could also put a manipulative connotation into the manner in which he uses his words:

"No, I won't come *with you*. I have other things to do today."

We might interpret this as a double message that he is not saying directly to Jane. He might be trying to tell Jane (but not directly), that he would go with someone else, but not her. Further, he might be manipulative if he says:

"No, I won't come with you. I have *other things* to do today."

Here he is not telling Jane directly why he will not come to the cinema with her—but he is hinting that he has something to do that supercedes her suggestion. In effect he is putting her offer down but is indirectly inviting her to show interest in what those "other things" might be.

Clearly the message here is that words alone do not carry the message of assertiveness. There is much more to it. What I am saying here applies to most of the scenarios in this book—I cannot detail the direction of gaze, the facial expression and other nonverbal aspects of behavior in each scenario and many, like the demonstration shows above, could be interpreted in different ways. So if you do not at first understand the point I am trying to make in a scenario, think about other interpretations that would occur if the intonation were different.

In the example of Jane and Markus above, I have emphasized the intonation and the qualities of voice and speech that demonstrate assertiveness and the other orientations of aggression, nonassertion, and manipulation.

> Think about intonation. Begin by saying the words spoken by Markus to Jane in the different manners indicated. Then speak some words of your own (you can use different words for each tone this time). Say something in an aggressive manner, then nonassertively, then, if you can, in a manipulative manner, and then say something in an assertive manner. Feel the way in which your voice is working.

There are some other qualities of speech that characterize the way people are feeling inside and also how they relate to others. They are tools that can be used to communicate nonverbally but we cannot generalize about the message being conveyed without knowing the context. Here is a list of them:

- How much is said in relation to others' speech.
- The loudness of the voice.
- The speed of the speech.
- The flow of speech—hesitant or smooth.
- The management of silence and the ability to use silence.

Not saying as much as another is expecting is often a matter of a nonverbal "message" being given—defensiveness, or deliberate blocking of communication —or it could be a form of aggression, manipulation, nonassertion, or it could be assertive—it could be that the speaker is feeling withdrawn and is behaving in accordance with this.

> Think of a situation in which you or another have tended to hold back and not say as much, perhaps, as someone else was expecting. What is going on? What is the message to the other?

On the other hand, saying too much can be characteristics of the nondirect and disorganized nonassertive person—and/or the person who is anxious.

Like the volume speech, the use of a louder voice than expected can also convey a message. Loudness is an interesting quality. You might think that being "loud" is the way to be heard in a group, but actually being quiet and persistent is often just as effective, or more effective so long as you get someone's attention to start with. Loud and demanding voices sometimes carry messages that are not interesting, but quiet and persistent voices may be carrying something that is worthwhile hearing.

And then there is speed of speech.

> Jan is a mature student, who has just started a degree program in early years education at Dindane University College. She has just had her first assignment back. The mark is not good, she does not understand the comments, and she is not sure that the marks have been added up properly. She manages to see her tutor. She has rehearsed what she is going to say but words come tumbling out. . . .

Rapid speech is usually a giveaway for anxiety, and anxiety in one person affects communication with another or others. With patience and time, Jan's tutor may hear her out and endeavour to help her to express what she wants, but there is a danger that he will not pay due attention and she will not be sufficiently assertive to regain his attention. In being assertive, it is often important to deliberately slow the pace of speaking.

> Recall a time when you or another person were talking more quickly than usual. What happened to the assertiveness in the situation? Can you be assertive while talking too quickly?

Another quality of speech is its smoothness or hesitancy. There are two elements to this—one is simply the style of speech and the other is the way it comes over in a particular situation. Until you know how someone speaks you may need to rely on other cues alongside with the smoothness of speech such as speed of breathing. The UK's ex-prime minister Tony Blair, for example, speaks fairly hesitantly but that is not necessarily a sign that he is not assertive.

Another quality is the vague use of what I call "fluffy words" that are meaningless but are spoken as a nervous habit. These weaken the power of what is being said. One example is "I mean," another is "really," and these may be used together. For example,

> "You ask me how I am feeling about the journey, well, I mean, really it is a matter of getting there. I suppose that I am all right—really—I mean—well I am worried about it really. . . . Yes, I suppose I am really a bit worried."

The last point is about the management of silence. I always think of silence in the course of conversation as being "owned" by one person or another. I might say to you:

> "I'm going to the computer lab for a bit. What are you doing?" (silence)

Or

> "Great—rain again. . . ." (silence)

In both cases—by way of question or comment—I have given you a silence and the expectation is that you will put something into that silence—a response or comment. On the other hand, if I speak in the following ways, the silence is mine:

> "I'm just thinking . . . (silence) . . . I don't know how you feel about this idea but it would be nice if you came along too."

Or

> "Well let me just think about your comment . . . (silence). . . . Well I do not think . . . (and so on) . . ."

Not taking account of someone else's silence is often aggressive behavior. Equally it can be an act of aggression not to take up silence that is given to you. I have a fairly painful anecdote to tell here. I was in my very early days as a psychology lecturer and I was working, probably not too well, with a smallish group of graduate students training to be art teachers. They were not impressed with their course in general and I had difficulty in getting them to respond to questions I asked them. I would ask a question and there would be silence. I would quickly deal with the discomfort by jumping in with an answer for them. I was being manipulated. One day I decided not to jump in and instead to play their game. I waited. The silence loomed—it was theirs. As they realized I was not going to ease the situation, there was a sense of hostility from them—a form of nonverbal aggression and this lasted for a while, and then it changed—perhaps a pen was dropped . . . something initiated the change, but it was not a voice. Then I think they were beginning to feel helpless. They realized that they were out of control because they could not break the silence and they needed me to ease it. It was my silence to do what I liked with. I did, of course, break it in the end—and interestingly they began to respond to my questions better. . . . Silence plays a large part in communication, and to be assertive you need to learn to use silence to your advantage. Used properly, it can greatly increase the impact of your words.

Think of a person who uses silence well in her communication. Try to make two statements about why her use of silence is effective.

We generalize about the nonverbal aspects of verbal behavior:

The voice of the person being nonassertive will be quieter; there may be a sense of holding back words and feelings. The speech may be quick and halting or hesitant with silences that do not enhance the communication. The nonassertive person may talk using a mass of disorganized speech.

The aggressive voice is likely to be harder, maybe even harsh and directed. It may be loud. Others' uses of words and silence may be abused. Some aggression may be expressed by the deliberate withholding of words or information.

The manipulative voice may often carry a whine in order to direct the attention of the listener to the subtext, which may often be at odds with the actual message. Alternatively the voice may be "put on" or disguised in order to cover up the real message or the speaker's real feelings.

The assertive person will tend to speak in a direct and relaxed manner, giving the right amount of information, and skillfully managing silence in order to give her words a greater impact.

Bodies and their Language

We go beyond the words now to look at other aspects of body and expression that are used when being aggressive, nonassertive, and assertive. I leave manipulative behavior out here because often the manipulator is deliberately disguising the messages of her communication so it is not possible to make generalizations.

In one of the boxes above, I asked you to speak in aggressive, nonassertive, assertive, and possibly a manipulative manner and to note the nature of your voice. Now I want you to pay attention to other factors in your body and your expression as you speak in these different ways. How does it feel? How were you standing or sitting and what was the expression on your face? See if you can make statements about posture and expression in being aggressive, nonassertive, and assertive.

I introduce body language and expression through a scenario (now, of course, recognizing the provisos about interpretation above). This is a longer scenario because I will return to it to illustrate other issues.

Frederick, Hans, Libbie, and Louise are in a shared flat. It is Reading Week at Collaston University and Libbie has invited some friends to come and see her, while the others have all gone home. Her friends were going to make arrangements to stay at the local pub, but when she realizes that the flat is otherwise empty, at the last moment and without telling her flatmates she emails her friends and invites them to stay in the house. She invites them to use all the beds because the others are away—they just must make sure that the beds are properly re-made before they leave. Her friends are only staying for two nights and none of her flatmates are due back for four nights. She is a little bit nervous about the arrangement but it will save so much money and the beds are not being used, and no-one will know . . . will they?

Late in the evening on the second night, the door to the flat opens and Frederick returns. He goes to his room and disturbs the person in his bed.
. . .

"What the hell is going on?" says Frederick. Libbie emerges from her room in her nightclothes. "What have you been up to Libbie?", he says, "I suppose this is you and your friends, taking advantage . . . I don't want anyone else in my bed, Libbie. How dare you set this up?"

Frederick is very angry indeed. The person in his bed gets up, tidies the bed, slips past the still-arguing Frederick and Libbie, and settles down on the sofa.

Frederick is legitimately angry and the event causes many exchanges of feelings in the flat over the next week, but things settle down. The main issue to emerge seems to be the fact that Libbie did not ask her flatmates if they minded if their beds were used. They all finally have a good discussion and agree that if this issue were to arise again, it is up to individuals to make their own decisions about their beds and that decision is to be respected—but there must be prior notice. We now shift to a situation that happens some weeks later. It is now the vacation.

Louise is staying in the house over the vacation. She lives abroad and cannot afford to go home. She has some friends from her own country who want to come and stay—and they are very short of money. She decides to ask the others if her friends can use their beds. She will change the sheets and do the washing. She feels it will be all right because the issue before seemed mainly to be the lack of prior consultation. She decides to tackle each of her flatmates separately.

She asks Hans while he is washing up in the kitchen.

"Hans, you know I'm here in the hols. Well, I've got some friends from home coming and I am wondering if I could use your room—well your bed—for one of them? They'll bring sleeping bags. I know we had all that trouble with Libbie's friends but that was because she didn't ask us before, wasn't it?" She goes on to reassure Hans that everything will be tidied afterwards.

Hans goes on washing up, grunts and half-turns to Louise. She says,

"Please, Hans, you know it would make such a difference to their stay,—and you are such a nice person Hans. . . ."

"It means I will have to clear everything up I suppose, doesn't it", he says, still not looking at her. "When is it that you want it, anyway? I may be back early myself. What do the others say? What about your floor, could they not sleep there?" He speaks quickly and carries on with the washing up.

Louise only answers his first question. "Oh they come at the beginning of the hols—early next week when you are not here. Go on Hans . . . , you know what it's like when you've got no money to say anywhere. I thought you'd let me use your room Hans—you, of all of them". She puts on a little girl voice and moves towards him. "You're such a nice guy, Hans."

Hans eventually says, "Well, I suppose so." He is not happy, but does not want to upset her.

Louise then goes to see Libbie and asks her about the use of the room. Libbie has just turned on the television in the sitting room. She looks up at Louise.

"Well actually, no, I would rather that you did not use my room, Louise," she says, looking directly at her. "I know that I made a mess of the same thing a little while ago—and I know I made a real mistake there, but since then I have thought a lot about it and I don't think I would want anyone else using my room. You all made me think last time—so—well basically, no."

Louise says "Come on Libs, fair's fair." Libbie says "No Louise, I am sorry I made that mistake, but no." She turns away and watches the television to stall further persuasion.

Louise finally goes to Frederick and asks him. She has picked a time when he is on the way out of the house and stands in the narrow space in front of the door. She hopes for a quick, positive answer because he is in a hurry. However, he overreacts because of the situation and because of the previous experience with Libbie's friends.

"Just going out, Lou—can't you see—come on now—let me out! Some cheek you've got to ask me just now. The answer is NO". He raises his voice. "We've been here before Lou and I hate the idea of some stranger settling into my sheets, under my photos, in my space. I pay for that space, it's mine and I'll let no-one—Lou—no-one else use it. Now just let me get out—you've delayed me enough already." He shoves past Louise.

There are many nonverbal behaviors that will have been displayed by Hans, Louise, and Frederick, as well as by Libbie in her somewhat manipulative attempts to get the decision from her friends that she wants.

> Think back to the three scenes in this scenario and list the nonverbal behaviors that might have been displayed by Hans in being nonassertive and agreeing to something with which he is not happy—Libbie in assertively saying "no," and Frederick in being aggressive. You might also think about how Libbie has been manipulative in her efforts to get what she wants.

Some of the nonverbal behaviors that might have been displayed by the four characters in addition to the various ways in which they will have used their voices and speech include:

- Posture.
- The angle of the head.
- The nature of eye contact or lack of it.
- Evidence of the attention paid to the other person.
- Facial expression and facial gestures that are not related to the communication.
- Breathing rate.
- The quality and degree of the movements and body gestures—dramatic or slow, smooth movements or "jabbing" movements, tight or expansive gestures, or no movement.
- Stray movements that may be unrelated to the communication (e.g. rocking).
- General level of confidence, portrayed in many ways,
- The use of touch.
- Other more personal forms of communication that are associated with the relationship between those involved.

It would take many pages to describe in full the various nuances of these signs and signals for assertive, aggressive, and nonassertive behaviors so I have added only a few notes at the end of the list. You, as a human being, will have a huge ability to "read" others' behavior and to learn more from it in order to fine-tune your own behavior.

The posture of a person is one of the most obvious ways in which behavior is displayed, particularly in the angle of the head. "Saggy" people usually look nonassertive, and in the same way you could say that assertive people hold themselves up to the world. In the scenario above, Hans kept his head down. He also avoided eye contact with Louise and did not show her that he was paying attention to what she was saying. The facial expression of an assertive person is attentive, bright, and open. An aggressive face has sharpened features. Breathing rate is another way in which we display how we are feeling—but again it will be "read" in relation to other signs. A person will breathe quickly when she is aggressive (ready for fight); but also when she is being nonassertive and frightened (ready for flight), as well when she has just been running! Then there is the quality of body gestures—a person might be rigid ("frightened rigid"), tight and immobile, or expansive, with arm movements that open away from the body—a movement that might describe trust and openness. The aggressor may use more dramatic gestures that have weight behind them or symbolize actual violence (thumping the table or jabbing the air). Sometimes gestures can indicate how a person really is when the words that are being said suggest some other state. For example, they may be demonstrating tension in clenched fist or tight lips. Then there are other giveaway gestures. It is difficult to be assertive and clear if you are restless and fidgeting, or constantly tapping a foot or hand, or biting fingernails. These are the gestures of a nonassertive, or sometimes of an aggressive, person.

Imagine you are in various communication situations and try out gestures, facial expressions, head positions, changes in breathing rate, and looking confident and less confident, still or fidgeting. How do you feel—assertive, nonassertive, or aggressive? What are the gestures that help you to feel assertive? A mirror might be useful!

Some "Whole-Person" Matters Including Personal Space and Relative Height

There are a some "whole–body" nonverbal communications involve spatial factors, such as:

- Whole–body movement—stepping nearer, or away from, the other, etc.
- The use of personal space—one's own and responses to others' personal space.
- Relative positions and heights—sitting, standing, and so on.

In a situation in which you want to display assertive behavior, it is often worth moving forward towards the other person. If you are standing at a counter, for example in a coffee bar, making a point about a cup of cold coffee, for example, then putting a hand flat on the counter in front of you—firmly but not forcefully—establishes your presence and "says" something like, "I am going to make my point here."

The example above has also something to do with territory and personal space. As humans we are aware of a space around us that we treat as our territory. We let intimate friends in, but most others we tolerate in that space only for short periods (a brief touch), or under sufferance in a crowd. Most people have an automatic reaction to others who do not respect their space, and they move in order to preserve the space. Some people are not aware of the personal space that is required by others and, by standing too close, they affect the communications that they have with others. The abuse of space can be confusing to the other person. It is often nonassertive people who get their judgments of personal space "wrong," but standing up close to someone else, in their personal space, can also be a tactic of an aggressor. It is important to bear in mind that sometimes people stand close to others because they have uncorrected sight problems. Here is a personal space story and it may be that you have had similar experiences. A long while ago I had a friend who did could not "read" personal distances. He stood too close when he communicated (and I was not the only one to experience this). I was very aware of this whenever I was with him and had tried to tell him— but in vain. One day he gave me a lift to a station. I was going away somewhere and had a large bag on the ground. In the course of the ten minutes during which we waited for the train, I backed around my bag three times, trying to preserve my personal-space zone. The nature of the communication was needless to say considerably distorted!

In terms of actual distances, there are cultural as well as relationship variables at play here. Rees and Graham (1991) suggest that for British white middle-class suburban people, the personal distance is around 6in (15cm) for those who have a close and intimate relationship. For those who are friends it goes up to about 18in (45cm). For others it is further. What do you think?

Pretend that you are having various interactions with another person in which you are aggressive, nonassertive, and assertive (you could base it on the scenario above). Coat-stands, chairs and plants may be called in to stand for the "other persons" in this role play. Experiment with personal space, taking a step forward, a step back, sitting, and standing. Then try measuring your personal space—how far it does it extend out from you at chest level (for example)? Ask a friend to stand in various positions near you, in the role of various others (your family members, teacher, peers, and so on—as well as her/himself).

There is also the matter of relative height. I am going to take a guess here and say that it is slightly more difficult for a relatively short person to be assertive, though some are extremely successful (and there are many tall nonassertive people). When you have to look up at another person, you are already in a position in which you are at a disadvantage. If you are successful, you will find other ways of making your presence have more impact. Some shorter people use "props" such as high heels or thick-soled shoes to increase their height. We may also make assumptions about assertiveness in people with different body shapes.

> Think about people you know—do you make assumptions about how assertive or aggressive they might be from their height or body shapes? You might find it useful to discuss this with a friend and see if you agree.

Sometimes the furniture that we choose or use can add to one's assertive or aggressive stance. This will be covered in the next chapter.

Finally we will look at the issue of clothes and assertiveness, and how the clothes you wear might "come over" to others and how they make you feel about yourself. Clothes can influence how people feel about the impact on or power that they have over others. There are, for example, those who wear uniforms—where the uniform indicates authority or a controlling role over others. The obvious examples are police, traffic wardens, and prison officers. Once there is a uniform, there is often also an indication of rank integral to that uniform. Then there are other forms of clothing that give messages—the wig of the judge is one extreme and the bunny girl outfit of nightclub hostesses is another—perhaps at the two extremes of assertiveness and nonassertion in terms of expected role at least.

Then there are the messages of non-uniform clothing. As a child, I always considered my father to be less approachable and less friendly when he was in his work suit. In the past, academics wore gowns as a "badge of office" that may have helped them to think themselves more in role. Now many academics wear clothes that are not dissimilar from students. At an academic conference, few men would wear formal suits now. However, it was not many years ago that I noticed that if I went to a conference it was not men who were in dark trouser suits, but women. For a time, dark suits had become the way of power dressing for women in higher education! The meaning of clothes changes.

Clothing can influence how you feel about yourself and the power you have in particular situations, and it can influence how others respond to you before you even open your mouth. It is worth being aware of how you choose clothes in relation to particular situations. When I go to speak at conferences, or run workshops for teaching staff, or work with students, I think about the impact I want to have through the clothes that I wear. Usually I want to present myself as relatively informal because that is how I like to be seen and that is how I like workshops to run, though sometimes I dress up. I am conscious that when I work abroad, I am not always able to predict the "rules" for dress in that setting.

The most important thing about dress is that you will generally perform better, look more relaxed, and be more assertive if you are comfortable with what you are wearing and in what you are wearing.

> Think of four situations in which you find yourself in work, education, and other settings (an interview if you like) and list the "rules" that you have informally set yourself about your clothing.
>
> You could discuss your personal "rules" for dress with a friend and see if you agree or disagree.
>
> How do other people's clothes influence you?
>
> Who do you dress for—yourself or others?

Thought, Emotion and Self-confidence—What Goes on Inside Behavior

Go back to the statement about the nature of academic assertiveness in the first chapter and you will see that most of it refers to what goes on inside. Here are some of the things that I mentioned:

- Finding an appropriate "voice" or self-expression.
- The willingness to challenge, to disagree and to seek or accept a challenge.
- The ability to cope with the reality or the likelihood of not being "right" sometimes, making an error or failing; effective recovery from these situations.
- The willingness to change one's mind if necessary; the openness to feedback on one's performance (academic or otherwise).
- The willingness to listen and take account of the viewpoint of others, awareness that others can make mistakes, and reasonable tolerance of their failings.
- Autonomy—a willingness to be proactive; to make and justify independent judgments and to act on them.
- An appropriate level of academic self-esteem.

Behind all behavior lies the thought, emotions, and self-confidence which make up who you are and how you are in different situations. There are volumes of books to be written about personal psychology—look at the bookshelves on "mind and spirit" in your local bookshop. I am about to squeeze a few salient points into a couple of sections in this chapter, to be then followed up by the practical material in Chapter 9.

The first thing to say is that whoever you are and however you are now is not fixed. You can change (Chapter 2, page 22). However, it may not be a matter of just deciding to be different—if only we could wake up and decide to be bright and cheerful today and every day . . . ! It is worth thinking about the operating rules that you follow, of which you may not always be conscious. As humans we have many of these operating rules and most date back a long way in our lives. The best way to help you to become aware of them is to give you some examples and then you can start to list some for yourself. Let me start by making some guesses about operating rules that are drivers to behavior in some of the scenarios earlier in this chapter. There was the scenario of Louise, Libbie, Frederick, and Hans, for example.

> Louise feels she has power enough to get around everybody in different ways. She might be thinking "I'll get what I want if I approach everyone differently." She has confidence in her ability to get what she wants, however unreasonable she has to be.

> Frederick is comfortable with losing his temper and showing his feelings to Louise.

> Libbie is very straight with Louise—and probably she is straight with others too.

> We might guess that Hans would not lose his temper very easily. He feels he must please Louise—and probably others too. From the manner in which Louise treats him, it would seem that he is susceptible to some social and sexual flattery.

The operating rules that people use to order their behavior are often couched in phrases that you catch them using. Some people, for example, behave as victims in life. They have a raw deal. They say things like . . .

> "Oh I couldn't do that—I'm not brave enough. I admire the way you just go out and do things."

> "It's always me . . ." or "Why me all the time?"

> "It's all right for you . . ."

Here are some more sayings that tend to reflect people's operating rules.

> "Oh well, that's life."

> "I'll put a brave face on it."

> "Grin and bear it."

You can almost hear the whine in the words. Some people always seem to be optimistic and happy, too. They "put a smiling face" on all the time and "take whatever life throws at them" or "take things in their stride," and so on.

> Write down some phrases that are like "operating rules" that you might use about yourself, or that others might use about you.

These operating rules relate to what we might call "life positions," which are to do with expectations and assumptions. Life positions relate particularly to the place we feel we have in relation to society and people around us. This "position" may be "fact" or "fiction." For example, when you are a student, the fact is that you are in a hierarchy of expertise that is related to status in higher education. If you are a Private in military terms, the fact is that the Major is "above" you in rank and so on. It is usual to expect children to obey their parents (OK—to some extent). However, there are also the fictions—the statuses that people attribute to themselves. There is no reason why Hans (above), as a colleague of Louise, feels that he should please Louise by being nonassertive. Some people feel that they are not sufficient as people to hold their own opinions (Belenky, et al., 1986). This is connected with self-confidence and self-esteem.

Life position also leads us to have expectations about interactions. You could say that Louise (above) expected to "get round" her colleagues in the flat in order to "get her own way" and it was as if Hans expected to give in to her from the start of the conversation in the kitchen. We have expectations about many interactions before we meet them.

> Allan's tutor has emailed him to come for a meeting. Allan has missed several seminars, without being in touch. He knows he has to deal with a person who is of higher status, and who is probably not going to be pleased with him.
>
> As a postgraduate student, Beth has just given a research seminar on her PhD studies on the interpretation by the media of the phrase "post-9/11". Participants were interacting and continue to express interest and ask deep questions after the session has ended. She is due to review the session with her supervisor in ten minutes and she expects him to be pleased with her, and to make positive and constructive comments.

Before we meet people, we have often reviewed expectations of the meeting, and at first we manage our behavior along the lines of the expectation. We can be wrong! Suppose Allan is confronted by a tutor who actually lavishes praise on him because the tutor has just marked an excellent essay of his. Supposing Beth's supervisor has strict ideas about how Beth should conduct her seminar and was very irritated by Beth's (albeit better) presentation . . . expectations can prepare us for something, but at the same time they can mislead us.

Bringing us back to the subject of assertiveness and associated behaviors, people who are habitually nonassertive expect to lose out, be dominated by or need to please others. People who are aggressive tend to expect to have to fight for their rights, or they treat others as irritants. People who are manipulative assume that they can only get what they want by being divisive and indirect.

On the Inside and Outside of Behavior and the Relationship between them

Now we need to look at the relationships between what is going on between the inside state and the outside state of behavior, and we will see that it is not a simple relationship of the inside "driving" the overt behavior.

> Does the way in which you feel about yourself in relation to your educational situation match or differ from the way you feel about yourself in other situations (home, social situations, when travelling)?

There is a constant interaction between how we feel on the inside and how it relates to how we behave and we use both together when we interpret the behavior of another person, though we are using guesswork when it comes to the inside thoughts, emotions, and self-confidence of the other. We cannot know what is going on inside the head of another unless the person communicates it to us. In this section, we are going to take a look at how the outside display of behavior relates to what is going on inside the mind of the person. Let us look at a few situations.

> Fran is in a seminar in her art and design course. She has been talking about the processes that she has gone through in creating an abstract painting. She is standing upright and her voice is strong as she talks, but she is saying things like "I don't think I really know what I was thinking of when I painted this (long pause) . . . it was sort of, well, like . . . I don't know. . . ." She continues to stand upright, looking at her colleagues and speaking with a clear voice. She says then, "I don't think I like it really. . . ."

There is something strange here . . . voice and posture do not match the approach Fran is taking to the presentation. If we were in attendance, we might be wondering what is influencing Fran's strangeness. We might have expected her to speak in an assertive manner from the way in which she is standing and speaking.

> Dave is lounging in a chair. He looks half asleep. In a languid voice he says "I'm really going to work hard next semester."

Do you believe him?

> Ben has just collected the marks from his last assignment. He walks quickly, looking about him with his head held high. He stops by the Canoeing Club notice board. Chas is looking at the board. Ben says briskly:
> "No more of this for me, Chas, I'm out on my ear—failed the retakes. Never mind. That's life and it is fine. There's a world out there. See you later." Before Chas can speak, Ben walks on at a fast pace.

Is it really fine for Ben? Probably not! There seems to be a contradiction in what Ben is saying and the manner in which he is acting, and Chas might well "read" into the situation that Ben is pretty upset and his method of coping is to seem all right. This may work for him or it may not. There are some philosophies of behavior that suggest that you should "let it all hang out"—in other words, you are always authentic, speaking and behaving in the manner that relates to the way you feel. Sometimes it works to try to be authentic—but sometimes you can be "jollied out" of feeling low or you can "act into" a better mood. The song that talks of whistling a happy tune when we are "down"—"I Whistle A Happy Tune" by Richard Rogers and Oscar Hammerstein—is sung by Anna in *The King and I*.

By "acting up" and appearing happy, sometimes we can shift a negative mood, or—as the song goes on to say, make ourselves feel more courageous. On the other hand, by pretending that everything is well when it is not may mean that we avoid taking actions that we need to take. Going back to Ben and how he was behaving before his retakes, he was saying:

> "Retakes? No problem. I got it wrong the first time because I was out partying too late the night before. I knew the stuff really. I've got a good memory—I know that from my previous grades—it's still there in my head. No, this time I'll just go in and write what they want and I'll be back on track—just keep off the drink the night before."

OK, Ben we will see how you get on!

Then there is Alex, who has a different way of handling bad results:

> Alex has failed an examination, and when Suzanne asks how she is she says "I'm fine" as she chokes on a tear and turns her head away. As Alex is walking away she is saying to herself "I am fine, I am fine. It was the doing of the examination that was not good. Me and my life are fine and I will get out of this difficult space. That is all it is. I will be all right in the retakes."

For more on managing failure, see Chapter 10.

So let me summarize this section so far. How you feel on the inside and how you display your behavior to others are related. Usually the inside feelings and the outside behaviors are in accordance. However, as you see above, sometimes there is discord. If you observe someone behaving in this disjointed way there may be a sense of strangeness about the person and her behavior—an inauthenticity. This may be a defensive mode (probably the case with Ben and Ali above), and it may be an intentional strategy (as when Anna whistles the happy tune). Alex is aware of being "down" and is talking herself up. We will be saying more about self-talk at a later stage.

> Think of an occasion when another person displayed behavior that does not seem to match how you think that person is actually feeling on the inside. What is going on, do you think? (You can only guess how another is feeling, of course.)
>
> Think of an occasion when how you behaved did not accord with how you were actually feeling. Why was there a mismatch?

Displaying Assertive Behavior—A List of Hints that Summarize the Chapter

I have said a lot in this chapter about the components of assertive behavior, and in order to make the points I wanted to make, I have described many situations in which the behavior was not assertive. However, there are many more hints, tips, and observations to make so I end the main text of this chapter by pulling these together. They are a mixture of behaviors and thoughts, emotions, and self-confidence issues.

- Assertive people speak directly to the person—they convey their message clearly. You do not need to speak with a strong or harsh voice—start gently.
- Be specific about what you want to say. Do not wander around the subject and generalize, and do not use fluffy and superfluous words like "I mean" and "really."
- Deal with potentially difficult matters as soon as they are an issue, and notice any tendencies that others have to delay, and the excuses they make. "Take the bull by the horns," as they say.
- Look the other person in the eye, not over her shoulder. Don't look down at the table or floor. Look as if you mean what you are saying.
- Your posture should be straight (no raised shoulders, arms pulled up, no hands fiddling with each other, and no standing on one foot).
- An assertive person looks reasonably relaxed. This may be difficult—but she has the capacity to pretend to be relaxed if necessary. It may come in useful to know that sometimes!
- Maximize the chances of feeling confident by being aware of the setting, the clothes that you wear, the whole manner in which you present yourself. Be yourself, but maximize the confident self.

- Check out whether you are smiling as you talk in order to placate the other, and quash any tendencies towards nervous laughter. This often occurs without intent, and it is important to avoid it. Such laughter is a way in which we learn to soften our messages to others when we are nervous of them.
- Assertive people avoid being sarcastic (other than the occasional playful "dig"), even when the person they are speaking to is sarcastic. Sarcasm is a form of aggression—a means of reducing the other person. If you respond to sarcasm with sarcasm you have become caught up in the same aggressive game and, in effect, this gives permission to the other person to behave as badly as she wants.
- You will need to be relatively organized about what you say in formal situations. Think through the line that you are going to take and any key points that you need to make, and make sure you hang on to your line despite the other person's efforts to distract you and take the interaction in different directions (to his or her advantage).
- Remember that you cannot control how things turn out when you are interacting with another person because you cannot make her behave in a particular way—you can just maximize the chance of things working out. We all make mistakes or things do not go according to plan; that is the way it is, and sometimes we have to leave knowing that we did not achieve what we intended. If I was feeling trite, I could say "That's life," but I won't. . . .
- If things go wrong why not take the advice of Anna in The King and I and whistle that happy tune!!

Activities and Journal Exercises

You may have used your journal already a fair bit in this chapter if you have engaged in the "boxed tasks". Those tasks are related to the content of the chapters. The exercises below are more generalized.

How You Present Yourself

Imagine that you have applied for a job as a care worker in a residential home where the job would require you to be reasonably cheerful and moderately outgoing. Dr Simons is your tutor and has known you for the last three years. You have named him as a referee and he is asked to give you a reference. He is asked to comment on the manner in which you present yourself. Write the reference as he might give you. If you want to imagine the words of your own university tutor, that is fine.

Ten Situations (1)

List ten situations in which you feel you need to be more assertive. This might mean that you feel you are currently nonassertive, or aggressive, or manipulative in those situations. We will be coming back to this list several times and you will have a chance to modify it. Are these situations predominately in one location (for example, home and family, social experiences at home, social experiences at university, job situations, academic situations . . . others)?

Apply What You Have Learnt About Behavior in Some Scenarios

Now is the time for people-watching. The ultimate task is to write four short scenarios that demonstrate people being assertive, nonassertive, aggressive, and manipulative. You may want to do this in one situation—such as the story about the flatmates Libbie, Frederick, Hans, and Louise (above) or they may be separate. They can be from your own experience, or from the observation of others, or made up. In doing it, remember to draw from details of posture, expression, what is said, the quality of the speech, how people are standing in relation to each other, and so on. You could write this in your journal or you could do the task orally with another person or a group.

How Assertive Are You?

On a hypothetical and averaged out scale of 1–10, how assertive are you? Rate some of your friends and get them to rate you!

The Journals of Christina and Tom

Christina's journal

Tues Feb 15th

Hey—got a valentines card from someone and I don't know at all who it is from . . . I like it. I hope it wasn't Dave—I don't fancy him but I think he likes me. That would be really disappointing.

Another session with Phil and Dee again today. It was cool. Do I really want to change? It feels like hard work.

I was going to write about today but I have just been reading what I wrote last week about the seminar on population biology. I'd read up a bit before the seminar today and I felt I knew more about the stuff we were doing on limiting factors and the regulation of populations and again was able to say a bit that the others did not know. Mo was really helpful. She knows my voice is not very loud and she made the others be quiet. Lots of tutors wouldn't bother. But—well—is it that my voice is not very loud or that I don't have much confidence in what I say? Today's acadass session (we call it that now) makes me think about that. In some ways, knowing a bit more than the others today in the seminar made me feel less withdrawn and what I said came out quite well. I felt good, too, to have contributed.

I am meant to think about what an imaginary person, a Dr Simons, might say about how I present myself. He is meant to be a tutor who has known me for three years. The job is for someone working in a residential care home and they particularly want someone who is cheerful and moderately outgoing—OK. How can he have known me for three years when I have not been here one year yet? I will pretend. I guess he is going to need to be honest, too and he may turn out to think that I am not suitable. . . .

> *I have known Christina for three years. She is pleasant and outgoing. I understand that she works in a bar in the evenings and she appears to get on all right there. She contributes well in seminars and seems to be reliable and pleasant. She smiles and seems to get on socially with. . . .*

No—that is not what I should be writing. No-one would say that about me . . . This guy is going to be honest now . . .

> *You enquire about Christina. She is quiet and I would say that is a sign of lack of confidence. She may be better in her work environment (a bar), where she seems to spend much of her time (note from me: I am better there). She deliberately sits as far back as possible in class and does not always listen in, and in some ways it feels as if she is only half there most of the time. As for being cheerful and moderately outgoing—I would say she is unsettled here at Somanton and not of a cheerful disposition.*

Thank you Dr Simons. They give the job to the wonderful Steph. PS I think you should talk to Mo about me. She will tell you I have been doing better lately. . . .

Thurs Feb 17th

The valentine card wasn't from Dave, I asked him outright—that was being assertive wasn't it. Cool. Felt quite proud of myself! Bit down tonight though. Had a row with Steph. She suggested that we should go out to the Bombay restaurant on Friday because it's her birthday. I felt really pleased that she had asked me and it was going to be just two of us. Well now she has invited lots more and I know what is going to happen—I'll just get into a corner and no-one will notice me. What's more Chris and Pete are going. They both think I'm stupid and ignore me.

Fri Feb 18th

Going to this meal of Steph's later. Loads of people going . . . I'm feeling a bit better about it now. I thought about what advice Dee would give me if I told her what I wrote in my journal on Wednesday. She would tell me to seem to be confident even if I did not feel that. She would remind me about the whistle a happy tune song and tell me to wear "confident clothes." OK so I'm going out to buy something new this afternoon between lectures (if Jules remembers about the tenner she borrowed—shouldn't have let her have it). Maybe I'll get something a bit bright—risky . . . something is saying "that is not me." But it'll be the new me!

I think of other things that Dee would say, like "Be cool" and "Feel the tension flow out of your face. Relax it." And she says all those other things that help you to be assertive because you feel more confident. Sal, this girl on the course, said to Dee that looking cool was fine, but what do you say when you are shy and when talking to new people screws you up? Dee said that the golden rule was to be interested in other people, find out about them. OK—so I will try it. . . .

Tom's Journal

Sat Feb 19th

Had another assertiveness session in the Union on Tuesday. Gemma goes on about it so I could not forget to go—though I am thinking that me and Gemma might have to part—she is just too full-on all the time.

Feels a bit strange, this assertiveness, but . . . maybe there is some useful stuff in there. We looked at how people display their assertive behavior. I never realized that there was as much to it. I have been watching other people and it is amazing how they give away where they're at. In the lecture on coastal geography on Wednesday, Dr Hammond was fiddling with an elastic band, stroking his hair, constantly pushing his glasses up his nose and I realized that this all interfered with the way he was putting his stuff across. It sort of weakened what he was saying.

On the course we were asked to list some situations in which we needed to be more assertive—well, that thing with Gem is one of them for me. I guess I have been there before when I had a girlfriend in the past. Last year I was with Pip for a bit after Freshers week. I guess we got together because it was easier for both of us to be with someone then rather than not. Pip dumped me after two months because she went off with Mervyn. She said that I was too quiet, except when I got angry. I didn't half get cross then. I was so shocked at what she said. I thought it was all right with us. I had an essay to do and I had to stay in to do it. Her course hadn't really got going. It hurt quite badly (feels hard to admit it). First experience for me I suppose. Me getting cross though . . . does that mean that I am aggressive sometimes? I was really upset. How dare she dump me? The more angry I felt, the more beers I had—what a disaster that was. I think Sam brought me back home.

Maybe I do need to think about when I get cross. Bit strange to be a quiet and an angry person, but I suppose I bottle things up.

OK—situations which I find difficult:

- Bust-ups and dealing with things in relationships.
- Times when a person is waiting for me to respond and I have clammed up. It gets worse.

- *Getting praised. In the cartography session, Tina, the demonstrator, came up behind me and said that my work was really good—the best in the class. I just did not know what to say.*
- *When Karl in our flat spewed all over the floor in the kitchen and did not clear it up. I was all nice to him at the time and then furious later but I could not tell him why I was so cross.*
- *When Merv and Pip came to the debating club and were all over each other right in front of me—doing it on purpose. I left and went to the bar and I had a pint or two too many probably. I think I was quite loud and cross there—Pete said I was, later. What else could I have done?*
- *Yeah I got really irritated in class the other day when mates kept talking to me and I couldn't get down the notes. It's always like that. I didn't say anything to them—didn't want to be seen as sad. I went to the library after but went on feeling irritable about it for the rest of the day. Of course it happened again.*

Mon Feb 21st

OK so I did the wrong thing about the valentine card—just found out I got it all wrong—Gemma has just said that she had three cards (not sure that I believe her). She said that one was boring—a picture of a pretty scene (mine)—it was like someone didn't know how to send a valentine, she said. And she said that the other cards were so cool. No, I really just think she got mine and was disappointed with it. I said nothing. At least I have learned to say nothing sometimes. . . .

The Origins of Assertive Behavior and the Effects of Circumstances

Introduction

This chapter covers the general topic of "contexts"—how place, atmosphere, situation, how we feel, and our histories influence the manner in which we behave. I have divided this chapter into two main topics—the first is about our histories—how we learned to behave assertively or not, and second I focus on the importance of place, situation, and location in determination of behavior. You could call it the "environment" of a situation. The focus will be on the academic situation as a context. There are, too, several small sections. The first is on the influence of the emotional context of an interaction and then there is a small section that relates to the whole chapter. It is on "triggers and barriers" to behaving assertively, nonassertively, or aggressively. I refer here to triggers that set off a sense of power or weakness in us, and barriers that can bar assertive behavior in a person in particular situations. Barriers and triggers are important both in looking at the history of your behavior and the way in which you currently behave.

The aim of the chapter is to help you to think about who or what influenced the way in which you behave, and contexts that are relevant to you. It will prompt you to think about the underlying message that regardless of how you have been influenced, you can be different now if you choose to be different.

Where Behavior Comes From—the Effects of our Histories

There are two obvious origins for behavior—it is genetic, or it comes from your own experiences—and it is not possible to disentangle the effects of these two. For example, Tom, whose journal you have been reading, is relatively nonassertive. Is it because he was born that way, or because of the experiences he has had? His genetic predisposition may have meant that he had a relatively soft voice and shy disposition. His parents may have cajoled him to "stand on his own two feet," or they may have told him to revere others, not to question their judgments and to speak only when spoken to. They might have said "Respect your olders and betters" or "Children are to be seen and not heard" and "You should always mind your p's and q's"—and so on. In school, Tom may have found himself in a social group of quieter peers and stayed withdrawn, or he may have been picked on as a quiet student and this may have encouraged him then to carry on keeping his head down. Genetic predispositions and experiences interact to create the current behavior. What is important is that you can change. I reiterate the message of Chapter 2 (page 22)—Dweck's idea—that people do change and that not believing that you can change is likely, itself, to be a negative influence on your life. You are not stuck with they way you are and it is not just a matter of waiting for different experiences to mold you by chance. However, change often takes deliberate effort.

If I draw a line between extremely assertive and extremely nonassertive behavior on the page (as follows) with a mid-line marker in the middle, where would you say that you fitted as a child? Mark a range somewhere on the line. Of course this will be a huge generalization.

Nonassertive behavior ————————————— Assertive behavior

Where do you fit now?

What has been behind the shift between assertive and nonassertive behavior?

Of course there are likely to be particularly strong influences on behavior from various agencies. For most of us these agencies would include parents, school, peer group, and work colleagues, many of whom would usually also be influenced by your common cultural background. Sometimes brothers and sisters in the same family might have different experiences of "being shaped" as assertive or nonassertive by parents who consider that boys should be "strong" and "go ahead" and girls should be more retiring and meek. These attitudes were much stronger in the past, and there is now more equality for girls in terms of the expectation of what girls can do with their lives. In some countries, though, the distinctions between the expected behavior of males and females is retained and enforced. In these places such attitudes can make as much sense to the population as our cultural attitudes to gender make to us.

You have seen in the previous chapter (Chapter 4) that I have been using commonly-used phrases to suggest the rules that we tend to follow (e.g. "Children should be seen and not heard"). There are thousands of them for many situations in our lives and they are usually shorthand ways of cajoling or expressing attitudes about someone's behavior. They are, like other matters in this chapter, influences on the way in which we are or are not assertive. It is interesting to bring some of those back from your childhood experiences—they may help you to see how others attempted to shape your behavior. Here are some phrases.

"That'll make your hair curl."
"Eat up! It'll make a good strong boy."

"Stand up for yourself."

"That'll make a man of you."

"What would the neighbours think?"

"You look like you've come through a hedge backwards."

"I don't know where we went wrong with you."

"Now [name], well now, *he's* a nice boy." (with emphasis as italicized)

"Stand on your own two feet."

"Faint heart never won fair lady."

"Go out and show them who you are."

In effect, many of these comments are attempts by one person, for right or wrong or unthought-through reasons, to impose her will on another. When I say "unthought-through," I have in mind particularly parents, who may transmit the same messages to their children as were transmitted to them by their parents—without reevaluation of the ideas.

> What would be the attitude of your parents—or those who had influence on you as a child—about the kind of person they would have liked you to be in terms of assertiveness, nonassertiveness, and aggression? You might want to bear in mind that many people think of aggression as equated with assertiveness and they may see assertiveness as "being selfish." You might want to take that into account.

In talking about the various influences on your life in terms of assertiveness, I need to say again that while it can be helpful to think about how others have wanted you to be and worked at shaping you, you are now responsible yourself about how you operate in the big, wide world. Your history may mean that you are well-prepared to stand up for yourself as an independent and effectively assertive person, or you may have a lot of ground to cover to become that person. Some therapies would suggest that your current behavior is totally related to the past and you need to go back to that event to resolve it and free you in the present ("She had a bad childhood and that is why she is as she is"). My work as a therapist has led me to believe that the past is an influence, but we can survive it and change. We hear about those who have trouble leaving the past behind. We do not hear the stories of the vast numbers of people who have come through extremely difficult times and thrive effectively in the present.

The Effect of Context

Now we move to the present situation. In this section, I am going to be looking at the way in which the environment we are in affects the manner in which we communicate. This includes the influence of the place and situation and who the people are (not just what they say). It also involves some less obvious features, whether or not we are conscious of them—time of day, year (anniversary), smells, lighting, ambient sound, atmosphere . . . and so on, though I am not going to try deal with them all separately.

We start with the matter of furniture . . .

A group of English literature students has been asked to develop a joint critique of the novels of a certain author. Because they live near each other, members of the group have decided to meet at Steve's house. They sit around the table but there are not enough chairs so Allan sits on a low stool at the table. Allan usually has plenty to contribute, but today he is quiet except when he stands up and wanders around (saying that he needs to stretch). Chen comments later to Allan, "You seemed a bit out of it today." Allan agrees, but it is only later that he realizes that it is because the discussion was going on over his head and it was his low-level position that had much to do with his inability to interact and contribute.

The way in which furniture is arranged can affect social situations as well as more formal situations. With a colleague, I was involved in interviewing someone for a research studentship recently. The room had been set up in advance and the interviewee arrived early and was already in the room when I arrived. My colleague was on his office chair, the interviewee was on a hard plastic chair and what was left was the soft, more casual chair that was a lot lower. Shifting chairs round at that stage was not appropriate. During the whole of the interview I felt acutely aware of sitting below the interviewee and as a result feeling ambiguous about my role there. It was difficult to question someone from below! Certainly in the past in some universities, the status of a student, a research assistant, a lecturer, head of department, or professor was demonstrated by the nature of the chair that was provided. I cannot say that this was related to the height of the chair (we all have legs that need to fit under desks) but higher status chairs had arms and were more padded. In old-fashioned sets of dining chairs, there is often one with arms for the male head of the family. It signified status.

> Can you think of other ways in which relative importance and power is demonstrated in the relative heights and qualities of furniture? This is particularly relevant to work situations.

The arrangement of a teaching room also has an influence on the kinds of interaction that happen. I run many day workshops with teaching staff and I frequently do rapid room rearrangements in order to facilitate discussion between participants. I always encourage participation.

Trying to disregard the influence of the tutor/lecturer, can you think of rooms that seem to facilitate interaction in seminars or tutorials and rooms that discourage interaction? Can you identify why that is?

Think of some of the rooms in which you have seminars or tutorials—where would you sit in order to feel you had the most "voice"? Where would you sit if you wanted to be least involved?

Where does your tutor invite you to sit in relation to her/him in her/his room? Does the seating position help or hinder your ability to express yourself?

As I have hinted above, desks have a lot to do with signifying status or position and creating patterns of communication. As a shortish person, I find talking over a high desk to some sort of official is difficult. Where does your doctor sit—behind a desk or beside it?

We step away now from the arrangement of rooms to the status of place. Do you remember how you felt about the idea of college or university before you arrived, and when you arrived? Here is what a mature student said about the prospect of going to university following an access course:

"There was a mixture of feeling when I came to university. I was excited but also very afraid. The fear tended to overcome the excitement. I felt I did not know the standard of work expected and I expected not to be able to reach it. I did not feel that I would be able to say anything in groups or that I would understand what was being said in lectures."

Maybe university seems more daunting because there are people alled "Doctor" or "Professor" or designated "Head of Department, Faculty and School." Colleges and universities have a strong sense of hierarchy and one of the functions of hierarchy is to make you feel you know your place. For most of you, when you first arrive you are not just a student, but a first-year student, and being a "first-year" notionally puts you into a lower position than students in later years. It is when you are a "first-year" that you most need to ask questions, find where to go, feel you have a "voice" in this new place—and ironically it is when the hierarchy of the place puts you at the greatest disadvantage, though this is always true of being new to something.

Damion is a first year student at the University of Central Northlands. He and his fellow students are given the names of the tutors to whom they have been allocated. Most of the others have tutors who are Dr this and that. Damion finds that his tutor is a Professor McKay. He feels daunted and wonders how he will have the courage to say anything—imagining this professor as old, grey, and serious. He dreads the first meeting. (Actually Professor McKay is younger than his mother, female, wears jeans, and smiles a lot. She tells her group of tutees to call her Sandy.)

Academia as a Distinct Kind of Context

Although I have described assertiveness in relation to nonassertiveness, aggression, and manipulation, the main "opposite" to assertiveness in this section is nonassertiveness. Nonassertiveness is displayed in many different ways and sometimes it appears as a form of non-engagement. For example:

- Avoiding challenge when facing it would be good for your learning.
- Not seeking information when you are unclear about something (or asking fellow students when you really need the advice of a tutor).
- Not speaking clearly and loudly enough to properly express yourself.
- In parallel to the above, not expressing yourself clearly in your written work.
- Not dealing effectively with disappointment (e.g. about marks).
- In a group, letting others dictate how the group is to be run (again, not letting your voice be heard).
- Giving way to temptations such as cheating and plagiarism—in other words, giving way to dishonesty.

In this section I want to get you to think about how you find various situations affect you and your behavior, so instead of just listing the situations I will provide a couple of examples of how people might be nonassertive and hopefully how to be assertive will be evident from this. Some of the situations, of course, will not be relevant to your stage in education or the manner in which your program is structured.

Can you think of any other academic contexts than these? There may well be some more that are related to your particular discipline (e.g. studio sessions if you are in the practicing arts, crits if you are learning to teach, and so on). See if you can add at least one more situation with two little scenarios to illustrate nonassertive behavior.

You will see that in academic situations, assertiveness includes the notions of accepting challenge, being prepared, taking difficult things head-on, being upfront and so on. You could see it as asserting yourself as a person, rather than assertiveness as just something in interactions. We return to this list in the exercises section of this chapter (pages 70–71).

Emotional Contexts for Assertiveness

Another context in which assertiveness sits is the emotional context. As with the other contexts mentioned in this chapter, the main task at present is to be aware of the influences of emotional experience on how assertive you feel you can be.

Table 5.1 Examples of nonassertive, or nonengaged behaviour in areas of academic work

Area of work	Examples of nonassertive behaviour in this area of work
Exams	• You are terrified and the emotion gets in the way of your ability to perform (we all get anxious about exams and you need to learn to seek help and learn to relax). • You do not get organized with revision sufficiently early. You make excuses when you do not do as well as you expected ("I learn better under pressure at the last moment"—rubbish—that is not good learning even if you pass the exam). For more information on these and other issues to do with failure and disappointment, see Chapter 10.
Seminars	• You give a paper in a quiet voice, not looking at the audience and not expressing yourself. • You say "I cannot be bothered to prepare for the session. It is boring," and you do not get involved with any discussion (but you would not be able to, anyway, as you are not prepared!).
Vivas	• You are daunted by Professor Zeal , your examiner, and are very conscious of being "only a student," and lose confidence in the research on which you are being examined. • Professor Zeal makes a minor criticism of your research methods and you promptly drop your voice and feel almost apologetic instead of trying to counter his comment (you had recognized that this matter might be raised and can justify your decision to do the research in this way).
Attendance at a lecture	• The lecture is printed out in reasonable detail on the web. You attend it, but do not listen very much because you say "I can get it afterwards." You probably will not do this because you are going out tonight. • Your friend is paying close attention and writing detailed notes. You tease her afterwards for being so attentive to what you declare is a boring lecture.
Peer and self-assessment	• Your general attitude is that your tutors are being employed to teach you and therefore should not be asking you to "do their work" of assessing (and actually you find assessing yourself or your peers difficult). • You have done a good piece of work and you know it, but you do not like to give yourself a good mark in self assessment ("It looks bad," you say). • Your friend has done a poor piece of work and you feel you cannot give it the mark you feel it deserves, when asked to assess it in a peer assessment scheme. Your friend might find out you were the one who gave her that mark.
Group work	• You have managed to get into a group for a laboratory task in which there are several students who are "on the ball" with regards to the current task. You feel pleased and settle back to listen, saying "I don't know anything, tell me what to do." • Your group is not doing very well in the set laboratory task (lasting over two weeks). You all get low marks, and you tell your friend that it is because you ended up with a dumb group.
Supervision situations (postgraduate)	• Your research is not going well—you just cannot get started. You blame your supervisor, saying she is not being sufficiently helpful. • Your supervisor is not giving you the time you have been told you should get with him. You do need his help, but you grumble to the other research students and do not do anything about it.
Research seminars	• Another research student critically comments on what you have just said in your paper. You realize that what she has said is a correct observation. You know you have actually made a mistake, but fudge around the issue, hoping to have avoided admitting you made the mistake.

	•	An outside speaker of some reputation is giving a paper. You notice that he has glossed over an issue that seems to you to be important. However, you do not like to query what he is saying because of his reputation and because he is a guest speaker.
Tests	•	You make an excuse for not doing well when you knew that you did not learn the material sufficiently.
	•	You have not revised for the test and you ring in to your tutor and say you are ill.
Written reports of lab work	•	Things went wrong in the lab and instead of giving a critical account of the things that went wrong, you make up a set of results.
	•	Your work did not go well so you borrow the notes of a friend saying you just want to see how she has written up the work, and you copy them.
Online discussion	•	Your tutor has said that the idea of the dedicated chat room is that you should be able to learn from your peers. You look at the discussion, but you feel that you have not got anything to say and do not engage with it.
	•	You are asked to read a given piece of text and then to comment on it in at least two postings. You read the text and seek out two minor issues in order to make the required posting.
Essays	•	Your essay title requires you to compare and contrast two theoretical approaches to something. You put the titles of the theories into Google and actually find that someone else has posted an essay on this. You turn off your own thinking processes and paraphrase the material. You reference it so you have not plagiarized, but you are guessing that that the reference will not be checked because there are 200 of you on the course. It was an easy way to do the essay.
	•	You know that your English is not very good (you are not dyslexic). You ask your husband to read through your essay and improve it for you. You hand in the corrected version without looking at it again.
Presentation of yourself in a CV prepared in careers session	•	You have been asked to write a CV in a careers session. You have little confidence in yourself and the CV reads as a listing of educational qualifications and a few holiday jobs. It has no "personality".
	•	You are in your second year at university. You have a good loan and are enjoying life. You do not want to think about careers or to bother with a CV at present.
Critical review of an academic paper	•	You do not like to make critical comments about a published academic paper ("I am only a student . . . how can I be in a position to criticize this paper by an academic?")
	•	There is a point that you could make that you are pretty sure is justified but since there are several more superficial points, you make them instead and do not take the risk (it would have involved some harder thinking, too).
Giving papers at a student conference	•	Well actually it is more a matter of opting out. Volunteers were asked to give papers and you thought it sounded like too much hard work.
	•	You give your paper in a hesitating manner and apologise for it at the end of the presentation.
Placement experiences	•	You are in a placement that you did not choose. You do the minimum that you have to do in the current placement but are clearly not interested and you blame this on the placement not being your preferred choice.
Written reflective work (e.g. reflective practice on placements; learning journals, etc.)	•	You have been asked to write a learning journal for a health studies module. It seems hard work to write up reflections on the course as required, so you wait "for inspiration." Suddenly you are asked to hand it in at the end of the week so you have to write it all up at once—and you begin to realize that it is not so difficult to make some of it up.
	•	You have been involved in a difficult incident at work because you made a mistake. It bothers you a lot and affects your work but you decide not to put it into your journal.

In the chapters on managing better (Chapters 7, 8, and 9—in particular 9) there will be a substantial discussion of ways in which to cope better with emotion. We introduce the idea that your emotional state is a context that affects the manner of interactions. We start here, with a couple of scenarios:

> Serena is an architecture student, working on her final-year project. She is designing a house to accommodate three single mothers and their children. It has been a bad day—things have gone wrong from the start. Her young son is unwell and she had to beg her mother to come round and look after him—and then the kettle broke. She is working on the computer model in the studio when Jerry, her supervisor, comes in. He asks her to talk about how she is getting on. The "bad day" feelings influence her and she gives a rather impoverished account of her progress (she is actually doing well). Jerry is evidently not terribly impressed—and Serena ends up feeling worse.

> Della is a fashion design student and is very competitive—she has always been like that. She is regarded as one of the best students in the cohort. At the end of her second year, there is a show of work that is meant to prepare students for the more formal show in the final year of the degree program. Della feels that she can outshine the efforts of the others, but several days before the show she happens to see the design created by Mike, a fellow student, and she ruefully acknowledges that Mike's work is extremely good. The confidence that she felt earlier evaporates and she finds it hard to organize the final presentation. In particular, it affects the manner in which she tackles the reflective account that she has to write. She feels a sense of irritation that Mike has stolen her thunder.

Here are some of the emotional influences that can affect the academic side of your life as a student:

- Falling in love.
- Other reasons for extreme excitement.
- Stress and worry about coursework, or examinations, or getting assignments in.
- Tight research deadlines (e.g. at postgraduate level).
- Extreme competitiveness.
- Failure or serious disappointments about grades.
- Negative feedback or serious criticism that you cannot cope with.
- Not feeling that you know what is expected of you.
- Feeling "down" for various personal reasons—for example you are ill.
- Feeling you are on the wrong course, and being unsure whether or how to change things, and so on.

We would not be normal if we did not experience some of these feelings at some times, but it is a matter of how much they affect us and how well we can carry on with the demands of—in this case—student life. Sometimes emotions will be so strong that anyone would crumble—and events that can cause that are not just deaths and dire events, but also the good fortune to fall seriously in love. In this and other very "high" states people can lose perspective on the world outside their own good fortune. Also, I need to bring back into this section the experience of aggression because sometimes people react aggressively when they are stressed by the kinds of situations mentioned above. I think that the word "tetchy" is useful for describing this kind of edgyness.

> Think of three occasions when your emotional state—positive or negative—has affected the manner in which you have related to others or your academic work—whether you have been more assertive, or less, or aggressive.

Barriers and Triggers

This section is relevant to all of the contexts that I have mentioned in this chapter. I want to make it clear that different contexts contain what we might call triggers and barriers that work differently for different individuals. Serena's bad day (see above) might have triggered her into feeling more aggressive about her work and more willing to promote her progress in conversation with her tutor. Some people thrive better as environments become more competitive. This might have spurred Della on. We cannot tell in advance what will influence others. What we can do is to learn as much as we can about what triggers us in disadvantageous ways. I am, for example, competitive but if I sense that someone is doing better than me, I am apt to crumble like Della.

Triggers and barriers lead you to behave in particular way, and sometimes make it difficult for you to shift from that stance.

Al and Derry are in the kitchen of their shared house. They were all in hall last year and they are all new to this state of relative independence—and they do not know each other very well yet. Al is preparing spaghetti bolognaise. Sheepishly he asks Derry how long it takes spaghetti to cook. She comes up with a fork and draws out a strand of spaghetti.

"Al, it is too soft already. You cooked it too long. Why didn't you ask me earlier? Now, how are you getting on with the sauce? Oh I see you didn't fry the mince first . . . you should do that for the flavour. . . ." She goes on. Al feels a sense of familiarity. He would like to tell her to "get off his back." This situation reminds him of his older sister's constant overseeing of his activities. He finds that when he tries to tell Derry that he is doing all right and can manage, his voice has shrunk—just as it does with his sister.

When Al sits in front of the television in the lounge later and Derry asks quite innocently if he enjoyed his meal, he cannot help but treat her with the defensiveness that he puts up with his older sister. "It was fine," he says, curtly. A trigger has happened and a barrier has gone up.

Of course there might be other triggers and barriers in this context. Derry might have a much younger brother who is rather inept at cooking and who welcomes her motherly attitude and involvement when he has to do some cooking. He rewards her with gratitude.

When it comes to it, it does not matter whether the origin of the barrier or trigger is historical for you or more recent, though sometimes the historical ones are harder to shift. All that matters is that you are aware of what blocks you or sets you off. Then you are in a position to do something about it.

Activities and Journal Exercises

Route Map of Developing Assertiveness

Find a way of plotting your route towards being more assertive. You might want to draw something or write something that is about how you would like to be. What is the route towards it (draw it, make cartons, write it, etc.)? See pages 72, 75.

Academic Situations in Which You Might Be Nonassertive

Look through the list of academic situations listed in Table 5.1 above and note which of these situations sounds familiar to you, because you are not happy with your level of assertiveness in those situations. Explore those situations in more detail in your journal.

Ten Situations (2)

In the last chapter I asked you to think of ten situations in which you feel you would like to be more assertive. This could mean that you would be more assertive because you feel you are nonassertive, or more assertive because you are normally aggressive or manipulative. Look back at your list now and edit it. You may want to change the list, restate things—deleting and adding to make up the ten. Since you have read the last chapter, you may have managed things better! Now put the list into an order. Allocate the first position ("1") to the most easy to change item and go down the list from the most easy to change situation to the hardest. Now comes the hard bit—this week, tackle that number 1 on your list. Be more assertive in the best way you can (bearing in mind that there are some more chapters to go!).

Academic Situations

This exercise focuses on academic situations (see Table 5.1, pages 66–7). List five academic situations in which you would like to be more assertive. In the "Ten situations" exercise directly above, you may have included some academic situations that you would like to improve—and you can include those in this exercise. Now put those five into an order of difficulty or—to create a new word—do-ability.

A Challenge a Day . . .

Facing new challenges may or may not always be the same as being assertive in the narrower sense—but it is good practice in helping you to become more assertive. See if you can tackle one new challenge every day. You might want to list it in your journal.

Observing Others

Watch for the assertive and nonassertive behavior of others in the academic situations that you encounter. As you notice these happening, learn from the good examples and think how those who are not being sufficiently assertive could manage better.

The Journals of Christina and Tom

Christina's Journal

Tues Feb 22nd

So it was the course again today—yes, it was good . . . what happened? It was to do with where assertiveness come from and how it affects you. Then we looked at lots of situations in university—like during classes so we could see where it comes in. We did an exercise for this session. We drew a map of how we got to the present in terms of assertiveness—like our histories. Dee called it a Route Map. She suggested that we could do it in our journals and we could compare our lives with that of the person next to us.

OK, done it. I was sitting next to Tom and had to compare my route map with his. I put a lot more on mine than he did and it seemed that his was all about how he was manly and strong and mine was a lot about the times when I did not feel strong. Maybe that is because he is male and me female. I said I liked doing it and he said he did not—funny that, when I put down the negatives, and he the positives.

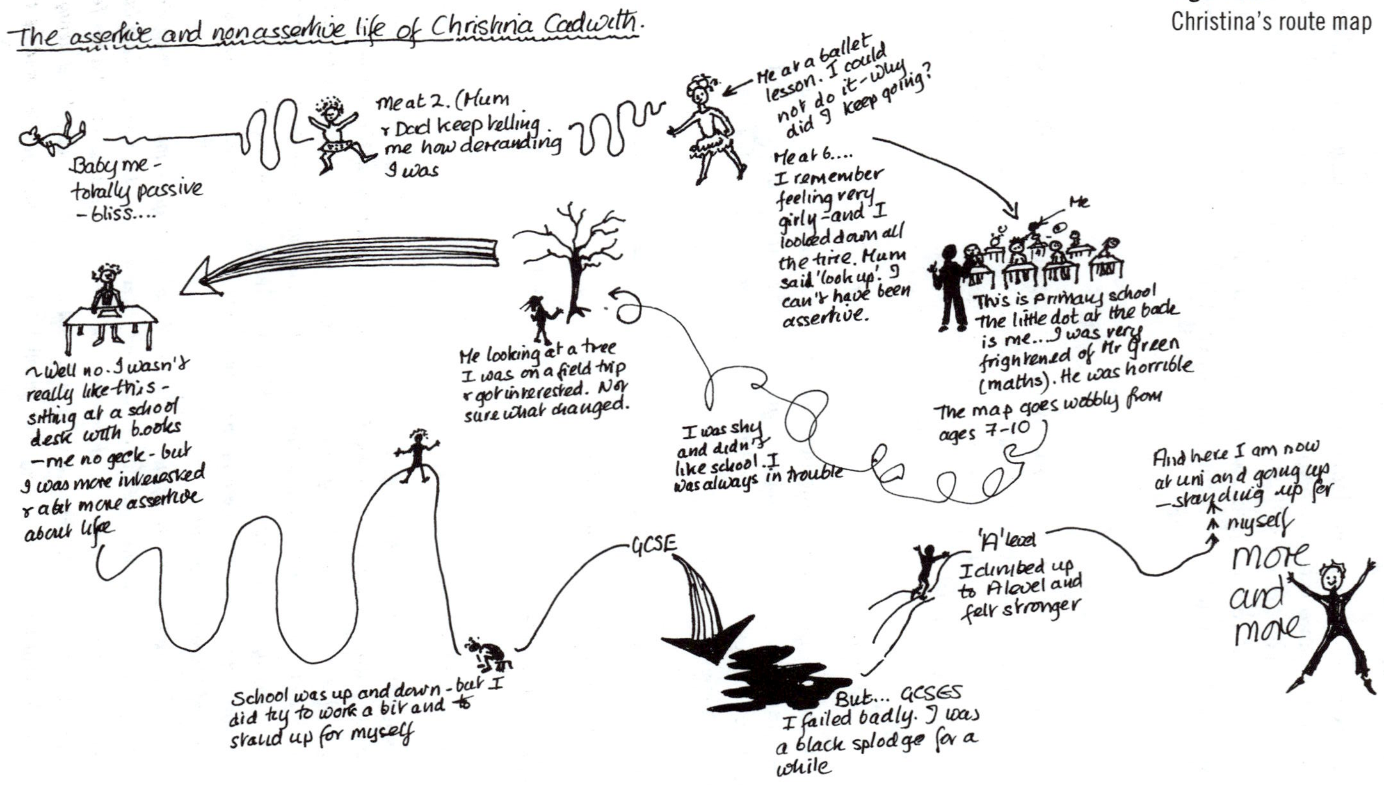

Figure 5.1

Christina's route map

The assertive and nonassertive life of Christina Cadwith.

Baby me – totally passive – bliss….

Me at 2. (Mum & Dad keep telling me how demanding I was)

I did no – I wasn't really like this – sitting at a school desk with books – me no geek – but I was more interested & a bit more assertive about life

He looking at a tree I was in a field & up I got interested. No sure what changed.

Me at a ballet lesson I could do it – why – not do it keep going?

Me at 6…. I remember feeling very girly – and I looked down all the time. Mum said 'look up.' I can't have been assertive.

Me

This is primary school. The little dot at the back is me…I was frightened of Mr Green (maths). He was horrible. The map goes wobbly from ages 7–10

I was shy and didn't like school. I was always in trouble

School was up and down – but I did try to work a bit and stand up for myself

'A' level I climbed up to A level and felt stronger

And here I am now at uni and going up – standing up for myself

more and more

QCSE

But… GCSEs I failed badly. I was a black splodge for a while

Fri Feb 25th

I had a look at the exercises we have to do this week. I am asked to think of times when I feel I could do with being more assertive. I will list them:

> *I have difficulty in group work. We do lots of groupwork in the lab and have demonstrators to help us with things. Sometimes the group does not really know what to do—like with staining the specimens the other day—and it is hard to get the attention of a demonstrator. I feel so helpless at those times. Even if I could guess at what we should be doing (and sometimes I do think I know), I would not dare to tell the group what to do.*

> *I've said about my difficulties with seminars, not wanting to talk and how Mo was so good. I guess that is a situation that is getting better now.*

> *In the library I often do not know where to find references and I wander round for hours looking. There are information desks but I am not very good at going and admitting that I don't know something because I don't know if others do know and it is just me or if it is a problem for everyone. Maybe I could ask that in this assertiveness course sometime. I am sure they told us all about using the library at induction and I obviously wasn't listening.*

> *Giving in our first assignment was terrifying—that essay on plant taxonomy. I'd no idea what was expected. Everyone else seemed so clever. I thought that they all knew everything and I was the only one who didn't.*

> *I found it hard when the marks came out from that first assignment. I did quite well and some of the others, with whom I was getting to be friendly, were really cold for a couple of days and called me a teacher's pet. Me, who was in so much trouble at school for years, a geek. Never!! I decided then I would not try so hard in the next assignment.*

I've written more than I meant to today . . .

Tom's Journal

Tues Feb 22nd

I have been to the academic assertiveness session. It was especially good since Gemma could not come today (she had a late class) and I realized that I got on a lot better without her sort of overseeing me. I felt more like a participant in my own right there—not someone who sort of fell into it by accident. We had to think about a list of academic situations and how assertive we are in them. This was useful as we have been looking at critical thinking in our tutorials and how to do it better. Our tutor, Zhang (from Hong Kong originally—he's really good), says that everyone talks about critical thinking in UK universities and that he did not know what it was when he came to the UK as a student so he is not surprised that we don't know. It's like everyone talks about critical thinking and we all nod our heads and say "Yes, we know what you mean," but inside our heads we are thinking, "Am I the only one who doesn't know what is meant?—I daren't ask—so I go on nodding."

Anyway Zhang said that what helped him with critical thinking were a few things—first that you had to understand that you tend to start at uni thinking that they will tell you lots of facts and you will learn the right ones and not the wrong ones—well you have to move on from that because things aren't simply right and wrong, but we might not know about them. If we don't know, we have theories and you try to decide which theory best fits what is seen or known—and for this you get evidence. The assertive thing then is that you have to get good at making judgments of the evidence and the theories and argue for what you decide you believe. That is critical thinking. So you have to be assertive because it is a challenge to do this, you have to argue your case. Zhang said that you also have to sometimes back off and say that someone else's thinking is actually better than yours—I guess that fits the definition of academic assertiveness that we had at the beginning of the course.

Now I have written all this down—about what Zhang said—I understand it better and it all fits this assertiveness stuff too. It's funny how you change—I thought uni was about learning lots of facts from lecturers who were experts and kind of knew the right answers. I do see it differently now. It is harder this way, but probably more fun.

Fri Feb 25th

I think Gem was a bit jealous because I said a lot about the acadass course.

I am looking at the exercise we were supposed to do. We had to do this route map thing of how we had learned to be assertive or something. Not sure that I can remember much. I'll try it.

Sun Feb 27th

I have been thinking more about situations and assertiveness. I need to get more assertive. For a start I need to deal with Gemma. She came round tonight when I was working—she knew I had stuff to get ready for tomorrow and she went on about how much she wants to go out and we could go into town for a coffee at least or go up to the Union. She was sort of hovering over me. I started to pack up my stuff— I mean, I do like Gem and I did want to go, but I thought—OK now is the time. I looked up at her and I said "Gem, sorry, I have work to do tonight—tomorrow night would be fine but not tonight." I really surprised her—never seen her look like that.

"Oh, you've turned into a right geek. Practising your assertiveness are you Tom? OK—fine. Well I'll go and ask Sam if he fancies going to Café Ele. I was chatting with him before I came up."

This was dodgy. Gem likes Sam and I think he likes her but I just about hung on and took a deep breath and said, "OK Gem—thanks for calling—must get on now".

Figure 5.2
Tom's route map

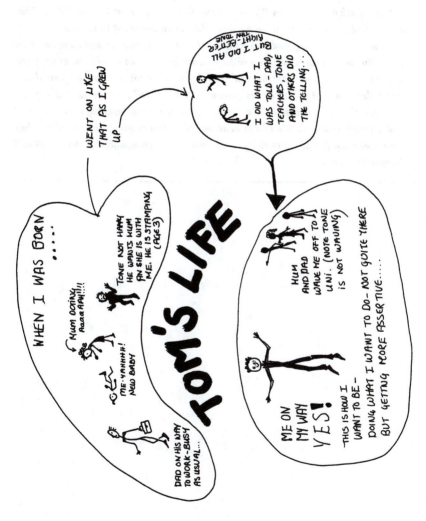

I was sweating and I felt very distracted from the work I was trying to do. Later I kept waiting for Sam to come back in. I kept thinking I should have gone and then I thought—no, I need to do the work for the seminar.

Mon Feb 28th

Another example of nonassertion today—not me, though. Assignments came back today—mark was 2.1—yes OK—but it was interesting about Dave and Pete. They got hauled up to see the Dean because they were supposed to have plagiarized. They were stupid. They had told us all that they were doing it and boasted about how silly we were to be working so hard. Dave got his whole assignment from this web site—don't know what he paid for it. Pete got a lot of help from one of last year's lot who had a similar assignment. It's like, well why are they doing this subject? Phil on the course talked a bit about assertiveness meaning that you would make an effort and tackle things head-on. They're just being passive about their course and not facing up to things sometimes being challenging. I wonder what'll happen to them.

6

As a Human, You Have
Rights and Responsibilities . . .

Introduction

This is a sort of turning point in this book. The chapters up to this point
have provided background to being assertive in the academic context. They have
covered what assertiveness is and how it is displayed. They have compared and
contrasted it to nonassertiveness, aggression, and manipulative behavior,
and looked at how you learn to behave the way you behave and how the context
or environment that you are in is likely to affect your assertiveness.

The focus of those chapters was the development of self-awareness and
awareness of the range of assertive behaviors. In the boxes in the text and in the
activities and exercises at the ends of the chapters, there has been some encouragement for you to think about you . . . but from now on the emphasis is on
change—on learning to manage better and on being different in your more
assertive behaviors. The shift in the text is not a major one—but if you are
following the sequence of this book through it is time to do more than observe
assertive behaviors! Starting can be the hardest part—once you feel more sure
of yourself as an assertive person, situations become easier.

In this chapter I introduce the idea of "rights"—what you could be seen to
have a right to do because you are a human being. The idea that people should
have rights by virtue of their humanity might seem to be a more obvious point
than most of the others expressed. Material on "rights" is a common feature of
books on assertiveness training. There are usually around a dozen "rights" listed
and they are broadly similar to the content of the Universal Declaration of
Human Rights (United Nations General Assembly, 1948—the United Nations
document is reprinted in Alberti and Emmons (1983)). The rights more or less
spell out what it should be to be human—and they apply, importantly, in
academic contexts. There is more than just rights to consider, however. If a
person expects her rights to be upheld, then she should take on the responsibility
to respect the rights of others to fulfil their rights—so always we are really talking
of rights and responsibilities.

The chapter is organized into four main sections beyond this introduction—
two substantial and two small but important parts. In the first section, rights are
listed and there are some general points made about these rights. The second
section mentions some important issues about rights. The third section is about

the human feeling of guilt which is often associated with standing up for rights. It is a mark of its significance that I have put it in as a topic on its own. In the rest of the chapter—the fourth section—I explore the rights in more detail. There are examples and illustrations of these rights in action in relevant situations and further discussion about them, with some tasks for you to do that will help you to think of which of your rights you may feel could do with more attention! There is then a short conclusion.

A List of Rights

There are some differences between the lists of rights in different publications; the rights included often depends on the people for whom the list is designed. For example in books written for those in work situations or specifically for women, the lists relate to work or women's issues. The list that I have developed is quite long because there seem to be many rights to discuss in the context of being a student, but I will deal with the items in groups. You will see that many of the rights have a direct link to the definition of academic assertiveness on pages 5, 10, 23.

Rights are listed below. In writing the list I have modified the words, because otherwise reading them becomes tedious! I have grouped the rights into "general rights" (those that have a general application) and those that have specific relevance to educational situations. This will enable me to manage the discussion (below) more helpfully. There are large overlaps between the rights.

General Rights

- You have a right to be respected as equal as a human being to other human beings, and as intelligent and capable.
- You have a right to be treated as a person independently of any role that you may carry.
- You have a right to maintain control over your body, the things that you own, and your time.
- You do not need to justify or excuse your own reasonable behavior.
- You have a right to say "yes" or "no" for yourself.
- You can ask for what you want (though, of course, you should accept the right of the other to decline your request).
- You can decline to care about something or—within reason—can decline to take responsibilities for dealing with the needs or problems of others.

Rights Relevant to Academic Situations

Rights that, in addition to general application, have a particular relevance to situations of academic work:

- You have a right to express your feelings, opinions and values in an appropriate manner and have them respected. You also have a right to withhold your expressions and you have a right not to make sense to others!
- You can make your own decisions and deal with the consequences.
- You have a right to be different. You can have needs or express opinions and values that are different from those of others.
- You have a right to privacy, solitude, and independence.
- You have a right to say that you do not understand something or do not know something and you have a right to ask for clarification.
- You can make a mistake, though you would expect to take responsibility for it.
- You can change your mind.
- As a human being, you have a right sometimes to fail at endeavours. You *will* sometimes fail at endeavours.

In constructing this list, as well developing my own approach to rights, I have drawn from Alberti and Emmons (1983), Back and Back (1982), Dickson (1982), Gillen (1992), Lindenfield (1987), Rees and Graham (1991), and Smith (1975). All thse books deal in some form with human rights.

At first glance, which three "rights" catch your attention? Why have you been attracted by them? Is it because of a recent event to which they are relevant—or to an issue of a long-term nature?

I particularly like the chance to discuss rights in the development of assertiveness. There is a certain comfortable sense of liberation that can emerge as one thinks through the list of rights and their implications. It is good, for example, to reflect on the fact that everyone makes mistakes or fails sometimes, and that it is not a cardinal sin but simply a normal part of being human. To be able to say "Sorry, I made a mistake" and feel all right about it can be liberating, particularly if you are under imposed or self-imposed pressures always to succeed.

Can you think of a time when you could simply have said "Sorry, I made a mistake" instead of drumming up excuses?

Some Important Issues About "Rights"

There are two main issues here. The first of these is so important that I have mentioned it already on the first page of this chapter—that if you take on a right, you should responsibly accept that others have that right as well. Sometimes two people's rights are in conflict and then it is a matter of negotiation, and a willingness to give-and-take, not just to "seize" them is an important feature of a truly assertive person.

> Lisa and Jilda are postgraduate students who share a room. Lisa wants to be alone in her space to do some writing. Jilda wants to discuss her research with another colleague in the same room. It is a cold night and there is no-where else to go. . . .

The other—and related—point is that the list of rights is to be considered with care. You should be thoughtful about your rights. I will explore some matters about rights that need particular thought.

First, since higher education institutions are becoming more and more culturally and racially mixed, there is a particular need to think of cultural and racial issues. The interpretation of rights can vary according to religious, cultural or national settings, and not everyone will feel that they relate to the same list. Another implicit right, therefore, is to uphold or decline to follow whichever reasonable rights you choose. It might be helpful to think of it in this way. The existence of the Universal Declaration of Human Rights implies that there is a list common to all humans, but through choice or chance of birth we become a member of groups that may restrict our rights in various ways. Gender, religions, nations and their cultures, disabled people, families, schools, clubs and associations, and higher education institutions are examples in their various ways. In the absence of a better word, I will call these human groupings. In being born into these groupings or in joining them, we adopt their rules and their attitudes to, and handling of, rights. There may be a "payoff" which keeps us in that group despite restrictions. For example, it is good to be part of a common culture, or in terms of higher education institutions as "a human grouping"; though it restricts your rights, you anticipate the reward of a degree. We may join and leave groupings and sometimes forget to leave the restrictions behind. For example, we leave school, but at first may take its restrictions with us and initially treat higher education like school.

It would be foolish if I suggested that to be assertive you should always adhere to these rights and restate them vigorously if they are threatened. They are to be applied or not applied thoughtfully. You will often decide not to take up your right because that is the appropriate judgment in that situation. Harry provides an example of this:

> Harry has had an accident when he was playing in the student basketball team. He is in a wheelchair for a couple of weeks. His parents visit him and they go out for a pub meal. Harry notices, to his horror, that the barman asks his father what Harry might like to drink. His father asks Harry and then tells the barman for him. Harry is only too aware of what is going on

and is about to tell the barman that he can speak for himself, and he will make sure that his father knows that too. However, he holds back. His parents have come a long way to see him and he wants to maintain a comfortable atmosphere.

For Harry, being assertive here is being aware of what is happening, and how his rights (and those of other disabled people) are being abused, and taking a reasoned decision not to say anything.

Because these issues about rights are so important, I will summarize them.

- If you expect to have rights, you should expect to have responsibilities to allowing others to have rights.
- Rights are to be asserted in a considered and thoughtful manner.
- There are different attitudes to rights in different cultures, religions, and racial and other human group memberships. The different attitudes are to be respected.
- You may often choose to forego your rights.

Looking at the list of rights, think of or make up a situation in which you, or another person, has deliberately *not* stood up for your/her rights because you have judged that the situation is such that it is better to stay quiet.

Guilt

I now deviate a little from the actual topic of rights to consider the issue of guilt—because when people assert their rights, they often, as a consequence, feel guilty. Because others can learn about how and when someone with whom they interact experiences guilt, guilt itself can become an important form of control. Others use it to get us to do what they want us to do.

Let us think about what guilt is. I see guilt as a "wake-up" call that is a response to a current anticipated situation. It seems as if an all-knowing "conscience" is telling me that I have made a wrong judgment and should think again. That conscience may be appropriate—but it may also be reissuing messages from the past that are associated with what parents or others might have said to me. Or it may be associated with what rules I have set for myself—or with moral or religious dictates that at some time I have taken on. On this basis, guilt can mislead us. In the context of rights, guilt may well be what others try to engender in us in order to get us to give up our rights and accede to what they want us to do. To summarize what I am saying here, treat the feeling of guilt not as a sure message that you have done something wrong, but as an alarm that has been triggered—and there are matters to which attention should be paid and judged to be relevant or not relevant to the present situation.

The other thing to say about guilt is that it is an individual experience. Indeed, it is often a physical sensation. While it is common to say "You make me feel guilty," actually no one can *make* another feel guilty. If I feel guilty, it is because I have put the feeling there myself. It is my feeling—even if I consciously did not intend to experience the feeling—it is all still me!

Think of an occasion when you have experienced guilt in a situation where the guilt was a leftover and not relevant to the current situation.

Your Rights and your Responsibilities

In this section I will take these rights and the associated responsibilities—sometimes individually, sometimes in groups—and I will illustrate them with one or more scenarios. I have divided the rights into those that are more general and those that have particular relevance to academic work and have used scenarios that are from the social experiences of student life for the first group and from academic situations for the second group. This is an arbitrary division and is just a means of focusing on the rights that are particularly important for academic situations. Any of the rights has relevance in any situation.

List of General Rights

You have a right to be respected as equal as a human being by other human beings, and as intelligent and capable.

You have a right to be treated as a person independently of any role that you may carry.

These are important and basic statements. They are not saying that everyone is equal in ability or job or in ambition—but that every human being is of equal value as a person regardless of individual differences. This means that people are equal in value regardless of physical differences, and so are people from different social and cultural backgrounds. This "right" runs into controversy in a number of social debates, such as that concerning abortion—does a foetus have the rights of a person—and what about a coma patient? There are still plenty of issues around the unequal treatment of the genders in modern society. There are many situations in which I think "I am treated like this because I am a woman." Sometimes I comment and sometimes I choose not to comment.

> Sara Jane is a student. She needs to get a job in the summer vacation and goes into a shop in the nearby town. They have been advertising for summer staff. The manager very pleasantly asks her to tell him a bit about

her background and experience and she says that she is a student. His face drops a little. "Ah well," he says, "I'm sorry but actually the vacancy has been filled." Sarah Jane is bemused.

"But you wanted summer staff," she says.

"The post is not available," he repeats. Sarah Jane leaves.

It seems that he does not want a student. Her role has determined her ability to get a job. She feels mistreated.

I could repeat the same scenario for many different people. Let us consider what Sara Jane might have said in this situation—which probably would not have changed the manager's mind, but might at least have helped her to feel better.

"The post is not available," he repeats, and Sara Jane considers what might be going on.

She says, "What is it about students that makes them unacceptable for this post?"

The manager does not expect to be confronted and does not seem to know what to say. Eventually he says, "In my experience, they are unsatisfactory as workers. They talk and mess around and do not concentrate."

She says calmly, "I accept what you are saying, and I realize that you do not want to employ me—but I think you are making a big generalization."

Sara Jane's friend later tells her that this shop owner has a reputation for liking to boss staff around. He seems to feel threatened by having staff who are brighter than him, and who perhaps see the realities of how poorly he manages the business.

A situation in which this right may be particularly relevant is for women with families, who choose to go back into education. They may find that family and others around them expect them to continue to prioritize their wifely and family duties over their studies, regardless of the role of the husband. Why should this be? They are people!

There are countless examples of situations in which inequality is demonstrated for those from ethnic minorities, people who are disabled, and those who look different or sound different from the rest of the population. Prejudice, lack of understanding, or fear may be one factor behind this.

Can you think of a situation in which either of the two rights discussed above were abused with regard to something that concerned you? Did you stand up for yourself? If you cannot think of a personal example, try imagining a situation in which this right was abused.

You have a right to maintain control over your body, the things that you own, and your time.

If you wish to be fat, you can be fat. If you wish to smoke, you can smoke. Others have a right to wish you to be different (and to breathe clean air). They may cajole you or try to educate you to be different. It may even be sensible for you to become different—but it is your body! In the case of smoking, others can decline to tolerate the smoke you produce, too. It is interesting to think about the processes going on at the stage at which you attained control over your body and how you clothe it, your hairstyle and more generally your emergence from parental control over body, time, and possessions. It is easy to forget the responsibilities that go with this right of control of yourself. The measure of your maturity and thoughtfulness will be reflected in your ability to negotiate a fair balance of rights and responsibilities with those others who are affected by your behavior. Parents are often rightly or wrongly worried about their children's behavior with regard to their bodies. Someone else's worry is like a nagging pain.

What can you recall of the ages at which you felt you had achieved your rights to dress as you wanted and have choice in your hairstyle?

If you were/are a parent, what do you think about the age at which children should be given rights to dress as they want and have the hairstyles they want? (Is it possible to just state an age or do you need to say more about the conditions of this granting of rights?)

Helen is in her second year at university and is home for the summer. This year, she has got used to going out without having anyone worrying about the time she gets in. If she goes out late, she sleeps in late—no problem! At home, Helen goes clubbing with her old school friends. They get in at 3.00 a.m. and Helen sleeps well into the next day. She is shocked to find her mother very angry about the time she arrived back home. She says she is concerned about Helen's safety and she is upset because Helen is still in bed at midday.

There could be several stages to this one. First, why should Helen's right to go out be infringed? She manages the consequences of late night and tiredness in the morning perfectly well at university.

Helen tells her mother that she is used to going out late without having to explain her behavior to anyone, and besides, she says, coming in late does not need to affect her or her father. Her mother comes back immediately with the argument that she could not sleep because she was worried about Helen and therefore she is affected by Helen's behavior. Helen tells her, "You don't have to stay awake—that's up to you."

Her mother is very upset now and argues back, "I worry all the time about you and your safety and your sleep. . . . You just try being a parent. Just try thinking what's like for me . . . ! You do what we say in our home. . . ." She walks off.

Helen is upset and thinks about the situation. She knows that her mother cares and worries, but she needs to feel she can act as an independent person. When things have calmed down, Helen talks to her mother. She explains her point of view but acknowledges their worry about tiredness and safety. She says she will tell her mother what time she is expecting to come in, who she will be with and where she will be, and agrees to phone if the details change. However, she says that she *does* need to sleep on in the mornings if she has a late night. Helen points out that she is living as an independent person—and that many of her school friends are in flats of their own and not living with parents. Helen's mother begins to understand a bit better. It is a compromise, perfect for neither, but at least one that they can both live with.

> What do you think about the rights and responsibilities here, and how would you handle it?

In the same way, what you do with your time is up to you, so long as you take responsibility for it. In other words, if you fail to get an essay in on time because you left it too late, you should recognize that your time management failed and you have to bear the consequences. We are good at finding excuses for being late for deadlines but it can be liberating to be honest here—and not to have the stress of making up stories that you know others see through. Try saying: "I got my timing wrong. It was my fault and I accept the consequences."

In terms of possessions I will take some personal examples. I give money mainly to Oxfam and Amnesty International—that is my choice. When other charities send letters or wave poppies in my face, I usually say, "I support Oxfam—that is my chosen charity." This allows me to deal with the charity boxes at Christmas and it feels comfortable to me. I do sometimes give to other charities if I feel a reason so to do. On the whole, I do not lend books either. So many times I have looked for a book and remember that I lent it to someone in the past and it has not come back. Not lending is my choice and again I stand firm on it. In the case of precious books that I like to lend, to hear what another person thinks about the book, I try to get a second copy for lending.

You have a right to say "yes" or "no" for yourself.

You do not need to justify or excuse your own reasonable behavior.

You can ask for what you want. (Of course, you should accept the right of the other to decline your request.)

Have you been in a situation where someone has said "yes" or "no" on your behalf? I gave a classic example of this above (Harry, page 80). The title of a UK radio program for disabled people (*Does He Take Sugar?* epitomizes the point). To respond to a communication for another, in the presence of the other, can often be a form of controlling behavior.

> Josh has a new girlfriend called Marie. He is pleased to be with her. They are out with mutual friends and one of the friends asks them to a party. Josh keenly answers "Yes please" for both of them. Marie feels a bit put out because he has not asked her if she wants to go or if she has the date free.

Marie might have felt put out, but not conscious of why she felt like that—or she might have held back from saying something because it would then have embarrassed Josh. She might have said, "Josh, please let me answer for myself—what was the date?". In our scenario she might let that occasion pass by but . . .

> Josh and Marie are at the party. Marie meets some friends there and talks with them. She introduces Josh. He dives in and takes over the conversation and ignores Marie—despite the fact that these are her friends. He seems desperate to impress them. They try to talk to her, but Josh responds. She feels like an appendage. It is hard to put into words how she needs Josh to treat her differently, but afterwards she tries: "Josh, you must let me talk in situations like that and—like when we were asked to this party, let me speak for myself. I feel a bit like a child when you talk for me and answer for me."
>
> "It is you, Marie, you're so quiet. Someone's got to answer for you. For god's sake don't be critical of me when I'm just being sociable. You're just like all the other stroppy females I have gone out with." His voice rises. Marie feels she has made a reasonable request of him and does not feel that it would be useful to get dragged into further confrontation. She says, as calmly as she can, "I just need you to let me answer for myself, Josh."

Josh may have some male chauvinism to be knocked off him, it seems! You might notice that he has also criticized Marie by generalizing about her ("just like all the other stroppy females . . ."). She might reasonably have said also that she is answering for herself in this situation and does not want to be associated with "all the other stroppy females" in his life. We look at techniques to deal with unjustified criticism in Chapters 7 and 8.

In the examples of Josh and Marie, I have illustrated all three of the rights that were listed above—but there is an important example that I want to add here that may be of more relevance to other females!

> Claire was at the same party as Josh and Marie. She ends up dancing with a guy called Warren. Warren seems to be keen on her and she feels flattered but a little wary. She wants to dance with him, but his hands

wander rapidly and after initially putting up with it, she pushes his hand from her breast. The party ends and she thanks him for the dances and says goodbye to him. He seems surprised at this and when she has got her coat he is still there waiting for her.

"I'm taking you home," he announces.

Claire is uneasy about his behavior. "Thanks," she says, "but it's all right."

"What's with you girl? You liked dancing with me. Don't tell me you're messing me around—come on . . ." He moves towards her.

"No—thank you—I want to go home alone." Claire looks around for somebody she knows, feeling a little fearful now. "I was happy to dance with you but now I want to go home alone. Please will you leave me alone." He becomes abusive, saying she does not know what she wants and calling her a cold and frigid bitch. . . .

You can see that this is becoming a potentially difficult situation. It is a more extreme example of many situations that involve sexual behavior—where one party for whatever reason does not want to get any more involved with the other. Claire's behavior is reasonable. So far as the example goes, she is managing the interaction by acknowledging his point (that she did dance), and by being clear what she wants now (not to want to walk home with him, and to be left alone). Claire's assertion of her rights does not, of course, guarantee that he will responsibly accept them. Situations like this are often complicated, as well, by alcohol—probably on both sides.

You can decline to care about something or—within reason—can decline to take responsibilities for dealing with the needs or problems of others.

I have included in this group of rights the caring about things and people. The "within reason" in this statement is important. If you are a parent, it would not be reasonable to say that you have a right not to care responsibly for your children.

We start with the "something" in the statement of right. People often forget that we each see the world from our own point of view, and that view is developed from the experiences that we, individually, have had.

Annemarie dresses in shabby old clothes all the time. The other girls in the flat cannot see why she does not do more about her appearance. They try to help her to see how she could dress better—but she seems quite content with the way she is.

Pete has a busy life. He is doing a vocational degree, working at the same time, and his job—in developing Web sites—has become much more interesting. He scarcely manages his studies, but has decided to carry on but not to try to get high marks. Erin, his tutor, can see that Pete has a potential for a first, but Pete is clear that his priority is his work situation, and he is content to get a second class degree.

These are situations in which Annemarie and Pete reasonably uphold their rights to care or not to care about things. If others feel that they are making mistakes it is all right to point this out but in the end Annemarie and Pete are responsible for setting their own priorities.

Caring for someone is usually a kind thing to do, but it is reasonable to set a limit because we need also to look after ourselves.

> Franco is deeply homesick. He constantly wants company and then just talks about home, and his girlfriend at home. His friends have spent many hours with him and have suggested that he should go to the counselling service but he makes excuses not to do this—and goes on calling up his friends. Bryan starts to decline to meet with him. He says that he feels guilty but feels as if he is being used—and then feels more guilty for saying that. The situation is beginning to upset him too.

Franco may be homesick, but there may be secondary gain for him in this situation—he likes the attention that he is getting and wants to make sure that he goes on getting it (by not going to the counselling service). Bryan is getting upset probably because he is being manipulated into giving more and more without having any sense that he is achieving anything. He also experiences guilt—which I have discussed above (page 81).

> It is worth thinking of the issue of secondary gain—there are many people around who moan about their lot because they enjoy getting the attention and sympathy of others. Most of us have been at both ends of this . . . can you think of times when you have been at one or both ends of it?

Rights That, in Addition to General Application, have a Particular Relevance to Situations of Academic Work

Clearly there is much overlap in my divisions of rights into two groups. I have said that I have made this division in order to focus on those rights that are particularly important in academic situations.

You have a right to express your feelings, opinions and values in an appropriate manner and have them respected. You also have a right to withhold your views and you have a right not to make sense to others!

You have a right to have your say, express your opinions, and to have them respected; but others might say or have said:

> "What nonsense you talk!"
> "Don't make such stupid suggestions."
> "Balderdash! It's utter balderdash."

"What utter rubbish you talk"
"Only a woman would say that!"
And lots more. . . .

Expressing yourself may not be easy because others may say negative things that put you down. Sometimes it is easier not to open your mouth—but then the consequence is that you do not have a presence in a group, or your view goes unheeded.

> Majella has never said anything in a sociology seminar. She feels that her peers speak in a more sophisticated manner and therefore seem to know more. The more she listens to them, the less confident she feels and she is less able to contribute. . . .

Majella may not have noticed that Tai, Naveed, and Miriam are sitting in the same group experiencing the same doubts about speaking. It is, in fact, only the loud voices that are being heard.

> One day there is a new tutor, Arlene. Arlene asks the loud-voiced students to quieten and, in a gentle way, she asks those who are silent to offer their opinions on the changing roles of parents in the family. Arlene is interested to get a multicultural perspective on this. Gradually new voices are heard. In subsequent seminars, these new voices gain strength—as does the respect for them in the group. Majella, Tai, Naveed, and Miriam are now recognized voices in the group.

Again, of course, there are conflicting situations when it comes to expressing or withholding contributions in a group, where you have opted into a group. A situation of immediate concern comes to mind. I am a tutor on an online, nonassessed short course. For some reason, several of the small number of participants have not engaged with the course—in fact, as I write, the course is made up of intense dialogue between two participants with the input and support of the tutors. In this online course, the intention is that much of the learning is from sharing views and discussion and some of the tasks include a requirement to respond to others' postings. If participants do not post, there is less value to all. The question is whether, having opted for the course, one should just be able to sit and read but not contribute, or whether there is some responsibility to contribute. You might want to think about this right to express yourself or not in relation to responsibilities to others. Of course, no one can make you speak out, it is up to you and your physiological processes!

> Are you a person who dives into interactions, or who tends to hold back? Or does it depend on the situation and how you are feeling at the time?

You can make your own decisions and deal with the consequences.

This is close to other rights that I have mentioned above, for example saying "yes" or "no" for yourself. That is, of course, a decision—so I am going to use this section to link in a more general idea that will affect you in higher education, which is the development of autonomy or independence as a learner. These words tend to float around undergraduate programs, particularly around the year or level of study. They refer to a shift from you (as a student) being told what to do and how to do it to the point where you make your own decisions and independent judgments in your learning. In theory you should be rewarded in the grading system for being more independent. This shift is handled better in some programs than in others. Sometimes students are told that they should be more autonomous, without appropriate support being given to them to get to that state, and sometimes they are simply not given the opportunities to make sufficient independent decisions in their studies. Not infrequently students are encouraged to be creative or different, and then are marked down for such approaches.

The factors that tend to militate against this progression to independence in your learning may often be related to the fact that teachers and their departments are rewarded for high ratings for student satisfaction about the teaching that they receive. If you—as a student—are asked what you have liked and disliked about a lecture, it is quite natural to appreciate lectures in which life is made easier for you—where lecture notes are put on the Web and where readings are made available and you do not have to search for them. In what is often called "spoon-feeding" of students, lecturers take away from you the need for the independent decision-making which you need to learn to do. They do not help you to face the challenges in learning. I have another way of putting this. I say that real learning is an untidy process and that the essence of higher education is that you have to learn to manage its untidyness. If it is all tidied up for you, you will not learn to manage it in future!

> Make a general statement about how much you are able to make decisions for yourself in your learning now and a year ago. Has it changed?

You have a right to be different. You can have needs or express opinions and values that are different from those of others.

You have a right to privacy, solitude, and independence.

I take these two rights together because the second provides a more specific example of the first. I start by suggesting that you read a well-known poem by Jenny Joseph—"When I Am Old I Will Wear Purple" (Jenny Joseph, nd). It says a lot for older people, or anyone—you can be comfortable to be different when you are not old too! You may be different in your student group because you are racially different, different in age, female and not male, smaller than everyone, happier than everyone, brighter than everyone—difference is a matter of degree only—and it is good to be different and not always follow the crowd.

Di comes from a family in which no one else had entered higher education. When she first goes to Subton, a traditional university, she knows very little about how her life will be (apart from what she has learnt from television soaps). She is very conscious of how different she feels. It seems that the other students speak with different voices. At home in the first Christmas, she tells everyone how unhappy she is, saying things like "I don't think people like me fit in there". Her friends at home encourage her to give up but she persists and things do become better. She realizes that her different background is only one of a mass of differences between her peers (Jenny is dyslexic; Hanna is lesbian; Chen comes from China; Jude is black). In the end her social difference is a source of pride for her.

There are many pressures to be the same in society or to "join in":

"Buy this in order to keep up with the neighbours."
"Get a hairstyle like this to be in fashion."
"Join the jet-setters."
"Keep up with the times."
"Don't be left out, listen to . . . , buy . . . , go to . . . , drink at. . . ."

Fashion is, after all, a measure of sameness. Stand by your differences! But, of course, there is comfort in being one of a group with some commonalities. You may need to stand up for your different opinion academically, too, particularly if you are a postgraduate. The following scenario illustrates this:

Abraham is a PhD student. Early on in his studies he has to write a piece for his supervisor, setting out his general approach and plans for the research. Dan, his supervisor, says: "Well quite frankly, I do not know if this is the start of excellent work or fairly fruitless speculation. I think you should take a different approach." Abraham is left in a state of unhappy uncertainty for a while but then decides to disregard his supervisor's advice. It is a risk, but he feels he knows what he is doing. He gets his PhD and subsequently writes the material as a book which is applauded as a new approach to the topic.

Asking for solitude, or to be alone, or to be independent is also a matter of asking to be different in many people's views. There tends to be a social pressure to join in and socialize, and those who want to be alone sometimes find themselves to be subjects of criticism.

A psychology assignment on abnormal psychology is set. The lecturer encourages students to discuss their experiences as a background to writing the essay, though they should do the actual writing alone. The idea of discussing a topic is new to Sali and her friends and they arrange to meet in the library project rooms on Thursday. Janine does not want to join them. The others do not understand why she says she wants to write this on her own. Actually it is because Janine's mother is currently experiencing a nervous breakdown and Janine wants to use the essay as an opportunity to explore what is happening to her family. Sarah also does not want to join the group. Sali comments sourly, "She always wants to do her own thing."

In this scenario, there is some resentment at those who do not want to join in and be part of the group. Those who want to do things on their own or who need solitude have to cope with such attitudes. As something of a loner myself, I have found the book *Solitude* by Anthony Storr (1988) helpful and also fascinating to read.

You have a right to say that you do not understand something or do not know something, and you have a right to ask for clarification.

You can make a mistake, though you would expect to take responsibility for it.

You can change your mind.

As a human being, you have a right sometimes to fail at endeavours.

All of the four rights listed above emphasise first that you are responsible for yourself and the way in which you function. Second they acknowledge that humans may be successful or fallible and that is simply part of the human condition. Pressure comes when we put ourselves into situations in which we agree to subject ourselves to conditions in exchange for a reward—as, for example, in higher education or work situations. We are then working to meet a set of expectations. Some people also demand perfection. Here are some relevant scenarios:

Jen and Calum are drama students. Calum is directing a short piece in one of their performance modules. Jen is trying to understand the instructions that Calum is giving her. She keeps on asking him to explain again and he is getting frustrated.

"Come on, Jen", he says, "Get your act together. On the booze last night were you—again . . . ?"

In an example like this, we do not know if Jen is not concentrating, or whether Calum's instructions are not clear. He is certainly tending to use implied criticism to get what he wants. There are some options for both of them—one is an aggressive response from Jen:

"For God's sake, Calum, cool it and get off my back. . . . I don't know what you want to do. You are not clear."

Or Jen might be nonassertive, saying:

Sorry, Calum—sorry, sorry, sorry, I'm not with it today—and no, I wasn't drinking last night but I just can't do it. Get someone else to do this part. Sorry. . . ."

Or she can be assertive, recognizing that she has a right too:

"I realize that you think I should be able to understand what you are asking me to do, Calum. Maybe I should—but I don't, and I need you to go through it again more slowly."

Being assertive, she is also not getting hooked into his implied criticism (Chapter 8, pages 126–33).

Here is another example that must be common to students for whom English is a second language:

Chen is an overseas student and is on a UK MBA program. In one of the early seminars, in a session on Master's level study skills, plagiarism is mentioned. He has never come across the term and is worried. It seems that it is important and it seems also that everyone else knows about it. When he asks what it means, the tutor is quite irritated that he could be so naive and gives a trite response that Chen does not understand. Chen asks one of his colleagues and gets a vague response that seems to conflict with the values that were prevalent in his first degree in China. It seems that one should not copy the work of experts—but that is what education is about isn't it? For the moment he does not ask again, but remains anxious, hoping that it will not affect his work.

And another:

Marianne is a new second year student. She has a tutorial booked with her new tutor. She manages to get a book that she needs from the short-term reference section in the library and becomes engrossed, forgetting the time. She gets to her tutorial fifteen minutes late. As she anxiously goes to her tutor's room, she is thinking what she will say. She had wanted to make a good impression. She could say that she had to finish using the book—or that she simply forgot the time or that she had a different time noted for the meeting (implying her tutor's lack of clarity?). She knocks and calmly says, "I'm sorry about being late, I was in the library and I made a mistake over the time."

Her tutor looks up—"Oh it's OK—don't worry, I had not noticed the time either." There are comfortable feelings on both sides and the meeting goes well.

It is often very tempting to make an excuse for mistakes, but, as I have said above, it can also be very liberating simply to admit that you have made a mistake and to take responsibility for it. Obviously, it would be reasonable for Marianne's tutor to express some concern if Marianne makes the same mistake time and again. At present she possibly thinks the better of Marianne for her straightforward admission of error.

In Marianne's situation, what would you have done—honestly!?

Marianne's tutor was forgiving. However, sometimes people are not even reasonably forgiving when you make a mistake.

> Deter is part of a group in a problem-based learning activity. The group has been given a case history that seems to relate to diet—with a list of clinical symptoms. They are required to produce a reasoned diagnosis and suggestions for treatment. They have discussed how they will go about it and have allocated tasks within the group. They have given themselves an hour to do this and then will return and pool their findings. Deter thinks that he has been asked to find out aspects of fat metabolism and potential malfunctions in this system. He returns with the information but as one of his colleagues talks, Deter realizes that they have investigated the same topic. It seems that Deter was not concentrating and should have been looking at the metabolism of carbohydrate—and this is now not covered. Salim is angry.
>
> "Deter, you bloody well should have listened," he says. Deter apologises and agrees that he made a mistake. Salim will not leave it.
>
> "You're useless, mate, we would have done well on this and now have not covered a major part of the work". Deter repeats, "I apologise again to all of you. I was not concentrating and I made a mistake—I take responsibility for my mistake. Have you any suggestions as to what I can do to make up for the error?"

Deter may be able to make up for the error—or may not. He is probably experiencing some guilt (Salim may be intentionally or unintentionally punishing him by doing his best to stir up guilt feelings). There is actually no point in Deter burdening himself with guilt feelings—it will not make the situation any different. Deter could go off and do more work—or the group can accept that it has not completed the work—or perhaps there is the possibility of asking for more time.

Then there is failure. Before I start to cover failure in the context of rights, I want to draw your attention to Chapter 10, which deals with failure in more detail.

Humans sometimes fail at things that they try to do—that is the way it is. Failing can be a disaster but it is also one of the roots of being successful. Few who are successful have not come through periods of failure—and because they are successful, we have to assume that they managed that failure and probably learned usefully from it. In the academic field the association of achievement and failure seems to be particularly close in art and design subjects. Because it is talked about in these fields does not mean that it is not important in other academic disciplines. Scientists often learn more from failed experiments than from those that work—but it is in their tradition that they tend not to write about failed experiments.

Many who fail will say that failure ultimately has been a very positive experience and it is unfortunate that we tend to regard it with such negativity. Also we find it all too easy to allocate the notion of failure to the whole person, instead of identifying the task.

Joe did not reach the pass mark in an examination. His tutor is irritated with him because she knows that Joe has the ability to do well.

"So I see that you are among the failures this time, Joe," she says. Joe feels shocked to become "a failure" because of his tutor's careless use of language. He thinks himself into the identify of a failure and is very depressed for some while.

Think of a time when you have experienced failure. Were others around you helpful to you and your recovery in the manner in which they spoke to you, or handled it?

Conclusion: Being Responsible to and for Yourself, while Taking Account of Others

Remember that an overriding right is that you do not have to use your rights if you do not want to! They are to be used thoughtfully.

Sometimes it is useful to think of having a local list of rights that are associated with a situation in which several people find themselves—such as sharing a flat or house or working in a group. Gillen (1992) provides a suggested list of rights and responsibilities for managers in work situations. Sometimes this list will be called "ground rules". The important thing is that everyone involved has signed up to the list and usually will have had something to do with forming the list.

Imagine that you are sharing a house with three other students. As a group, you decide to write a list of rights and corresponding responsibilities. What rights and responsibilities might the list contain?

Activities and Journal Exercises

Do Some Thinking About Rights

Think of an example or a scenario to illustrate three of the rights that are listed in this chapter—whether the rights were abused or whether you or another person were able to uphold your rights.

Look at Your Own Rights

Take two examples of rights of yours that you feel that you do not uphold enough for yourself, record your thoughts in your journal—or talk with another person about how you might start to ensure that this right is maintained in the particular situation.

Think About the Rights of Others

On your own, or with others, think of two occasions that have involved you (or make them up) when you have had to acknowledge that others have rights and you have had to be responsible for allowing for the rights of others.

What Do You Want to Have Working Better in Your Life?

With reference to the material on rights in this chapter, what four things do you want to achieve, or make better? Try to make two of these things quite specific.

Watching Others . . .

Watch for others maintaining or not maintaining their rights, or abusing the rights of others or being or not being responsible about the rights of others.

The Journals of Christina and Tom

Christina's Journal

Tues March 1st

Wow—March already and over half of my first year gone. I wish I could keep up this journal every day—I am sure it would be so useful. We did stuff on rights today. It never occurred to me that I have rights . . . (and responsibilities of course—how could I nearly forget that bit, it was said so often!). This week I am going to write in my journal a bit every day and I will do bits from two of the exercises—thinking about my rights and the rights that I could get better at asserting, and I will watch for others' rights.

Wed March 2nd

OK, today I spilled milk all over the floor and inside the fridge. It sort of was my fault because I was in a bit of a hurry (9 o'clock lecture) and I pulled open the fridge door rather roughly and Mel's soya milk was on the top and it fell over. What a stupid place to put milk—everyone knows that the fridge rocks when the door sticks. Well I was about to make excuses out loud—like "What prat put milk there?" and "Why couldn't the landlord get a better fridge for us with a non-sticking door?" when I remembered the rights and I slowed down and I said "Oh sorry everyone, I've had an accident. It was my fault" and I cleared it up (wasn't too bad). I felt cool after that and the others were fine about it. In fact they helped me to clear up. I bought some more milk for Mel.

Thurs March 3rd

Still on rights—OK—we got our essay titles today in the seminar. The one that I wanted to do wasn't very clear. So I asked Dr Steel what was meant and what was wanted in the essay and how much writing I should do for each of the subsections. I don't think he had even noticed me before and he said he would go over it after the seminar, so I waited at the end. There were several others who waited too and an older woman called Dory (funny name) said that she was so pleased I'd asked because she wouldn't have dared and yet she needed the same information. Yes!!

Sat March 5th

Missed my journal yesterday—oh well, can't be perfect. . . .

When I'd written that line down, I looked at the rights list and it tells me that I don't have to be perfect. I do find this quite useful, though, so will try to keep it up. So today—ah well today I think I infringed the rights of Kath. She was going up to the library this morning—I mean—on a Saturday—and I reminded her that she had promised to come shopping with me and help me find a present for my Mum (she knows my Mum. She lives in Castlemere too.) I suppose I felt a bit peeved that she was going to work (I mean I've got work to do too—but a Saturday—no) and so I made it difficult for her not to come with me and afterwards I didn't feel good about it. I felt guilty. She was so nice about it too and it made me feel worse.

I have a right to hold different values from others. Well cool—I was in the bar on Saturday night before we went clubbing and I suppose we'd had a few drinks and Charlie and Anna started to talk about the election and it turned out that both of them came from families that voted Conservative. I had always thought of Conservatives as those with money and Mum and Dad always voted Labour—so that is what I did when I voted last year. I could not believe what Charlie and Anna were saying about socialism as "nannying everyone." I did not say anything. Next time, I must say what I think—but maybe I need to think a bit about what I do think instead of repeating what Mum and Dad have said.

Tom's Journal

Thurs March 3rd

What do I want to have working better in my life? I still want it better with Gemma but that's not going to happen, is it? I think she went out with Sam again this evening, though she's not said anything to me. She said she was meeting some of her coursemates at Rostie's at 8.00 and guess what—Sam left the house at ten to eight. So I think it's time me and Gem have to part. Then I might think about Donna—still like her a bit. So in terms of the exercises that we were asked to think about on the course, it fits with "What do you want to have working better in your life?" I want to have my love life working better. I shall do something about it. There are two things there. There's me and Gemma and then, if she's seeing Sam, in the house, I'll have to cope with her being with Sam, and cope with Sam himself. I feel angry with them both—well, that's assuming she is seeing Sam.

I guess also I want to be a bit more like the "going places" me I drew in the route map last week (Figure 5.2, page 75)—a bit more "up" and bright and happy and talkative and open. I'd also like to be a bit more cool—things make me upset and angry so easily.

So there's this stuff on rights too. I never thought of it as rights—like I have a right to make a mistake. Sounds odd but I tried it yesterday. We've got a new tutor for the cartography module. I'd only seen him briefly—he was introduced in a lecture and then I had to find him to give him a map I'd borrowed and was told belonged to him. I saw someone from behind in the corridor and thought it was him and went up to him and handed him the map. He looked at me as if I was really strange and I realized it was not him. I didn't just say "sorry" and buzz off with my head down, but I said, "Oh, I've made a mistake. I thought you were Geoff." He told me where to find Geoff and said that I was not the first one to make that mistake. They both look similar from the back. It was better than just saying "sorry." Perhaps I say "sorry" too much.

I guess that Gemma has a right to change her mind about liking me too. I have to accept that. As Phil would say, it is the way it is. But then I don't have to hang on to her either.

7
Managing More Assertively:
Tools and Techniques

Introduction

For this chapter and the next two, I have used titles that include the word "managing." The chapters are all based on the idea of coping better through being more assertive, but they deal with different aspects of this. I have tried to be as logical as possible in dividing up the material in the chapters to put the ideas in the most helpful way. You may well, though, end up shuffling between the three chapters (there is plenty of cross-referencing). I start in this chapter with some behavioral techniques for managing better. These deal with the words and approach you might use in a situation, and we might call these some of the tools of assertiveness. In the next chapter I shift upwards in scale to consider the management of some situations that are characteristically difficult, for example situations in which you give or receive criticism or receive compliments (Chapter 8). In the third of this set of three (Chapter 9) I will be looking at the management of the thoughts and emotions that influence the way in which you behave, particularly in the difficult situations described in Chapter 8. Half of Chapter 9 is a listing of ways of coping with thoughts and emotions and half of it is about the basic idea of being confident and having reasonable self-esteem. Self-confidence and good self-esteem supports and is supported by assertive behavior.

Some Tools and Techniques in Assertiveness

This section is mostly about techniques, but a few principles will emerge too. The techniques are summarized in Appendix I (page 200) for quick reference or revision. As you read about the techniques, you will find that you already use many of them without being aware of them. I name them in order to talk about them and provide examples of them in action, but then, once you can put them into operation they can sink back into your unconscious ready to be triggered when needed.

It is important to remember that these techniques are not intended as ways of manipulating people so that you get what you want regardless of others, though they could be used in that way if the nonverbal signals indicate aggression. They are intended either as ways of protecting or asserting your rights or those of others in situations in which the rights are threatened, or where account is not being taken of rights. However, as I have said before, there is more to assertiveness than simply what you say. Your words need to be supported by appropriate body language. It is difficult to assert yourself if every nonverbal signal indicates acute anxiety. These are assertive techniques when you use them in a calm state, looking as relaxed as you can. You may not, of course, feel relaxed (see Chapter 9).

Broken Record and the Principle of Persistence

In a confrontation there is often one person who feels (perhaps mistakenly) that she is "on the right side," or who tends naturally to be aggressive. It is then in this person's interest to work to achieve domination over the rights of others early on and then have the matters cleared up quickly to her satisfaction. This might typically arise in bureaucratic situations where "officialdom" is involved. But also it arises in groupwork:

> A group of three dental students have been given a problem to investigate by their tutor. They have to return in two hours with information towards a solution of the problem. Marissa is in this group and she is notorious for loudly dominating groups in which she works. She is often on the right track so tends to be listened to, but then others in the group feel frustrated. They do not want to have the work done for them. The three of them in this group agree on areas for individual research and later come together to discuss the material. At this stage, Marissa, as usual, takes the lead in coordinating their material. Karl has a different way of seeing the issues but Marissa sweeps aside his ideas and ploughs on. . . .

We will come back to them. Here is another situation, which does involve officialdom:

> Aiden is a media student and, as is usual practice, has borrowed a camera from the store in the department in order to pursue a project. He knows that he took out the camera at 1.40 p.m., and he knows that he has brought it back within the allowed 24 hours. The technician who was working yesterday is off today. The store technician today says that the camera is being returned late and it was due at 11.40 a.m. There is therefore a fine to pay. Aiden is taken aback. He knows that this man has a reputation for not trusting students. . . .

The easiest way out for Karl and Aiden (in these two examples) is to be nonassertive and to give in, but they are not going to let that happen and will persist, doing just what their adversaries do not want them to do. If you feel that your rights are being negated, persistence is important. You could say that persistence is a principle of being assertive—but you should also remember that you may not "win". You may have to give in. Do what you need to do in order to feel right with yourself. "Broken record" is a technique that concerns persistence. It involves working out what it is that you need to say and staying with that line, using more or less the same set of words (see later) regardless of what the other says and regardless of how the other tries to knock you off course. The aim of the use of broken record is either to achieve the right that you believe yourself to have, or to reach a point of negotiation.

So the scenario with the dental students (first example above) might have gone:

> Karl: "Marissa, I have a point to make. I would like to say what I think about this problem. You are just pushing on with your own ideas."
> Marissa: "We have only got twenty minutes to get this done. Let's just get on with it . . . As I was saying. . . ."
> Karl (calmly): "No, Marissa, I have a point to make and I want to make it now".
> Marissa snaps: "Oh shut up Karl! We've got all that we need to sort this problem. We don't need anything else. Are you not wanting to get this done in the right time?"
> Karl (as calmly as possible and leaning forward): "Marissa, I have a point to make and I have a right to make it."
> Marissa scrapes her chair back angrily and says, "If you really have to have your say, but make it quick. We haven't got much time."
> Karl sits back and gives himself and the situation a moment to settle and then makes his point.

That moment of silence is important when things have got heated. It is not unusual that where the broken record technique is used, the person at whom it is directed gets frustrated and uses "put-downs," or becomes abusive, trying to knock the other off course ("Are you not wanting to get this done in the right time?"). The constant pressure of the one message is very powerful.

We will look at how Aiden got on:

> Aiden: "I'm not late back with the camera. I booked it out at 1.40. No fine is due."
> Technician, prodding his finger at the page: "It says in the book it was booked out at 11.40 a.m. That is, I am afraid, what the book says, young man. The camera is late back and you pay me the fine."
> Aiden: "I got the camera at 1.40. It is not late and no fine is due."
> Technician: "I go by the book. Look—here it is, written here. You pay up now or I'll make sure you do not get a camera next time you need it."

Aiden notices the book that the man shoves towards him. The time is not written clearly and the man has evidently misread it. Aiden also notices also that the loan prior to his was at 12.30 p.m. He points this out and, very gruffly, the technician

acknowledges that Aiden could be right and he will check with his colleague.
Here are some tips about the use of "broken record":

- Be persistent with its use, even if it feels a bit odd. Do not let abuse or put-downs from the other knock you off track. Your use of the technique will frustrate aggressive people and they may react more strongly, but eventually, in their own frustration, you hope that they will give in and at least then listen to you. . . .
- However, recognize too that the other may not give in!
- Do not use broken record technique too often with the same people— it can become tedious and less useful then, and they begin to learn what you are doing.
- Broken record only works if you keep calm, with your voice firm but slow. You need to be in control.
- One of the reasons why broken record works is because it gives you a "line" to hold on to regardless of the way that the other may try to disrupt you.
- When you feel very unsteady in the situation, the easiest thing is to stick to the same set of words. However, when you feel more comfortable, you can deliver the same message, varying the words or intonation a little, without allowing yourself to be knocked off course.
- Do not be surprised if some of the following abuses are thrown at you. Just keep going! Sometimes the other person will ask you questions in order to shift you from your message (as did Marissa). You do not need to answer them!

"Listen to yourself."
"You sound stupid saying the same thing all the time."
"Why do you keep saying the same thing?"
"You sound like a broken record."

Can you think of a time when you have used the broken record technique—even if you did not know what it was called? Can you think of a time when you could usefully have used it?

Graduated Response

This is more like a principle than a technique, but it is easier to include it with the techniques. I am putting "graduated response" in here because it is well-illustrated in the two scenarios above. It applies to all situations in which you stand up for a right or try to be heard or have to deal with some sort of confrontation. The principle is that you should graduate your message, starting calmly and gently at first and raising the pressure as is required. While you only see the words said in the scenarios on these pages, you can probably "read" into them that Karl and Aiden are increasing the pressure of those words as they go through their encounters. Start gently and do not use all of your power of assertiveness at one go. Anne Dickson (1982) talks about "using your gears" for this—it is a good term. Remember, however, that the idea is also to stay in control.

Situations of Criticism and "Put-Down"—A General Note

There are several terms that I am going to introduce here that are concerned with situations of criticism and "put-down" which are dealt with in more detail in Chapter 8. They are negative assertion, negative inquiry, and fogging. I do not like the names for the terms here but names provide a label and sometimes labels are useful. I need to say a little about criticism first.

Criticism can be used in the "best" interests of the receiver (constructive) or it can be designed to manipulate or hurt. In the latter case, it belongs to the category of manipulative behavior (Chapter 3) since it is negative comment dressed up as "something that you should know". How about the following? You have to imagine the "underhandedness" whine in the tone.

"I just thought you should know that. . . ."
"And—err—by the way . . . you might like to know that. . . ."
"You know, I really feel I should tell you. . . ."

Often some manipulative material is piled in with legitimate criticism as a sly means of adding weight to the legitimate message (and, yes, we all do it). How about . . .

"You always leave everything to the last moment. . . ."

Is "always" correct? Is "everything" correct?

> Think of two situations in which you have been criticized, or have criticized and "weight" has been added to the legitimate criticism by a bit of exaggeration.

"Put-downs" are also a form of manipulation. They are situations in which one person makes a (usually) indirect comment about another where the content or insinuation of the message is designed to hurt, degrade, or violate the rights of the other. An example is:

Susie has made a joke and Celia does not laugh. Susie waits a moment and they says, "Oh well—I suppose I am just used to being with people who have a sense of humour."

Or think about these statements. They are put-downs, designed at least to disarm:

"Come on—loosen up."
"You are beautiful when you get so angry."
"Some of us get our work done on time."
"Typical of a female, that is!"

Can you think of personal examples of these? Try to find three and I will ask you to use them later (see page 106).

Again, it is not always *what* is said, but the way it is said that is significant. As I go through some of these techniques, bear in mind the important distinction within criticism that it can be constructive and legitimate or it can be designed to put another down—and that separating the two forms is not always easy.

Negative Assertion—Accepting Legitimate Criticism

Negative assertion deals with criticism where it is valid and justified. It is really to do with your management of being criticized and involves the simple acknowledgement of the truth in what is being said. Barbara's work has been criticized by her tutor. Barbara says:

"You are right to say that my written work is sloppy. I know I can do better than that—I guess I just need to be a bit more organized and read it through and use spell-check. I have not needed to use spell-check before."

As a technique, negative assertion works for you and the criticizer because it is honest. It avoids the burden of having to think up creative excuses. Humans are fallible—we make errors and we all do work that is less than that of which we are capable (we have considered that in Chapter 6 when discussing rights). If you are assertive you know you make errors or mistakes and therefore why should you not acknowledge them? That does not mean to say that negative assertion is an easy way out or is cost–free. People who criticize others—even constructively—will often expect defensiveness in response to the criticism and not the simple acceptance of error. Negative assertion works particularly because it is unexpected and surprises the criticizer. The change in emotional atmosphere often leads to a reasonable discussion of the issues. Acceptance of error also allows for greater clarification of the matter in a calm manner:

Julianne is a mature student in the first year of a Foundation degree program in beauty studies. She has failed a class test and is upset about it. Her tutor, Molly, goes through the test and comments that it seems that Julianne has simply not learnt the material. Julianne is immediately defensive and a little aggressive, saying that it is not her fault that she did badly, because she had not been told what to learn or how to learn it. How could she be expected to learn from the vague waffle in lectures?

"Anyway," she then says, "I am not sure that I want to continue with the course."

Molly sits back and says, "Julianne, that is serious." They talk about Julianne's possible departure from the course. Suddenly Julianne sits up and says, "Molly, I don't want to give up. I think I can acknowledge now that I did not do adequate work for the test. I know that I have to learn to learn from lectures. That is what I am here for. Failing the test was no one's fault but mine."

Molly feels that now she can actually help Julianne with the work.

Imagine a little scenario from your own experience. You are criticized legitimately (by your partner or parents) and regardless of what you actually did or did not do, imagine that you respond with negative assertion—agreeing with the criticism. Where does the interaction go then?

And another exercise . . . in order to be ready to acknowledge your own faults, it is worth starting to think about those aspects of yourself that are worthy of criticism by others. Start writing down a note of anything that you can think of on which you could legitimately be criticized. There will be more to do on this later.

Negative Inquiry

Negative inquiry is a very useful technique that is valuable in situations of criticism and put-down—both where the criticism is justified and where it is unjustified. In using this technique, the person who is being criticized asks for more information about the subject of the criticism.

Uri is a demonstrator in a physics lab, who tends to be rather serious about his duties. Matt, Chandra, and Shaun are not taking the lab session in thermodynamics very seriously, partly because they are not really sure what they should be doing. Their equipment is in something of a mess.

Uri comes up and says, "How do you think you can do good science when things are in that kind of a state? I told you last week to sort yourselves out and it is now worse."

The three look down, and he continues, "You do not deserve to be in this class. Talking and messing about like this are not appropriate behaviors in the lab. Get yourselves sorted out and don't let this happen again."

He starts to walk away. Matt swallows and calls after him: "Uri, perhaps you could show us how we should arrange our equipment on the lab bench so we can get ourselves sorted out?"

Matt has accepted the criticism to some extent (though Uri may have gone a bit far). By asking for information, he has softened the situation and he has also put some of the responsibility back into Uri's hands. It is a useful part of the technique that Matt has used some of the words involved in Uri's criticism (getting "sorted out").

Negative inquiry can be a difficult technique to use if you are feeling low and lacking in confidence when you are criticized. However, it can defuse further unhelpful criticism and it can get the relationship between the criticized and the criticizer back onto an even keel, ready for constructive discussion.

Going back to the conversation between Uri and the students, Matt could have increased the effectiveness of what he said by using negative assertion at the same time—saying for example:

"Uri, we know that we have everything in a bit of mess, but perhaps you would show us. . . ."

Using negative inquiry in situations of put-down makes important use of its disarming function:

"Are you sure that this module on Aristotelian philosophy is the right one for you to take? It is, well it is one of the hardest."
"You feel that I am not capable of it? What difficulties might I have?"

Or:

"You may find it difficult to get them to take you seriously in the interview if you dress like that."
"It is possible that they are not interested in serious people. . . . Maybe you would tell me what you mean by 'not taking me seriously'?"

I have asked you, above (page 104), to think about personal situations in which some put-down has been in operation. Taking one of the put-downs, work out a scenario where you use negative inquiry. What happens?

Fogging

Fogging is used when you are being criticized and where the level or the content of criticism is unjustified and possibly manipulative. For example:

Cherie and her friends are going to the cinema and they have arranged to meet in Market Square. Cherie has had a phone call just as she left and is a bit late, though normally she is fairly punctual. Glen is irritable tonight and stamps around and grumbles as the group of friends wait for Cherie. When she arrives, she apologises. Glen says, "You're always late Cherie. We've been waiting for hours and it's cold. You're fouling up the night already."

Cherie is late this time but it is not reasonable of Glen to say that she is always late. I said above that it is quite usual when people criticize another person for them to exaggerate or generalize the criticism beyond what is directly relevant. Fogging is a simple technique of agreeing to elements of the criticism that are actually true and thereby separating them out from those that are not true. It frustrates the power of the criticizer.

Cherie looks directly at Glen.

"I am late this time and I have apologised, Glen. It is not true and not fair of you to say that I am always late." She says no more.

It might have been tempting for Cherie to disagree that she is "always late" and to start mentioning times when Glen was late—in this way getting "hooked into" his way of seeing the situation. Her simple acknowledgement of real error is more likely to be effective.

(I have used the term "hooked into" here. It is a useful term for what aggressors try to do to those whom they attempt to dominate.)

Self-disclosure

Self-disclosure is a powerful technique in many forms of social communication, not necessarily just situations of criticism. It may be simply used as an expression of "this is where I am." However, as a technique, I will deal with it here in the context of criticism as it is often used in the acceptance of reasonable criticism as I have been discussing above. It involves one party being open and saying something about how she feels—or providing a personal philosophy or explaining how she is thinking. The effect is particularly powerful when it is a person in an authoritative role who self-discloses. The effect is often to facilitate the appropriate part of the communication. To illustrate this, I go back to the situation of Uri and the students in the science lab, and continue from where Matt has asked Uri for some help.

Uri walks back to the lab bench where Matt, Chandra, and Shaun are standing.

"OK, guys, I feel I was a bit hard on you and I agree that the guidance you have been given on this series of experiments has not been good. I will go through it again, but then you must settle down and get on with it."

In making this self-disclosure, Uri has cleared the atmosphere and has made it possible for a reasonable instruction and discussion to ensue.

However, there are limits to self-disclosure as a helpful technique. People who go on and on about their shortcomings can be boring and difficult to deal with. They may also seem to exude an aura of "goodness" by constantly noting how inadequate they are, or playing for your sympathy by seeming to be a victim. These may be ways of manipulating the feelings of others. You will have to judge what is going on when a person seems to be self-disclosing about inadequacies too often.

> Can you think of a situation that you could ease by disclosing something more about yourself than you have already said?

Signposting Statements, Clarifying and Summarising

Again these are powerful techniques in social communication. Uri has demon-strated signposting in the paragraph above. He says "I will go through it again, but then you must settle down and get on with it." He is clarifying what will happen and laying out what he is going to do and what he expects. In this case he is in a place of authority. It is often a person who is in authority who will use signposting because it means that, in this case, Uri is setting the agenda. However, the signposter does not have to be a person in authority. To illustrate this we will go back to Molly (tutor) and Julianne. Julianne has used negative assertion and has accepted the criticism of Molly and has agreed that it was justified. What happens next?

> Molly is about to lean forward now to start advising Julianne on her patterns of learning and how to cope with lectures. However, Julianne sits up in her chair and says, "It would be helpful for me if we could first talk about taking lecture notes. I have never done it before and I don't know how to do it. Perhaps there is a book you can recommend? Then maybe you would go through the actual test so I can learn from my mistakes."

Julianne has taken the initiative and, in an appropriately assertive manner, has "signposted" how she would like the conversation to go. This is helpful for Molly because she can now see how best to meet Julianne's needs. In this conversation, you might see that there is also some self-disclosure that further helps Molly.

It could have been that Molly, if she had spoken first in the paragraph above, might have summarized the situation as a means of creating a further break between the difficult phase when Julianne was defensive and aggressive and the new phase of the giving and receiving of help. She might have said:

> "OK, Julianne, let's just think about where we have got to. You are saying that the test was a problem for you partly or totally because you feel that you do not know how to learn from lectures—and that no one has helped

you with this. (I can understand, by the way, why you might find that difficult.)" Julianne nods, and Molly then continues.

"Then you said that you were thinking of leaving the course anyway. We talked about you leaving. But you changed your mind and said that you do not want to leave, and you want to overcome the difficulties that led to the problem with this test." Molly looks directly at Julianne. "Is that how it is now, Julianne?"

This summarising takes the conversation to a helpful stage, but with Molly— who was earlier criticized, now asserting appropriate authority. In a sense she took over the power in the interaction by summarising it (i.e. signposting).

Making Empathetic Statements

Showing empathy is another way of making communication flow, particularly when it is stalling in a situation where one person is in authority over the other, or where a criticism has been made. I might say that it "oils the works of communication"—but there are exceptions, which I will mention below. To show empathy is to show that you have some understanding for the other person's situation. Molly makes an empathetic statement in the passage above when she comments that she understands why Julianne is having difficulties with learning from lectures.

Other statements that might indicate empathy are:

"I realize that you are not feeling too well today."

"I understand why you should have got that impression."

"That must have been a horrendous experience for you and I am not surprised that you are anxious now."

"It must have been a very difficult time for you."

Empathy is also a technique that may be used by a person who is telling another to do something or who is criticising another. Sometimes it will be helpful—but sometimes it may not be helpful. Here are some examples . . .

"I realize that you must be feeling pretty fed up with all this work, but you really do have to pass these exams."

"I know you think you know all about this metal and its qualities, but I still think that you should go to the lecture."

"I know what I am saying is upsetting, but I think that last essay of yours was very poorly written. It was very stilted."

In these latter examples, empathy has been used to make it easier to assert authority; in the third case, the speaker is using empathy either to make it easier to criticize the other—or possibly is using it to enhance the weight of the criticism by suggesting that the writer of the essay should be upset. In other words, empathy can be used in a manipulative manner too.

Deliberate Use of a Name

Have you noticed how powerful it is when someone uses your name in conversation? It is a useful technique when you need to be direct with someone (not always in the context of assertiveness). Of course, you can add to the power if you use a formal version of a person's name rather than a nickname or a shortened form. Many people have memories of parents using full names when they want to make a strong point. An example of the power of use of a name is given in the scenario involving Cherie and Glen, above, where Cherie uses fogging. She says "I am late this time, and I have apologised, Glen." Feel the power of the use of the name!

> Make a resolution to use peoples' names today—three times, in order to see how it feels.

Shifting into Process Talk

This is an important technique and one that can be used in different kinds of situation. It can be very similar to several of the other techniques mentioned above. To use it you need to recognize the difference between the content of a conversation and the processes involved in the conversation (what is going on behind the words). The technique involves making a deliberate shift from the content and talking about the process. You will see a bit of self-disclosure in the example below, and that again I have used the term "hooked into". I commented on the use of this term above (page 107). It is a useful term when talking about processes.

Adele and Tan are in the coffee bar. Adele is really down—she has boyfriend troubles and also is finding the modules that she has chosen to do this year very difficult. She has been talking about leaving university, going home and getting a job—and she has been talking like this to everyone she can find to listen to her. Tan feels concerned about her, but feels she has listened to the same things over and again and has made many suggestions, each of which Adele seems to have turned down.

Tan says, "Why don't you go home next weekend and relax and go out with your home friends. Put all of this out of your mind for a weekend. You might be able to sort it out then."

Adele sighs and says, "I could do that but I need to get this essay finished. Anyway there's nothing to do at home, like I might just as well be here."

Tan points out, "But you talk of going back to live at home."

"That's different, I would get a job. . . ."

"So OK, Adele, maybe you should go home and get a job today. . . ."

"Well, I might, but then everyone says I should finish my degree . . . and it's not really completely over with Tom. . . . It might still work out."

Tan now sits back. She says, "Adele, it seems like everything I suggest you have an answer for, and we go round and round in circles. I feel hooked into this stuff. It is not helping you and I feel useless and frustrated. I think that we should not have any more of these discussions."

We do not know where the conversation goes from here, but it will take a different course or it may end. Tan is taking a risk in making this process observation but she feels that she is involved in a kind of game that is frustrating to her. Games are fixed sets of interactions where there is a pay-off for one party at the cost of the other (Berne, 1966). In this game, which, we gather, Adele uses a lot at present, it could be that the pay-off for Adele is the attention that she is given by her friends as a consequence of her "misfortunes". In that case she will have no interest in actually taking action to solve her problem.

Here is a lighter example of the use of a process comment:

Ian says, "Going out tonight again Jan? Not back until the morning again, eh?"

Jan says, "I feel as if there is some teasing is happening here."

So I would say that making a process comment is often a technique to use when you feel that a current conversation is not getting anywhere. Getting nowhere often happens because there is a mismatch between what is actually being said in the words and the other messages that surround the conversation. You might find that you use process comments when you are being criticized, but also you may use it when you are in the role of giving constructive criticism that is not being received well, or when you are confused or disturbed about what someone else is saying and you are not sure why you are confused.

Think of a time when you have felt stuck in an interaction and could perhaps have taken a risk and made a process comment.

Activities and Journal Exercises

Practicing Techniques

I have mentioned ten techniques in this chapter (broken record, graduated response, negative assertion, negative inquiry, fogging, signposting, self-disclosure, use of a name, making empathetic statements, and shifting into process talk). Some are used in everyday conversation and some are limited to situations of criticism—so you may have to wait to be criticized or to criticize in order to use this exercise! The aim of the exercise is to get you consciously to try out the techniques. First list the techniques down the side of a page, leaving at least two lines of space at the top. Then across the top put "Use of technique" and then head another column "Situation" and then another "How it worked". This latter column is for a few words on how it worked. You may have room to put in notes about several uses of the technique. Now go out and use the techniques where appropriate, and make notes on them.

Observing the Behavior of Others

Listen for others' uses of the techniques listed in this chapter. As you will see from the ways in which the scenarios above often illustrate several techniques, the techniques are happening all the time in everyday conversations without any sense of a "technique" being used. They are part of what it is to have conversation. So, this time, set up a page as above, but listen for others' uses of the techniques.

Some Scenarios For You to Expand

Add more to the scenarios that I have given to you below, illustrating the use of the techniques from above and imagining the conversation and the development of the situation. You will probably find that several techniques will fit each senario:

1. Joanne is a student who has a part-time job as a waitress in a restaurant that sells inexpensive meals. One day she serves two rather prim looking women with jacket potato and cheese. A few moments later, one of the women calls her back and says, "I am not happy with the quality of the food in this place. This potato is not cooked properly and the salad consists of two leaves and half a tomato—hardly a salad is it?" The other woman agrees. "Pretty poor it is," she says.

   Joanne can see that the potato has not been cooked sufficiently, but the complaint about the salad is unjustified because the item on the menu only says "salad garnish". How might Joanne handle this situation effectively?

2. Sam has a pint of Old Maggie's in the Union bar. It does not taste as it should (he drinks it regularly). He takes it back to the bar and tells the barman the problem. The barman says that it is a new barrel but that no one else has complained. "Perhaps your taste-buds are having an off day," he says. How does Sam deal with this?

3. Sylvie, in her second year, is working in a group on a project on the history of agricultural methods. The individuals in the group have agreed to research particular aspects of the topic and to come together. Sylvie has a row with her long-term boyfriend (who lives in her home

town) and does not make much effort with the work. The others are extremely hard on her as it means that they must do more. This situation has not happened before. The annoyance of the group leads them to be unreasonably critical of Sylvie and her sense of responsibilty. What do they say, and how does she respond? (Sylvie has done some work on techniques of assertiveness.)

How Could You be Criticized?

I asked you above (page 112) to begin to think of ways in which you could legitimately be criticized. This will lead to you doing some practice, in the next chapter, on accepting these "faults" and that makes it easier to engage in negative assertion (as described above). So now start to make a more formal list of legitimate criticisms of yourself. Please be honest (and do not criticize yourself for being obese when you are really a size 12 or 14). You might find it helpful to follow Gael Lindenfield's (1987) exercise that suggests that you put your list under the headings of natural handicap and imperfection, mistakes, and faults. Once you have got a list, asterisk the three most important of these at the present time in each of the three categories.

You might want to note any of the criticisms that you have listed that are ambiguous. For example, "I feel I am independent but I actually like being independent. However, the fact that I tend to want to do things on my own and make independent decisions can be difficult for those who live with me."

The Journals of Christina and Tom

Christina's journal

Tues March 8th

I had a headache today and nearly did not go to the course. I went to Gary's birthday at The Seven Saints yesterday and it was late when I got in. Managed to get out of bed for the 10.00 lecture and went back to bed after it. Woke at midday and dragged myself to the lab session this afternoon. It was a hot day too and I had winter clothes on (actually writing this on Wednesday).

Well in the acadass session we got loads of different techniques. I was a bit curious when Phil talked about techniques—I thought it would be like "this is what you have to say" and a sort of script, but it wasn't like that at all. They were common-sense techniques and when I think about it I sort of do some of them anyway but it was really useful to see how they work when we role played them. The class split into lots of very small groups so we all got to try them out. It was cool. I could not remember them all but maybe, as Dee said, they sort of just come back when you need them. We had a good laugh in our group and, in fact, my headache had gone when we finished. Amazingly I liked taking the role of the person who was criticising and I felt, like, really strong and my voice felt loud. I quite surprised myself (an "aggressor in disguise," one of the guys said). Gemma, in our group, was really good at standing up to me when I was having a real go at her—well it was good until we collapsed in fits. Gemma was looking at a list of the techniques and getting back at me using one tool after another—fogging and negative inquiry and negative assertion and so on. But I supposed we learnt about them that way.

Thurs March 10th

It was hot today even though it is early in the year. I dug out some shorts and a top, got my sunglasses, and went out into the yard with my laptop to start the essay. It was OK until I went to sleep and woke up with a red cheek on one side and not the other because of the way I was sitting. Then my Uncle Tony turned up (he lives locally and I think my Mum has asked him to keep an eye on me). He had cycled round and was sweaty—I could smell it. He does what my Mum says—how pathetic. My Mum can be very persuasive—even bullying. I had not seen Tony for a while. Anyway he had a go at me lounging about in the sun and expecting to pass my exams. I thought about what I had learned yesterday, and when he started being ridiculous I used negative inquiry. I said, "Tony, can you tell me what is wrong with working out here in the healthy fresh air instead of inside in the stuffy dark room?" It was cool. He sort of backed off. Then I said, "You are critical when you come round to see me. I know Mum sends you. I am working." He kind of backed right off then and muttered something more about my Mum. This is typical of her. I felt really angry with her but saying something to her will not change things. I have tried it. It might change if I make it clear that I am going to make up my own mind about my life and that her nagging and bullying won't determine what I do now.

Tom's journal

Tues March 8th

OK, so what could I be criticized on? Natural handicaps:

> *Not good at sport, never was and never will be—so tough Mr PE teacher-at-school, that's the way it is with me. I'm never going to be like you.*

Imperfections:

> *Spots—yes they had a lot to do with not feeling good at school and it was worse because Mum fretted about them, had me put on creams, and lotions, saw the doctor, the homeopath, the herbalist and nothing worked. Tone, my brother, had a clear skin—that didn't help.*

Funny hair—kind of won't do what I want.

Smelly feet—well that's what Susie in the house says—unless she is joking.

I got worried about having smelly breath too—so I have lots of mints on me and it's sort of a habit now.

Mistakes:

I make lots of mistakes. Sometimes I think being with Gem was a mistake, though it's been better this week.

Tone and me being in the same family was a mistake—but maybe that is not what this is meant to be about. . . .

I made a mistake when I got that very low mark last year because I got too interested in the assignment and did not follow the criteria.

Faults:

I guess I get angry—where does that fit? If it is a fault does that mean I am stuck with it? I don't want to have this reputation as an angry and difficult person but I know they think that in the house. Before she says anything to me, Susie says, "Now I know this might make you feel irritated but . . ." (ah! a bit of empathetic statement there, I recognized it!).

I am shy—well that is what I thought it was—but maybe it's me not being sufficiently assertive. OK—so I am nonassertive, or am I aggressive because I get so angry?

Fri March 11th

We were asked to observe examples of the techniques happening. Great example in the house tonight—Susie often borrows Emma's clothes when she goes out. She seems to expect to do it—must've done it before she came here. I don't think Emma really likes it but she goes along with it. I'm glad that I'm not expected to lend my clothes. Well Em bought this little number last weekend for the politics ball and Susie says that it's just what she needs for her date the next night—some sort of posh dinner date with someone she knows outside uni. She starts on at Emma about borrowing it. Emma gives in. Well, off Emma goes. Susie came down this morning, pretty hung over, with the dress—with a stain on it. She said she would take it to be cleaned, which seemed reasonable. I tell you, Emma lost it. She went mad. She let rip at Susie about all sorts of stuff far beyond this dress. She called her names, she said Susie was untidy, said that the dress smelled now, said how she felt abused by all the borrowing of her clothes how Susie had even borrowed some of her work (they are on the same course). Hey—that's pretty harsh. They nearly went for each other and Karl hung round to keep them apart. I thought about how Susie could have used lots of the things we learnt about assertiveness that involve acknowledging the actual things she had done wrong, but not those things that were over the top, and understanding how and why Emma felt upset. In the end I think I helped them towards making up. Susie would take the dress to the cleaners today, and if it was OK then there was nothing more to say, but if the stain remained she would buy Em a new dress. Susie agreed that she would not borrow clothes again. Em agreed that she had gone a bit over the top and said sorry about one or two of the things she had said that were not really true.

8
Managing Difficult Situations

Introduction

This chapter is about the management of difficult situations. It deals with:

- Saying "no" and other forms of declining.
- Coping with persistent questioning.
- Seeking a workable compromise.
- The giving or receiving of compliments.
- Giving and receiving constructive feedback or criticism.
- Angry situations (expressing anger and being at the receiving end of anger).
- Coping with a range of "wind-up" situations.

In discussing how you might cope with these situations, I will be making reference both to the previous chapter that described assertiveness tools and techniques and the following chapter in which I describe ways of anticipating and dealing with thoughts associated with difficult situations. However, these are situations in which you will need your full range of basic capacities for assertiveness, and hence I start by returning to those.

A Reminder About Basic Assertive Communication

This is a reminder of the characteristics of a straightforward assertive communication. In Chapter 3, I said the following:

> Assertive behavior is confident, open, direct, honest, and appropriate. The assertive person does not violate the rights of others, but recognizes that she has responsibilities to them. She does not expect others to know magically what she wants and she does not freeze up with anxiety. If her communication is affected by anxiety, she may well say that this is how she feels. That is fine.

When the going gets tough or when you know a situation is going to be difficult, here are some of the basics:

- Start cool, calm and relaxed. If you do not feel this way, fake it!
- Manage your thoughts (Chapter 9).

- Be persistent and stand up for your rights (Chapter 6).
- Say what you need
- Remember to use nonverbal methods to enhance your message (learning forward, looking directly in the eye, talking firmly and slowly, etc.).
- Graduate the strength of your message if you need to exert pressure (i.e. use a graduated response) (page 102).
- Remember that if you feel guilty that does not mean automatically that you have done something wrong. Guilt is a feeling, and not any sort of ethically-driven judgment (Chapter 6).
- Remember also that it can be an assertive act to decline to stand up for your rights, or to recognize where there is a situation that cannot result in a satisfactory conclusion for you—and be prepared, then, to withdraw.

I shall refer to this list as "the basics of assertiveness."

The Situations

At the end of the discussion of each situation, there is a list of "hints and tips" for dealing with it.

Saying "No" and Other Forms of Declining

I could say that saying "no," or declining to act, is simply part of generally being assertive and one of your rights (Chapter 6). However, I have included it here because it is a persistent difficulty for many people. Indeed, it provides Manual Smith with the title of his classic book "When I say No I Feel Guilty" (1975). So some of the difficulty is that saying "no" can often generate guilt (page 81). Another difficulty is that people who bother to ask you something usually expect a "yes" answer!

"Simon, would you. . . ."
"Darling, you wouldn't just. . . ."
"Please would you. . . ."
"Would you be as kind as to. . . ."
"I would be so pleased if you. . . ."

You might notice a bit of manipulation creeping into some of these requests (I will see you as kind if you . . . ; it would please me if you . . . but I will not be pleased if you do not. . . . etc.). Of course, it is not always a matter of *saying* "no":

Della and Jon meet at a dance. Jon walks back to Della's house after the dance. Nothing is said, but by his actions, Della picks up that Jon apparently expects to sleep with her. Della does not wish to sleep with Jon tonight.

Sometimes it is more difficult to *say* "no" when the "request" is implied in actions as in the scenario above. Della has either to be "up front" and make the position clear early on (and then run the risk that Jon had no such intentions) or she has to wait to be certain that he intends to stay before she can decline. In either situation, she might feel uneasy because it will displease or even embarrass Jon (and she might like him a lot), and she runs the risk of being seen as cold.

The issues about saying "no" are common. For example:

- Being asked to lend something to someone.
- Being asked to come to an extra seminar when you had arranged to go shopping.
- Being asked to give time up for something.
- Being asked to go somewhere; to help someone; to go and get; to give; to donate; to buy a charitable magazine; to give to charity; to purchase something via television advertising, internet advertising . . . and so on.

> List at least five situations in which you would like to say (or have said) "no" but where you tend to say (or have said) "yes".

I will give you some hints and tips about saying no:

1. Remember the basics! It is all right to say "no."
2. You do not have to justify your declaration of "no."
3. Be appropriate in your use of nonverbal messages. If you are saying "no" to something, try not to appease the other person with a fixed smile!
4. It can help to use an empathetic statement (pages 109, 201) such as "I understand that it would make things easier for you if I (leant you . . .; went with you . . . ; helped you . . . ; gave you . . . etc.) but the answer is 'no'."
5. You might want to soften the "no" on occasions with "not at the moment," or "not just now" or "no, but I will let you know if the situation changes," and so on.
6. Think hard about any apologies that you might feel like giving—are they to assuage your groundless guilt or a bit of self-disclosure (pages 107, 203)?
7. You might want to find a compromise that suits both of you (e.g. "not now, but later . . .") (pages 121, 203).
8. You may find that the response to "no" is a lot of "why" questions about your decision. Some help in dealing with these kinds of questions is provided in the next section.

Look at your list of situations in which you would like to say "no" and practice saying no to them. You could just read each statement and respond verbally (out loud—because then you hear what you say as well), or get a friend to take the role of the other person to whom you then answer "no."

Coping with Persistent Questioning

One response to a "no" from you may be a lot of "why" questions that demand reasons for your decision and usually contain strategies to undermine your decision. Where these strategies are not obvious and direct, they will be a form of manipulation. Children are expert at "why" questioning! They know that it winds up their parents (page 137) and that, as parents get exasperated, they often get what they want—so beware!

"But Mummy, why do we have to go? But why? But why?"

It is your choice whether or not you respond to a request for reasons "why" you said "no." In giving a reason you may be inviting persistence by your questioner because she may then question your reasons!

"No, I am sorry but I do not lend books"
"Oh. Why is that then?"
"Well I just find that I have lost so many. They just don't get given back."
"But you can trust me. I have never not returned a book. Between best friends, surely you don't have to be so rule-bound. . . ."

And so on. Manipulation rules here—and notice the put-down in the last line! The simple phrase "Because that is the way it is" is very useful when a "no" is questioned. Another technique to use, if the questioning seems to be taking off, is to stand back and make a comment on the process (a process statement—see pages 110, 203). So you might say (with a bit of self disclosure too—pages 207, 203):

"I notice that whenever I say no, you ask me why. When I answer, you shoot me down, and I do not like that."

Or

"I said that I needed to get on with my essay tonight and I said that I could not go out but might come round later. You have now spent the last twenty minutes trying to persuade me that I should be going out with you. Georgie, I know you want me to come but I cannot, and the more you go on persuading me the less chance there is of finding some time to come round later."

Some hints and tips about dealing with persistent questioning:

1. Remember the basics at the beginning of this chapter.
2. Be reasonable in your giving (or not) of reasons for saying "no" or declining action, but beware of getting hooked into manipulative "why" questioning.
3. Remember the useful phrase—or an equivalent—"that is the way it is."
4. Remember that it can be useful to stand back and use the process statement as a tool to disrupt persistent questioning.

Seeking a Workable Compromise

For an assertive person who is involved in a situation in which there is some conflict with various rights and wants or needs involved, the aim will be to seek a workable compromise.

> Two students have moved into a house for the year. Jody is fastidiously tidy and cannot bear to have anything left in the lounge. Emma, on the other hand, wants to be relaxed about this and have her things around her. She says she does not want constantly to be clearing up her things. There have now been several confrontations between the two students and the issue is spoiling their friendship—which is usually close.

In this sort of situation, where those involved want to make a viable solution that they can live with, the key tactic is that both should endeavour to be optimistic about finding a solution, and should show empathy (pages 109, 201). In other words, each shows that she understands the other's point of view. There is then the opportunity to work out a set of ground rules that can be helpful to both. For example, it might be possible to agree here that there is one surface in the lounge on which Emma will put her things, and that will be tolerated by Jody— or they might buy some storage boxes. Alternatively the agreement might be that the lounge will be tidy at the end of each evening, but that it does not matter during the day.

Hints and tips towards seeking a workable compromise:

1. Relax—when people are tense, it is difficult to see the point of view of the other.
2. Try to introduce the idea of working towards compromise at an early stage, so you know where you are going in the conversation.
3. Use empathetic statements (pages 109, 201) to let the other know that you understand how she feels.
4. Be willing to give and take.
5. Find out if there are issues that need to be clarified.
6. Summarize frequently (pages 108, 203).
7. Keep to the point and be aware of the danger of drift onto other issues, especially if the going gets difficult between you.

The Giving or Receiving of Compliments

There is pleasure in giving a compliment as well as in receiving one. The active valuing of each other facilitates all forms of communication. Alberti and Emmons (1983) describe how they asked some university students "what makes them feel especially good" (p. 91) and many of their responses were about the expression of warm feelings towards or from someone else. The popular psychology literature tends to call this the giving and receiving of "strokes". Many people do not give strokes or get strokes, and feel sad as a result. Alberti and Emmons talk of giving compliments as a form of reaching out and it is just that—by giving a compliment, you will have created a warm space between you and the other.

> Janey is quiet and timid and does not easily engage in socializing, though she would like to have friends. Her fellow students on the Biological Sciences course think of her as a bit of a geek because she does well and is assumed to be working every evening. One day Anna notices that Janey is wearing a new skirt and compliments her on it (even though, as Anna says to her friend Samantha, the skirt is "seriously middle aged"). Janey feels warm and accepted by Anna and comes up to her the next day and asks about an event that is on in the Union that night. The compliment has opened up enough warm space for Janey to break through her timidity and perhaps to start to make some changes.

It is worth remembering, too, that you may think that others know how you feel about them, their clothes, appearance, and so on, but actually this may not be the case. This assumption can be an issue in long-term relationships.

First think of one or more occasions when a person has paid you a compliment that has been positive for you. What were the feelings that you experienced? Were they specific to the compliment or did they generalize to other things that day? Try giving at least three compliments today and tomorrow, and notice the effect on you of doing that. They do not need to be big compliments.

Like so many other assertive activities, giving a compliment is much easier when you are relaxed and feeling open and not defensive. You may sometimes feel that a compliment would help communication with another person (as it did for Janey) and then you may need to think about what it is that you could compliment (and yes, this is a form of manipulation, for a positive reason!). If it is someone you do not like or respect, it may be hard to think of something to compliment—but there will be something.

One of the reasons why people do not pay compliments is that they are concerned about the reaction in the receiver, who may show embarrassment or awkwardness, or they may fear that the receiver will feel threatened by potential manipulation ("buttering up," "preparing the ground for . . .," "softening up," and so on). So there is a certain subtlety required on both sides. The level of precision is an indicator of situations in which the compliment is serving as a lever or form of manipulation. Most manipulative complimenting is generalized because it is not genuine. You will also have an indication if there is manipulation from the weight or volume of the compliments. For example:

Tara looks across the refectory table at Dan and says, "Dan, you always look so smart when you come into uni." Dan smiles. He has always fancied Tara and she normally does not take any notice of him. Soon she is complimenting him on his seminar presentation and a bit later on his style of presentation and then she asks him to give her a lift to London next week when he goes up. Dan is not stupid and he now realizes that there was nothing in the compliments—they were meaningless manipulation.

If Tara had wanted to compliment Dan genuinely, she would have stopped at the smart appearance. Now Dan recognizes the game and does not, for the moment, offer the lift. So if you really want the receiver to value the compliment, you are likely to make it one that will be comfortable for the person to receive. You might think about the volume of compliments too. Is it that one or two genuine compliments carry the same weight as ten further compliments, so that the more compliments are made on the same day, the more the original complimentary messages are devalued? You could think on this one!

There are also status issues with the giving of compliments. It is usually easier for a person in a dominant position or a position of authority to give a compliment than a person in the lower status role. If we think about teachers and students it is interesting to consider that the school student is probably less likely to compliment her teacher on the clarity of her teaching than is the higher education student. The PhD research student may find it even easier to compliment her supervisor. We can probably put this trend down to a lessening of the gap between the students and teachers in these different situations. Sometimes, however, it is nice to buck the trend and compliment someone who is in higher authority—tell your lecturer, for example, that the lecture contained interesting information or clear explanation.

So how do you compliment someone? You relax, look the person in the face and say what it is that you like, or what is or was good. Sometimes the use of the first person ("I") makes the statement more powerful—it certainly changes the meaning:

"I really like the colours that you are wearing" as opposed to "The colours you're wearing are attractive."

Or:

> "I like the style of your essay writing," as opposed to "The style of your written work in essays is good."

The best compliments are those that are specific and clearly identify the feature that is being addressed.

> "The manner in which you have thought critically about this question is good, as opposed to "Well written" jotted in the margin or said about a whole assignment.

We are tending to shift onto the ground of feedback here—but some elements in feedback are kinds of compliments.

> Can you think of a time when someone has constantly complimented you? Did you value the continued complimenting or did it become tedious and difficult to manage? Did it retain its meaning?

There are sometimes strange compliments where you do not understand what is really being said. With apologies to sheep farmers, I will give you an example. I was at a ceilidh at a music festival recently, talking with a man who had asked me to dance. While were were dancing, he said, "Outdoor girl, are you?" I was not sure what lay behind this. I said "yes" because I like being active and outside. "Sheep farmer, are you, something like that? . . ." I still ponder on what he was getting at and whether or not it was meant to be a compliment on my tan or a put-down about my appearance. I did not ask him to dance when I was looking for a partner!!

In receiving a compliment many people seem to try to reduce the power of the compliment, possibly in order to manage the receipt of it better:

> Gemma compliments Jen on her new jacket. Gemma offers the compliment as a genuine expression of liking. Jen says (as is such a common habit in this sort of situation), "Oh I just bought it yesterday in a sale—it was only a couple of quid." (She might well have said that she bought "this old thing" at the charity shop "years ago".)

It can be interesting to think what this response from Jen does. Most obviously it reduces the value of the clothing or the implied skill in its selection, and it reduces the potential power of the compliment. Or perhaps Jen is quietly saying "and am I not a clever person for selecting the jacket"—in other words egging the compliment? I will leave you to think on that one! The best response for Gemma would be that Jen would simply look her in the face and say "Thank you, it is nice of you to say that." Usually "thank you" is the best response with which to reply to the giver of the genuine compliment though a little bit of elaboration might help, such as "It is one of my favourite jackets."

It is useful to practice receiving compliments. I have included an exercise at the end of this chapter, but for the moment think of three situations in which you have been complimented recently (imagine them if you cannot think of them). What did you say? Could you have received the compliment any better?

There is another common pattern that occurs on receipt of a compliment:

Pablo is in the house, working on a hand-written learning journal about his current fieldwork (the excavation of a Roman fort) and Ali is watching him. She says, "I just love watching you write, Pablo—you've got such beautiful hand-writing—it just flows out."

Pablo looks up at her and says, "Nice of you to say that Ali. But I envy your ability to type."

Instead of just saying "thank you" (in effect), Pablo has needed to reciprocate with a compliment back to Ali. It is a shame that it has become so usual to feel a need to pay back compliments. Again it reduces their value and it often gives the sense that the receiver has not really heard the compliment before she is feeling obliged to find a return compliment.

Some hints and tips about giving and receiving compliments:

1. To give a compliment, relax and engage with the person by looking her in the eye before you compliment her.
2. Design the compliment to be in a form that you judge will be appreciated by the receiver if your interests in complimenting are genuine.
3. Do not overdo compliments, as they can then be doubted or mistrusted.
4. Make sure that the level of the compliment is appropriate.
5. Be specific about what it is that you are complimenting.
6. Try not to leave the person you compliment in any doubt as to your intention (i.e. avoid any implication of manipulation).
7. In receiving a genuine compliment, gracefully accept it with a "thank you" and possibly a few other words that amplify the thanks.
8. If you feel you have to reciprocate one compliment with another, do it later.

Giving and Receiving Constructive Feedback or Criticism

In this section, I am mainly dealing with criticism or feedback that is justified. I talked about ways in which to deal with unjustified criticism in Chapter 7—using negative inquiry, negative assertion, and fogging. It is worth reminding yourself of these techniques because it is not unusual for justified criticism to slip into unjustified areas. I will start off with situations in which you are giving feedback or criticism to another person.

> Sal is a first-year postgraduate student doing research on English literature. She has been asked to work with some individual first-year undergraduate students who have had difficulties with an oral presentation that they had to give. She is working with Ben. This situation is new to Sal and she has just listened to a practice presentation from Ben. They are in the post-graduate students' common room and there are others coming and going.
> "Ben," she says "Where do I start? It is really not much better is it? You are just too timid and hesitant. You are not confident when you speak and I cannot hear you. You are just not clear enough." Sal has a fixed smile on her face as she is talking. Ben grunts and inwardly he sighs. He hangs his head. He has heard all this said about himself before. Sal goes on, "You have to speak up and say things clearer. Try to be louder next time. To be honest, Ben, I really don't know how much more I can help you—and—ah. Sorry Ben, I need to rush off to my seminar—hope it goes better next time." She leaves.

Ben goes out feeling even less good about himself, and even less confident about a third attempt at this presentation. It is really getting him down and it could begin to affect his other areas of study.

How could this feedback situation have been improved? We are looking here for ways in which Sal could have given Ben feedback that would help him to manage the presentation better. He needs support that tells him what to do differently and that gives him confidence.

> Before I start to suggest some ways in which this feedback or criticism could have been improved, cover up what I say below and try for yourself to identify four things that Sal could have done differently.

The following could have been managed better:

- Sal could have chosen a better location. It is not easy to give a presentation or feedback in a busy situation such as a common room. The situation where criticism or feedback is given needs to be one of calmness.

- She should have been better prepared. She does not sound as if she really knows enough to be helpful to Ben. She has little credibility.
- We are told that Sal has a fixed smile on her face. The fixed smile is a common feature of those who are giving feedback or criticism. It is usually a sort of appeasement.
- Sal directs her criticism at Ben and not his presentation. She has told him that he is not confident or clear. This is a common error in such situations. By directing her comments to "you," she is telling Ben that *he*, rather than his work, is inadequate.
- She is vague and unspecific. Her comments are directed to the whole of the presentation and not to details. It would have helped Ben if she had given examples of the least well-presented areas, and those that were better. She should have said what it was that was not clear.
- In being more specific, Sally could have told Ben more clearly what it is that he needs to do better next time by giving him helpful examples, hints, or tips.
- Sal is not calm and relaxed, and indicates her impatience. This is not appropriate for helpful feedback.
- Sal has not used any positive comments at all to help Ben to build his confidence. It is often appropriate to begin a session of feedback with some positive comment or empathetic statement (page 109), and certainly to end on some that send the person away feeling strengthened and able to make constructive improvements.
- If Sal had been doing her job properly, she would also have asked Ben if he had anything that he wanted to ask or say, and how she could best offer support. She could have turned the feedback session into a form of constructive discussion.

Clearly there is much that Sal got wrong in this situation but Ben could have improved the situation himself:

- He could have acknowledged the problem that he has with presentations (self-disclosure, page 167)and clearly requested help (rather than hanging his head and grunting).
- He could have been specific about what help he wanted.
- He could have asked questions of Sal and ensured that the session was a helpful dialogue. He might have been able to use negative inquiry (pages 105, 202).
- Recognizing Sal's lack of time and interest, he could have asked her where he could get more help—or when he could see her again—and so on.

Some situations of giving feedback involve much more emotion, and there is not necessarily the "protection" afforded by the different roles of the individuals as in this case where Ben, as a student, expected critique and Sal, as a post-graduate in the tutor role, expected to be "in charge" of giving feedback.

> Think of a time when you have wanted to criticize one of your friends, or a fellow student. What have been your considerations in this?

Here is an example:

Eddie's long-term girlfriend, Kay, regularly drinks quite a bit more than others and then is silly and argumentative with Eddie. Eddie has commented on this many times, but now it is coming to a head. He anticipates and fears that Kay will get mad with him.

What advice would you give to Eddie? All that I have said in the example of Sal and Ben, above, is relevant but there are some additional points. He needs to choose the time and situation very carefully, and in this sort of situation it is good to start with an empathetic statement (pages 109, 201). That might be something about how he anticipates she will feel about being criticized (e.g. "I think that what I am going to say will upset you"). He could also say how he feels and why it is in his interest to say something now (self-disclosure, pages 107, 203), and he may want to provide an example of one occurrence of the problem (e.g. "I am feeling increasingly upset about the way you treat me after you have had a few drinks. I felt very uncomfortable when you had been drinking yesterday"). Giving an example is a matter of being specific. Eddie needs to tell Kay what would be acceptable behavior to him—in other words, specifying the changes—and it is important that Eddie mentions the consequences (for example, "I am saying this because I am not sure if I can stay in our relationship if this goes on"). He may want to reassure Kay that he does actually want the relationship to work in the longer term (being positive).

Eddie needs to guard against letting this session of criticism go beyond the point at issue (Kay's drinking), even if Kay starts to bring in other issues (e.g. "That time at Sam's party—you were so drunk I could not get you home. . . ." Or Kay might try to deflect the issue, "OK, so let's talk about the way you treat me—spending hours with Gail the other night when you were meant to be with me . . .," etc.). Of course, Kay may feel that Eddie is being unreasonably harsh and use negative assertion ("I did have too much last night, but I don't agree that I have too much on a regular basis"—pages 104, 202). Both need to listen to each other, and to decide what is reasonable and what needs to be done (see "seeking a workable compromise" pages 121, 203).

The general principle of graduated responses (pages 103, 202) lies behind the giving of criticism. Eddie has mentioned this issue several times before, so this time he needs to be a bit heavier in his approach and his spelling out of consequences. Going in early on with all guns blazing is not generally a good idea.

I summarize the issues around the giving of criticism or feedback with some hints and tips:

1. Think about the appropriate time and place.
2. Talk about the behavior of the person, do not criticize the person.
3. Express your feelings about the situation.
4. You need to be specific and give examples, and mention when they occurred.
5. Ask for specific changes.
6. Use positive comments and empathy judiciously.
7. Keep calm.
8. Keep to the point and do not let the other person change the subject.
9. Check that you have not got a fixed smile on your face.
10. Graduate the message—do not go in early on with the heaviest consequences unless this is warranted.

So what happens if you are receiving criticism? There are many situations in which students receive feedback. Often you will get feedback in tutorials or seminars, usually from a tutor, but sometimes from your colleagues as well. This is much more likely to be the case in subjects included in art and design, where they may be called "crits." In many professional subjects at undergraduate or postgraduate stages, you may receive criticism from tutors or supervisors on your actions in professional contexts (e.g. teaching a class or dealing with a patient). Research students need to learn to cope with criticism in research seminars and vivas.

In order to consider issues around the receipt of criticism, let us imagine that you are in a situation rather like Ben's, though in a class setting. You are about to receive some criticism and feedback about an oral presentation that you have made in a class situation. This will come both from your fellow students and from your tutor. We will assume that you will need to be able to demonstrate the ability to give an oral presentation for the purposes of a level 2 module in personal and career development, and that this was a practice presentation. You know that you were not very organized in the presentation, that you read too much from your notes (you had been told to speak as much as possible directly to the audience of your fellow students) and that there were things wrong with the sequencing of the material. In fact you think that you could have done better if you had put more effort into it. This is an opportunity in which you can learn but it will be hard, because taking criticism is hard. So what is important for you in this process?

> Using the ideas above and prior experiences of being given legitimate
> criticism, see if you can predict three bits of advice that I might be about to
> give below.

So here are the bits of advice. First, try to treat this as a learning experience and
focus on the opportunities to learn. You may not agree with all of it, or it may
even be contradictory. It is up to you to accept or decline to accept (privately or
openly) points with which you disagree. There sometimes seems to be an ethos
in these situations of "if someone says something, it is a fact, and you have no
choice but to accept it." This is not the case, so evaluate what you hear carefully.
You may have a chance to say what you agree with and what you disagree with.

Second, do some thinking in advance about how you will cope with the
situation of criticism (Chapter 9 has suggestions) and do not be surprised to
be nervous—few people can be criticized without feeling nervous. It is normal
and you have to keep the nerves in their place (Chapter 9). They will be helping
you by keeping you very alert! Relax as best you can and then work on looking
even more relaxed than you are (check that you have not put on that fixed smile,
for example!).

Third, a key point in receiving feedback is listening very carefully. You may
want to make short notes—and this is a way of showing those who are giving the
feedback that you are taking the process seriously and they may then make a
greater and more interested effort, which is to your advantage. If you disagree
with something, it is fine to say so, but wait until the moment feels right for
this—and do not dive in straight away. Show that you have thought about the
issue. In Chapter 7, we looked at skills for disagreement with criticism where
what is said is unreasonable or over the top. If criticism becomes unreasonable,
you may want to use some of these techniques. Be willing to ask questions. You
will want to be clear about what they are saying—so ask for clarification or
further information if necessary. Again it shows your commitment to learning.
Sometimes being given feedback or criticism can be so disturbing that your
mind can go blank. You might want to say how you feel at this stage, depending
on the circumstances (self disclosure, pages 107, 203). Under these circumstances, it can be useful to ask if you can talk with someone later on or come
back for more guidance. If you are in a situation that is particularly difficult, it
can be valuable to have someone else taking a note of what is said.

So I summarize this in hints and tips about being criticized or given feedback:

1. Relax and manage the nerves as well as you can—or pretend to be
   relaxed. Get rid of the fixed smile!
2. Try to overcome any bad feelings.
3. Listen and perhaps write notes.
4. If you are going to disagree with anything, do it thoughtfully.

5. Ask questions for clarification.
6. Direct the feedback or criticism process so that you get the most from it.
7. It may be relevant to talk about how you are feeling about the process (self-disclosure, pages 107, 203).
8. If it is useful to you, ask if you can get more help later.

Angry Situations

A lot could be written here about anger and its appropriate expression, but I have limited what I am going to say. If anger is a particular issue for you, read Rees and Graham's (1991) book, which has more specific advice about anger management.

Anger is a natural human emotion and is associated with the energy that drives us in everyday living. It is not a sin to have angry feelings. Some of what I will be saying here might seem to contradict social attitudes that anger is bad and to be suppressed rather than expressed. There are a number of sayings that attempt to patronize or to put a person who expresses anger down, without any regard to the legitimacy of their anger:

"Keep your hat on."
"He lost his bottle/rag."
"She lost it."
"Keep your cool."

There is a sense, too, that to be angry is to be undignified as a person or "unladylike" as a woman. Indeed, there is a gender issue here. On the whole it is more acceptable socially for a man to be angry than a woman—but generally there is a fear of the expression of anger.

Supposing you are in a supermarket, and above the general sounds of trolleys and conversations there is an angry raised voice. What is your reaction? What do you feel about the person who has raised her voice? Do you assume that that person is in the wrong—or that something is wrong for that person that she has a need to express herself with anger?

Think about your reactions if the voice is male, and your reactions if it is female. Are there differences for you?

Anger and aggression become confused, as do anger and assertiveness. I have talked a lot about aggression, and anger is not the same as aggression. Aggression is a behavior and I have described it as a behavior that is about getting what you want without regard to the rights of others. Clear expression of anger is part of healthy assertive behavior when it is appropriate. It is not all right constantly to "bottle up" anger and leave it unexpressed. Anne Dickson (1982) expands on this idea eloquently. She says, "Facing your anger, taking charge of it, learning to express it cleanly without smearing it over everyone else's face is certainly a challenge." She also says that it "takes courage and encouragement to take that first step" to be angry in an open way (p. 74).

Here is an example of what can happen when legitimate anger is not expressed:

> Eileen is a mature student at Sowat University and is studying for a degree in social work so that she can move on in her career (she has been a carer). She has a husband, Steve, who works as a carer too, and two children under ten. Eileen and Steve agreed that it was a good idea for Eileen to get a social work qualification and they openly acknowledged the difficulties that would occur. The first semester seemed to go well and Steve enjoyed the greater contact with the children. However, it is now the second semester. Eileen is tending to stay longer in the library in the evenings because she has found she is constantly interrupted at home, and Steve is beginning to resent the extra time he spends in the house. He is missing his evenings in the pub. Because they accepted that there would be difficulties and sacrifices, it makes it harder now to admit that things are not working well. Neither is saying anything about the feelings that are gradually developing but they are prickly with each other.

This kind of scenario, which involves unexpressed frustration between people living in close quarters, is very common.

> Can you think of a time when there have been unexpressed frustrations between you and others living in close quarters? What happened?

In the scenario above, it would have been much better if Eileen and Steve had talked on an ongoing basis about the growing tensions. Ironically they seem to have blocked that discussion from taking place partly because they thought that they had done the work on anticipating the difficulties. Sometimes new couples block the expression of anger or frustration by developing a myth about "we are a perfect couple, totally in love." A perfect couple or a perfect partnership has room in it for expression of anger or frustration, and for dealing with it.

So what might happen with Eileen and Steve?

> Steve feels that his self-esteem is suffering. He is not used to being restricted by child-minding duties. He is beginning to resent having to come home and cook a meal for the children and he gets cross with them. He will not play football with his son as he used to in the evenings. When

Eileen comes in late he says things like "It's all right for you, swanning off into your books, doing as you please, coming in when you like. . . ." When Eileen tells Steve that she has a good grade for her first essay, he says "Good for you but look at what it's costing me and the children."

After several sessions like this, Eileen stays even longer at the university in the evenings and goes to bed late, withdrawing contact from Steve. Sometimes in these late hours on her own, she sheds tears. She is starting to note with satisfaction that the children have been complaining about the food they are getting for tea. She adds it to her armoury of "unreasonableness" with regard to Steve's behavior.

Trouble brews. . . . Unexpressed anger gets channelled into a range of psychological states and behaviors, for example into depression and low self-esteem, or hyperactivity and manic behavior. More overtly it can be expressed as indignation ("How could he . . .") or self-righteousness and judgmental statements that are confirmed in "backchat" with others (Rees and Graham, 1991). Anne Dickson shows how a range of punishing behaviors can result. These are mostly forms of manipulation. Dickson talks about the "disruptor" who deliberately lets slip angry comments to others about the person with whom she is angry. There is also the "spoiler" who deliberately damages pleasant occasions in her frustration. Steve is an example of the "deflator"—in the way he deals with Eileen's good news about her essay. The "stoker" complains endlessly, demonstrating how she is a martyr to the success of the other.

When did you last express anger? How was it? How did people react?

Expressing Anger

So it is good to express anger appropriately—not, as Dickson says, smearing it on others' faces. There are some things to say about anger. Expression of genuine anger usually has the effect of releasing stress and increasing openness, but used inappropriately it can terrify, cause others to "go over the top," lead others to run away, and so on. Let go, but do it with due regard to the others involved and the likely consequences.

How do you know when you are angry? How do you feel? What are the sensations? Do you have ways of managing such feelings?

First, it may be useful to choose the situation, but sometimes it is appropriate to express anger where and when it is provoked. You should be clear that you own your own anger. No one else can make you angry. Anger is your expression. It is not, therefore, appropriate to say "You make me angry." This goes along with the notion that anger is bad and it also focuses on the person and not the behavior of the person. To say "I am angry" is to make a powerful statement—and sometimes just this statement may be enough. Most of the techniques of assertiveness are introduced by the notion that you stay calm and relaxed. As I have said, you need to manage your expression of anger and make it appropriate, but the situation is not necessarily going to be calm! If you are expressing your anger at something that has not been done, for example, it can be important to graduate your response (graduated responses, pages 102, 202). Do not go in with all guns blazing, but be prepared to let them blaze if you need to.

Another thing to remember when expressing anger is to retain clarity. You need to tell the other person what it is that you are angry about, and you need to be honest and open. You also need to listen to the other person and sometimes it can be helpful to make empathetic statements (pages 109, 201) that show that you are listening ("Yes, I realize that you feel upset because I have expressed my anger at this situation but . . .").

Sometimes a person is angry and frustrated but there is no one to whom to express that anger. It might have arisen because of a whole lot of little things not going well, or there might be no one who is directly responsible for a frustrating event. I have just experienced a common example of such a situation. I thought I had booked and paid for a flight on the internet. When I tried to print the confirmation, there was an error note. To contact the company involved calling an expensive helpline, yet it was their fault. I felt frustrated but there was no one to whom to address my feelings. The anger spilled over and disrupted my writing for a while (it is sorted out now—in case you were wondering!). In such situations it is useful to have a set of personal strategies for dispelling anger, frustration, or tension. Some of these are directly mind-based and will be mentioned in Chapter 9, but there are others that are physical. Going for a walk or a run is one I use.

> Write a list of five things that you could do to dispel anger or tension when there is no one person to whom to express it.

Here are some hints and tips for dealing with your own anger. Many of these are similar to those of giving criticism:

1. Think about the place and time. It may or may not be appropriate to delay an expression of anger (so long as you do express it!).
2. Manage your anger with calmness, but express it and do not bury it.
3. If it is excessive and you may not be able to manage it calmly, dispel it by going for a run using tactics described in Chapter 9 (page 143).

4. Own your anger. It is yours. Say "I am angry."
5. Be clear what your message is to the other.
6. Keep to the point you want to make.
7. Say what it is that you need or want to happen.
8. Listen to the other.
9. You may feel that you can be empathetic (pages 109, 201).
10. Try to reach some form of resolution of the issues, or agreement to continue the communication.

Being at the Receiving End of Anger

Here are several situations:

On a geography field trip second year students are staying at a hostel. They stayed up late and made much noise last night and it is now 1.00am and they are there again, with plenty of cans and loud music. Don is a lecturer in charge of the group. He cannot sleep and storms into the common room very angrily.

Marie has borrowed Phil's textbook and Phil needs it back urgently. He has reminded her three times now and he is not sure if she is forgetful or if her action is deliberate. He sees her just before the physics lecture and goes mad.

Declan is part of a small research group that arranged to meet to discuss a proposed change of direction in their research. Declan elected to lead the discussion. The others have travelled a long way to get here and Declan eventually arrives one and a half hours late, giving a flippant and lame excuse, and then he takes lead in the conversation. There is a stunned silence at first, then Carol speaks out with anger at Declan's casual attitude.

James has made it very clear that he fancies Adrienne. She has made it clear that this is not reciprocated and has already told James to leave her alone. When she comes out of the house to go to visit a friend and meets James just outside the gate, she says fiercely "For god's sake, James, leave me alone. I've told you and told you I'm not interested" and she storms off. James had got the message a few days ago and was actually visiting Sean, another friend of his in the next house along.

It has seemed that Millie has been generally angry with everyone in her house this semester. The others know that she has problems at home and is not coping too well with her work. She comes in late one night from the library and her housemates and friends are having a bit of a party with loud music, plenty of booze, and dancing. Millie feels acutely left out, finds Sam, and goes into a state of blind rage.

These situations are different. In some there is a group at which anger is directed. There is one where the anger is misdirected, and another (Millie) where anger is "over the top." In dealing with anger directed at you, there is much in common with the situations of receiving criticism—and as with that, the basics at the front of this chapter should operate (i.e. relax and listen, etc.). As with receiving criticism, there is first the issue of whether the anger is correctly or incorrectly directed. If it is incorrectly directed, then use negative assertion, fogging, negative enquiry, and other techniques in Chapter 7. If the anger is appropriately directed and at an appropriate level, it is likely to be a matter of accepting the responsibility for the matter and apologising. Marie, for example, might say, "Yes, Declan, I will go back and get your book directly after the lecture. I am sorry that I have been so slow in getting it back to you. You are right to be angry with me." Learning to accept responsibility for making a mistake is an important coping skill in situations like this. (See also Chapter 6 on rights, and Chapter 10 on failure.)

Often anger is "over the top," in other words it is stronger than is warranted by the situation. This might be because the anger that is directed at you is about many more things than the situation in which you are involved (e.g. the scenario of Millie). In cases like this, or where the person has fully lost her temper, it can be useful to use the person's name (deliberate use of name, pages 110, 201) and a short phrase like "Millie, listen to me for a minute," and repeat it quietly and calmly but strongly enough to be heard. Then make eye contact and an empathetic comment such as "I realize that you feel very strongly about this—I would too—let us talk about it when you are feeling easier." You might also find it useful to make a self-disclosing comment like "I am frightened when you are angry like this" (pages 107, 203). These are suggestions made in Dickson's book (1982). She talks about this as "disarming anger." She suggests that such "disarming" will become easier when you can overcome a general fear of anger, and this will be achieved by learning to express anger yourself.

If you are the subject of someone else's anger, it is not always going to be within your power to defer the interaction to a more appropriate time and place—but it may be. In the last example above, Sam might have recognized that Millie was in quite a state and she might have led Millie into a quiet room in order to pursue the interaction. Sometimes you will know that you are going to be the subject of someone's anger—whether or not it is legitimate. Then you have the chance to do some work on your anticipation of the situation (Chapter 9).

Whether or not you can resolve the matter, try to end on a positive note or at a point from which you can develop further discussion or negotiation.

Here are some hints and tips about being on the receiving end of anger:

1. If you know that you are to be subject to an angry attack, prepare for it (Chapter 9).
2. Relax and try not to fear the anger.

3. If you need to, and can, suggest a different time and place to discuss the issue, do this.
4. Disarm the attack if necessary.
5. Assess whether there is a real basis for the anger and deal with unjustified anger as you would unjustified criticism.
6. Accept any anger that is justified—an empathetic statement may be useful.
7. Be willing to admit error or mistake.
8. Try to end on a positive or useful note in order to negotiate further or work to some form of compromise (pages 117, 203).

Coping with a Range of "Wind-up" Situations

I am going to incorporate a range of antisocial techniques under the general heading of "wind-up" situations. They are mostly forms of manipulation and many are described as games by Berne (1966). The common element is that the intention of the perpetrator is usually a form of put-down or degrading of the other, usually in order to enhance the status of, or amuse, the perpetrator. The put-down is achieved through a manner of winding-up or unsettling the other. The list is long and it includes:

- Teasing that goes beyond friendliness.
- Taunting.
- Hooking people into argument by raising issues or saying things that will "get them going."
- Using "crumple buttons" to manipulate (Dickson, 1982). We all have areas of sensitivity to issues, events, or emotions. When the button is hit, we react and can easily lose ability to cope with a social situation (e.g. being criticized).
- Gender, racial or cultural prejudice.
- Deliberate creation of states of confusion.
- The communication of disapproval.
- Patronising another person; by oversimplifying a situation, we give the message that the other person is less adequately equipped to deal with some matter.
- Questioning the other's choice or decision (for example, "Do you really want to do that?" "Do you really think that?").

There are clearly some substantial issues here. As is so often the case, it is first important to separate what is true in what is being said, from what is not true—what can be accepted from what is unreasonable. Where points are not true, use the variety of techniques for this as described in Chapter 7 (including negative assertion, negative inquiry, fogging).

In these wind-up situations what is going on is likely to be disguised and will be communicated not necessarily in the words used, but in the manner in which they are used. To be aware of what you think is going on and to communicate your awareness to the perpetrator is a key means of dealing with such situations because the wind-up may not work if you show that you know what is going on. Sometimes the perpetrator may not be aware of what she is doing until you show it to her. The best way to do this is to use process statements (pages 110, 203), empathetic statements (pages 109, 201), and self-disclosure (pages 107, 203). You show that you can see what is going on, how you feel as a result, and you then simply express that you do not like it.

> Matt often teases Sarah about her blonde hair, about blondes being dumb. She usually giggles but also feels uncomfortable. One day she turns round and looks him in the eye and says, "Matt, I know that it amuses you to say that I am a dumb blonde, and I know that I usually laugh it off, but I really do not like being teased like this. It makes me feel unhappy. I like being blonde, and as you know, I am not dumb."

Sarah has deliberately used Matt's name, an empathetic statement, and self-disclosure here. Often the perpetrator will deny that she is demonstrating the behavior but will actually cease it because you have demonstrated your awareness of it. Sarah has also demonstrated another way of dealing with these wind-ups. She has turned the negative characteristic (being blonde) into a positive point in her favour. She says "I like being blonde." She could amplify this and say that she receives compliments about it.

Some hints and tips for dealing with wind-up situations:

1. The first thing is to think about what is going on.
2. Ask yourself if it is reasonable or unfair. Teasing might be all right for a while and, after a while, too much—and therefore unfair.
3. Think about what is in the statements being made that is true or untrue.
4. Look the perpetrator in the eye.
5. Use the person's name.
6. Use empathetic statements, self-disclose, and process statements to demonstrate that you are aware of what is going on.
7. As appropriate, use the various techniques—negative inquiry, negative assertion, and fogging.

Activities and Journal Exercises

How Could you be Criticized?

Going back to the list of self-criticisms that you made in the last chapter (page 113), review it and add or take out items and then get a friend to make these criticisms of you out loud—or you could record your own voice. You respond in agreement. This is good practice for dealing with criticism and negative assertions. If you cannot get a friend to do this for you, read the criticisms out to yourself and respond. At the worst—write the exercise down and write your agreement with them.

Handling Non-legitimate Criticisms

Now, using your list of legitimate criticisms of yourself, get a friend to read them to you, but also to slip in one or two unjustified criticisms. Use your techniques of negative assertion, fogging, and negative inquiry to respond to these—or say something like "That is not fair"—or "That is not justified."

Review a Situation of Criticism

Jot down some occasions on which you have received criticism. It might not have been a big event and it might be from a long time ago. Think through each and now you know more about giving and receiving criticism, how better could you both have handled this situation? What was helpful about them and what was not helpful or made you feel bad?

Observations of Others

Take a situation of criticism that you have observed happening with others. Write notes on what actually happened and then see if you can write a dialogue in which one person deals better with the situation (page 145).

Journal Exercise on Re-evaluation

Teasing and criticism, constant disapproval, wind-ups and put-downs, where they come from people who matter to us (e.g. parents or a group of peers or a partner), can shape the way in which we think of ourselves, even over quite a short period. For a while I had a friend who made it clear that he considered that I had no "style" and could not judge "taste" (though I never managed to discover what those were!). While I was sceptical of his attitudes and argued back, deep down I found I had begun to doubt myself. It is important sometimes to reevaluate the messages people give to you and the manner in which you have responded, and to do some sortings out of what has been a wind-up or put-down, or ignorance foisted on you. Some will be from childhood or from broken relationships. You should then reevaluate your own image of yourself. Your journal is a good place to do this.

Scale Your Management Capacity

On a scale of one to five—with five being the positive end—scale your ability to manage saying "no" when that is what you mean, giving and receiving of compliments, giving and receiving criticism, management of your anger, and of coping with the anger of others.

The Journals of Christina and Tom

Christina's Journal

Tues March 15th

The course.

We have been asked to write a list of things about which we could be criticized.

I am untidy in my room.

I am not good at getting my work done in good time. I always say that I do it better under pressure, but really I think I am making an excuse there.

I feel I am not very friendly towards Mum sometimes when she keeps telling me how to live my life (ummmm—not so sure that I should be criticized on that).

I am not very good at talking with other people. I don't know what to say sometimes.

That will do for the moment. We had to give the list to someone in the group (it was Susie) and then acknowledge the faults. It felt funny, but in a way it is good to hear myself saying "yes, that is part of me". Dee reminded us that we are not perfect because the "rights" say that. Later the person reading our lists back had to add some things that are not true and we had to disagree. Susie said "You are bad at keeping time. You are always late," so I said, "You are not right that I am always late. I am good at being on time for things" (not quite true actually). Then she said, "You speak very loudly and forcefully to others," I said "No, Susie (good bit of using a name there!), I speak reasonably quietly and clearly." Then she said that I mumble. I said "I do not mumble" and then I said that it is actually true that I mumble and I should have put it in my list. I went away thinking about it and I have decided to try to be a bit more positive in what I say. It's like I should just take a moment longer before I say things, then say them more definitely.

Fri March 18th

This is an exercise that we were given to do—take a situation of criticism and think how well you handled it—how could you have done it better? OK, well three years ago the family went on holiday for a couple of weeks to France with the caravan. It was just assumed that I would go with them and I did not question it. We were fairly near the sea and every day they all went to the beach, but I did not want to do the beach thing with the family so I stayed in the caravan. It would've been all right if there was someone of my age to be with—but my brother, Steve was no good to be with. Who wants to be with a 12-year-old boy all day—boring. I was missing Rob, my boyfriend, too and I wanted space (and not to be with family). Well my Mum fired off at me every morning when I said I wouldn't go with them. She got at me for the way I was behaving, and how I was spoiling it for Steve (I don't think he could have cared less), and how much money they had spent on the holiday and how I was spoiling it for them and how I was making her worry about me and not enjoy the beach. I either fired back or didn't say much (probably grunted!) and turned away. It all made me want to be with them even less. I was perfectly safe on the caravan site anyway and I just read and wandered about and texted Rob.

So when I think about all that, what could I have done differently, though I could not have done anything different then? It's hard when you feel angry all the time, like I did at that time.

> *I could have said to Mum, "Well, I know you feel upset with me but you chose to pay this money for the holiday."*
> *I could also have said that I knew that they were worrying about me, but their worries were theirs. I did not make them worry. That is a difficult one to say but it would have helped me to understand how she was getting at me. It was like, "Well, if you choose to worry about me, it is up to you. I cannot stop that. I am old enough to be here alone and am safe. I realize that it breaks up the happy family holiday, but things change." Yes—that's cool.*
> *I could have said that I had no responsibility for entertaining Steve—so how could I be "spoiling it" for him?*
> *I should have said that it was assumed that I would go on holiday with them. I was old enough to be consulted (but they wouldn't have known what to do with me). I could have stayed with Kate.*
> *I know it wound them up, the way I was on that holiday and that I was not their little girl any more, but as Dee says, that is the way it is . . .*
> *Lots of stuff there . . . I could not have done all this assertiveness stuff then.*

Tom's Journal

Tues March 15th

The course, and after the course, the fireworks . . . I dumped Gemma. She was patronising in the course, pushing me around in the role play we did (we ended up in the same small group because I was not quick enough to find another). She was putting me down and criticizing me all the time. I did my best to ignore her. I liked the others in the group and they sort of tried to make it easier. Christina's one of them. Afterwards, when Gem had gone to get something from the room, I talked to Christina for a bit and said thanks to her and how I had appreciated her efforts. She could see what Gem was doing. She's a first year. Think I might ask her to stay on for a coffee next week.

So anyway Gem came back and said, "Your place or mine?" and I said, "No Gem, this is it. I've had enough. I go to my place and you go to yours and I don't want to see you again. She looked really shocked and then said in a smarmy but really angry way said, "How assertive we are tonight!" I wanted to answer but did not. I just turned away and crossed the road, as coolly and calmly as I could. I think I'll miss her—but at the moment it's a big relief. Maybe I really am on my way now.

Wed March 16th

Missing Gemma—but it's not that bad.

Dee said that sometimes we have to reevaluate ourselves, because if others treat us critically or put us down or have it that we are dim or boring, we can take that on and think like that. Well I have a lot of rethinking to do, then. Tone's attitude, for example. He treats me like I know nothing. When I did that route map (Figure 5.2, page 75), I realized how he must have felt at the age of 2 or 3 when I was born and suddenly took all of Mum's attention (Dad was too busy to be very bothered—or maybe he made himself busy because Mum had no time for him either, or something like that). Well, ever since then, it seems, Tone has been trying to prove himself better and I never seem quite to have met Dad's expectations. Dad wanted a doctor or a lawyer for a son. Well Tone blew that first but I was the last chance so got the flack for being disappointing. I'm on my way to being a meteorologist and I am doing quite well in my program. I seem to have a few good friends and I've sorted out the Gemma situation for the moment. I feel as if Christina might be interested in me. Yes, it's OK. I seem to know a bit more about how to feel comfortable in situations now.

Thurs March 17th

I sat with Donna in the refectory today. I decided to ask her out and not Christina. I paid her a compliment—saying that I like what she wears. I felt good—and she seemed pleased. We talked for quite a while and agreed to meet up there later today—my chance now. . . . When I came into the house, Em had just tidied up the living room and hoovered and I said how it was good that she had done it and she seemed pleased that I said that. She said I looked as if I had had a good day. Yes, today's been a good day.

9
Managing Thought, Emotion, and Self-Confidence

Introduction

This chapter focuses on the personal aspects of assertiveness—not about how you relate to others, but how you relate to yourself. Of course there are many references to attitudes, emotions, and self-confidence in previous chapters, but there are some more general issues that I want to cover here, both to pull these previous ideas together and to give you some helpful techniques. This chapter completes the three chapters that have been about managing assertiveness. Points and techniques in this chapter relate particularly to the contents of the last two chapters, in which I have covered assertiveness techniques (Chapter 7) and ways of coping with difficult situations (Chapter 8). As I have said earlier, you may end up shifting backwards and forwards between these three chapters and you will find that the chapters come full circle.

I have not used the text boxes in this chapter, the activities and journal exercises because the whole chapter is full of them.

Some Techniques and Activities for the Management of Thoughts and Emotions

One of the problems about difficult situations is not the situation itself but the anticipation of it, or the influence of difficult prior situations. Quite often we are more worried about the feelings of anxiety or fear that we experience in a situation, than the danger or difficulties of a situation itself. It is always worth asking yourself whether, when you are anxious, what you are anxious about— your experiences from a prior experience, or the actual event. This might be the case with Amy, Barry, Brad, and Gemma:

> Amy left school confident that she could manage her studies at university. She did well at school, better than many of her friends, so why should it not continue like this? Unfortunately she copied down the instructions for the first assignment wrongly and got a low mark, then, reeling from the low mark, she had to do a presentation in class and performed poorly. She is now reaching the end of the first semester and she is very anxious about the possibility of getting low marks. The assessment, this time, is by way

of a classroom test. She goes into class feeling shaky and sick with anxiety, and it is likely that this will affect her performance.

Although normally confident and proficient, Barry does not seem to be getting good marks for his teaching crits.* His tutor says that he is just not engaging with the class. Barry has a crit later today and is uneasy and feeling less sure of himself than at the beginning of his teacher education program. (*A crit is where a tutor watches and comments on a teaching session.)

Professor Slink has a reputation for being cold and critical. He has been allocated to Brad for supervision of Brad's Master's dissertation on the chemistry of soap manufacture. Brad has some ideas that he wishes to pursue, but those who have met Prof Slink before have warned Brad that he will have a rough time putting forward his own proposals. Brad is anticipating difficulties, now with building anxiety.

Gemma shares a flat with several others, among whom is Aaron who comes from Nigeria. Gemma would hate to feel that she is prejudiced, but she finds some of Aaron's behavior difficult because it differs from her own rather narrow background. She finds that as a result she cannot treat Aaron in the same way as the others. She worries about ending up alone with him, for example in the kitchen when she is preparing a meal, because she does not know what to say.

The anticipation of a difficult situation can sometimes be more stressful than the situation itself. Amy, Barry, Brad, and Gemma may find that there is little problem if they can prevent the anticipatory anxiety from affecting the actual tasks that they face. I am not saying that we should always be anxiety-free. Some anxiety ("nerves") keeps us on our toes and facilitates performance. It seems that different individuals perform better on different levels of anxiety. You have to get to know yourself.

What techniques might help Amy, Barry, Brad and Gemma? Here are some activities to help with positive thinking. Most of them work at dealing with anticipatory worries and preventing your thoughts from stopping you being assertive. You may find it hard to get down to these techniques (saying to yourself, for example, "It won't work—why bother?"). As I have said, they do work but you need to persist and most take some effort on your part. More elaborate forms of these methods are used in many types of therapy for anxiety disorders. Most of them are forms of what is generally called "stress innoculation." Choose whichever one suits your occasion.

Most of these activities are best done in written form—so your journal is an ideal place to try them. Though I suggest sometimes below that you can throw away once finished, the material can make very interesting reading if you re-read it later.

Give Yourself Advice

This method will work best when you are facing a difficult event or situation—such as an interview—and it might be useful to any of the students in the scenarios above. Imagine that you are a supportive advisor, mentor, or counselor, who understands the difficulties inherent in the situation that you are about to face. The advisor may be someone you know and respect, or someone you can imagine. As the advisor write down some advice and guidance for how you can manage the situation. This is likely to include advice about relaxing and looking confident. Read it through several times once it is written—perhaps before you go to bed. When it comes to the event, do not try to remember any detail unless there are some valuable points or phrases that could be useful.

You can use this method when:

- You need advice about something that bothers you.
- You have a difficult situation to face.
- You have a difficult meeting ahead of you.
- You have a viva or interview.
- You feel nervous about an event (sport or social event, etc.).
- And so on.

Dialogue Methods

I talk about this technique in many courses that I run. It has a wide range of uses because it is so flexible. Basically the method consists of you having a conversation on paper (or screen) with another person. We will start off by assuming that you have a difficult meeting coming up like Brad (above). Brad might write a dialogue (on paper) with Professor Slink. It will look like a short play script. It is a good idea to start by writing a brief statement about the issue with which you will be dealing in the dialogue, so Brad might write a statement about what he feels will be difficult in the meeting—what he fears most. He might start the dialogue from when Professor Slink says "Come in" to Brad's knock at the door. Brad says why he has come—but then he writes what he imagines Professor Slink will say—and he replies—and so the conversation runs.

When you are imagining what the other might say just wait and see what comes into your mind. Sometimes the words that come to you that seem the least likely, make very interesting sense when you read it through later. Let the dialogue run for as long as it needs to run. You may find that someone else comes into the conversation—or you may find that you are having a dialogue with the wrong person and need to start again. Once you have written the dialogue read it and put it away—or even throw it away. It is an exercise that works mostly at the emotional level and you do not try to remember it (unless there are useful ideas). It may sound odd to imagine what another person will say—but all I can suggest is that you try the exercise. It can effectively take the heat out of a situation and can enable you to face it in a more controlled and less anxious manner. But there may well be other surprises in what a dialogue brings!

The dialogue exercise, however, can also be used with groups or imaginary figures. You might choose to have a dialogue with an organization with which you are trying to deal (e.g. the university, the loans office, the basketball team, a religion), or it might be a religious person or figure of wisdom in your experience or from myth or history. Or you might have a dialogue with an object that frustrates you—the essay that you are having difficulty getting down to, the dissertation that you are stuck on, and so on. Or you may have a problem that niggles at you—have a dialogue with that. When I run this activity as part of a course, people look at me as if I am talking stupidly and then they do it and usually someone looks up with bright eyes and describes how she has solved a long-term problem or found a way around a difficult area of her research.

You might use dialogues when:

- You anticipate difficulty at a meeting in the near future.
- You are in disagreement with someone about something.
- You have a problem to sort out.
- You are stuck with your research.
- You have a philosophical issue that you want to sort out or explore.
- A moral or ethical issue is under consideration.
- You are unable to get on with your essay or other aspect of study.
- You are stuck with a painting, work of art, or design.
- You need to explore ideas for something more generally.
- and so on.

Thought Stopping

This is a method for dealing with something that bugs you—something that you cannot get out of your mind and that gets in the way of what you are thinking about or what you are doing. Amy might use it to deal with the bad feelings that were generated in her previous test. Barry might use it to deal with the time when his tutor said to him that he was not engaging with the class. The technique is best used when there is one single thought or emotion that causes you difficulty. The method is simple. It will work but you need to persist at it and I am sorry that I cannot explain why it works! Whenever the thought or word image comes into your mind, say out loud if you can—or otherwise under your breath, "Go away" or "Stop" or "Get out of my mind and life," or whatever words you choose. You may, as do I, have less polite words in your vocabulary that I cannot repeat here. Say the message sharply—even using physical gestures of pushing away if you are in a situation where this is possible. Persist. At first it will seem as if it is not working and the thought will keep coming back, but the more you do this, the more you will find that you can push out the offending thought. At first it will go for a few moments and then for longer. You may find that you can use images to help you—like a great big mouth that will gobble up the thought, or something to bleach it out, or a way of squashing it flat so it has no identity. At first, as I said, it is likely that the mouth will spew it back out—or the colour return to the bleached thought—push the idea back, bleach it again. . . . You do not need to be concerned about the image or the language that you use—no one else will know!

You can use this method to help you to get rid of offending ideas or images when, for example:

- You have said something embarrassing and it keeps coming back into your mind.
- Someone has said something that causes you pain.
- The image of your recently departed "ex" keeps appearing.
- Something on your mind keeps bothering you when you need to concentrate on other things.
- Something in the future preoccupies you—but you do not want to worry about it just now.

Mental Spring Cleaning

This is another exercise that will sound odd—but again one that can have profound effects. As with thought stopping, it relies on using imagery. You might use it (like thought stopping) to clear away thoughts that bother you, or fears, or your reactions to something or elements in your behavior with which you feel uncomfortable, though keep it simple to start with. Basically it involves conceptualizing the thought, fear, reaction, or behavior in an image, and finding a good place to throw it away, thereby clearing it out of your mind. Then you should think about how it is now, with the offending thought not around—shake yourself clear of it. If it comes back towards you, use thought stopping and push it away using physical motions of pushing away if you can. This needs an example:

Jay has known Del for a while but they are at different universities. They have been in contact by email. He is keen on her and she is keen on him, but she has felt defensive and irritable with him at times. However, it is summer and she has chosen to spend a few days with him, but is concerned about her uneasy reactions to him. Jay goes for a walk each morning, and stops at a special place where she can look out over water. She often uses this place to clear her mind of difficult thoughts and does just this with her irritability with Del. It is as if she bundles up the bad feelings and bodily throws them out into the water and then goes on, imagining meeting Del openly and easily. She repeats this exercise every morning for a couple of weeks. When she meets him, she feels easy, open, and comfortable—such that she is amazed at the difference.

That example was based on my own experience. The exercise is drawn from previous work on counselling and therapy and it works—but you need to work at it.

You could use this exercise to deal with any of the uses suggested for the thought stopping and, in addition, it is good for dealing with:

- Difficult feelings about a person.
- Fears or discomfort about an event in the past.
- Fears or discomforts about a future event.
- Bad feelings that are there for any reason.
- General irritability.

Burying Discomforts

This exercise is a variation on the last one. In a ritualized manner you dig a hole in the ground and bury the difficult thoughts or elements of the past that you wish to leave behind. In this case, however, you can use an object or even a piece of writing to symbolize what it is that you are going to leave behind. It is a particularly useful exercise for situations where thoughts and images of a person keep coming to mind—for example, after a relationship breaks up. Once you have done the burying, do something that is positive and celebrates your freer situation (jump for joy, stretch, shout out, dance) or visualize a celebratory act. In case you should feel terrified at the symbolic act of burying something for ever, you can mark the spot so that you could retrieve it.

This exercise is derived from American Indian practices. I learnt it at a summer camp many years ago. A close friend had gone to live abroad and I was feeling bereft and needed to "move on." We were asked to find symbols of leaves, twigs, or natural things to symbolize what it was that we were leaving behind—and to write something on a slip of paper. I buried the suffering. We had jointly built a totem pole and celebrated around it. The effect, for me, was a dramatic improvement that I have never forgotten.

This activity works for the uses listed under thought stopping and the mental spring clean activities. You could use it for:

- The painful end of a relationship when you want to let go of the other person and the thoughts keep on returning.
- Feelings that you are psychologically tied to something or someone and need to be free (e.g. missing home).
- Leaving behind a bad day with its associated feelings.
- Managing reactions to a bad experience.

Unsent Letters

Unsent letters can be a useful activity in situations where you anticipate having a difficult time with someone. Brad might use it prior to his meeting with

Professor Slink, for example, or Gemma might use it as a means of working with her difficult reactions to Aaron. The activity is simply what it says—you write a letter but you do not send it. You write honestly and openly about how you feel and the dilemmas and difficulties in the anticipated meeting or in the relationship. You write to a person involved, or to someone else about the event, expressing your feelings. You might want to keep the letter to look back at, though your journal could be a good place for it. Alternatively throw it away. The act of throwing away can be powerful in the same way as the mental spring clean or burying activities that are described above—so it is worth thinking about how you could ritualize this act as well. As with dialogues, you do not need to remember the content of the letter unless there are useful points that emerge. The writing of the letter works at the emotional level and will usually have an effect of making the event easier for you—as I said in reference to dialogues, it can take the heat out of a situation.

This activity is particularly useful when:

- You are anticipating a difficult meeting with someone.
- You have a difficult relationship with someone that you need to sort out.
- You have experienced a painful parting. It can be a way of saying goodbye at the emotional level.
- You leave anything behind in your life.
- You want to welcome something challenging into your life.

Work with Imagery

Many of the activities that I have described above involve working with imagery, but here I am suggesting the use of imagery and relaxation to cope with an anticipated difficult situation—such as those that face Amy, Barry, Brad, and Gemma. Find yourself a comfortable situation where you will be undisturbed—and relax. You might try putting on some relaxation music. There are many books that deal with how to relax—find the way that works for you. Think of a time when you have felt strong. See yourself looking as if you are strong. Feel your voice to be clear and direct. Feel how it is to feel assertive. Imagine yourself going into the situation that you are working on in a relaxed and confident manner—Brad knocking at the door of Professor Slink, for example. Meet the person or the situation—and check that you are still relaxed. Hear what is said and check that you are relaxed again. See yourself dealing with the situation calmly and confidently. If it goes wrong take an imaginary rubber (or whatever symbol works for you), rub out the bit that has gone wrong, and run it again.

Like the other activities, you need to persist with this one. Run though the situation in a deliberately relaxed way several times and then make it portable and run it through in your mind on the bus, as you walk, as you wait for a lecture to start. . . .

This exercise works well when you are good at imagining and when the situations are in images rather than words.

Positive Self-Statements

What do you say about yourself and your ability to do things? Do you assume that you can do things or do you assume that you cannot? The ways in which we talk about ourselves and our capacities is something that is learnt in childhood. Some of us assume that there is a way around problems, a way in which we will mend that dripping tap or sort out issues about a student loan or a relationship mess. We are proactive. Others of us assume that we cannot sort out these things and we play victim or wait until someone else comes along to help or to take over the situation. I have a friend who hates where she lives and has been trying to move for fifteen years, and has not yet succeeded. I think I know what her messages to herself say.

So, first, find those negative messages. You may find your messages in the form of thoughts or in little statements that you say to yourself, or in what you say to other people. For example, do you hear yourself saying:

"I always leave work 'til the last moment and then panic."
"I am, by nature, a lazy person. I don't do work in the evenings. It is not possible."
"I can't do examinations. I always do badly."
"My bad memory stops me from getting good marks."
"I don't do exercise."

Sheehy and Horans (2004) give some good example of typical negative self talk in first year students:

"I am only as good as my grades."
"I must study all of the time."
"I can't have a social life."
"I must be at the top of my class to be successful."

And so on. Now change those messages. They are generated by no one other than you, and you are the only person who can do anything about them. They are blocks in your life. You might choose to put a positive spin on the messages as they turn up in your life—or to have a go at it as an exercise in your journal, writing down those negative statements that you can think of and then the positive correlate. You could work with a friend, helping each other—and even verbalizing the positive statement to the other. Voicing the messages helps to establish them. If you reverse the message completely (e.g. "I can't cook" to "I can cook"), you may find yourself wanting rather rapidly to add qualifying words (e.g. "I can cook a bit"). That reaction is useful as it may cause you to reconsider some of the myths that you live by. You could stick the new list on a wall where you can see it.

You will notice that many of your messages are critical. You could conceive of the origin of them as a sort of "inner critic" and do some work on that "inner critic". What does your inner critic look like? Who influenced you in the development of this character? To what extent is the inner critic useful to you, and to what extent could you think of extinguishing these messages? You have many activities above that you could apply to this issue—for example, thought stopping, working towards extinguishing the critic though a mental spring clean, or burying . . . and so on.

Use this exercise when you find that you have sets of negative words about yourself that you say on a regular basis to yourself or to others—words that get in the way of how you could be.

What are You Waiting For? Beware of the Lurking Saboteur

This is based on some material in Anne Dickson's book (1982). Dickson lists some of the excuses that you might hear yourself making as a means of avoiding doing something. As Dickson says, what are you waiting for?

- For someone to say they are sorry.
- For the children to leave home.
- For someone to show you the way.
- For the sun to shine.
- For someone to do it for you.
- For someone to make it safe for you to jump.
- For someone to mend the stepladder.
- For someone to offer.

(Dickson, 1982: 149–150)

Think of a few excuses that you use about not wanting to do something new. It might be legitimate of course. In your role as a student you might be saying, "I can't come because I have got too much work to do." I spent all my first degree saying just that, and missed out on some wonderful activities, and I did not get a good degree, either.

Once you have dug out some excuses that you make for not doing something, you can throw out the excuse (thought stopping, mental spring clean and other activities above), or you might want to deal with the saboteur herself/himself or itself (unsent letters, dialogue, spring clean, burying, or batter her/him in imagination)!

Use this activity when you notice that you are using excuses to delay or decline invitations to do things, get involved, etc.

Talk to a Friend or a Counselor

There is talking to a friend, and there is talking to a friend. . . . Talk to someone who will listen and be supportive, who can give her attention to you. This will not be someone who says "Oh yes, it was like that for me, too." If the issue is bad enough, or the fear is such that it gets right in the way of everything, go and see a counselor. If you cannot find one yourself, ask at the student union what professional services there are for the support of students.

Keep a Journal to Support your Assertiveness

I have already suggested that you should keep a journal of your development in assertiveness, but maybe you did not start a journal at the beginning of this book—so here is another encouragement. A journal will help you to develop self-awareness and will demonstrate your progress towards a more assertive stance, as well as helping you to be more aware of the behaviors of others. It is also a place for doing or describing the outcomes of activities such as those above—and many more. It might be little more than a notebook. My book on learning journals (Moon, 2006) is a source of many more of the kinds of activities that are described above.

The Building Blocks to Confidence and Self-esteem

You might say, "Why cover confidence? Surely, to be confident you have to be assertive and that is what this book is all about." I reply that to be assertive and to use some of the principles and techniques that are described in the earlier pages, you also do need some level of self-confidence. Work on your confidence and your assertiveness will grow. Equally, work on your assertiveness and your confidence should grow.

I am going to present this material in the form of hints and tips, and there will be things for you to do. In such a way, this section will act as a form of summary for self-confidence related material in earlier chapters. It is important to recognize that confidence and self-esteem is an individual thing. You will build confidence and self-esteem in your own way, and I can only offer you these points to think about. For the same reason, there is no particular significance in the ordering of these points.

You can use this material in whatever way suits you:

- Ignore it ("I am self-confident enough!!").
- Read through it as a summary.
- Read it slowly and use the prompts to think a bit.
- As a checklist ("Where are my strong and weak points?").
- As a short course to instigate some changes.
- As a basis for, and stimulant to, learning journal writing.

A Starter

If you think about your general level of confidence and self-esteem, what is your general diagnosis? You are not likely to feel the same all the time, so in your response, you may want to note the times when you feel more confident and those when you feel less confident or have lower self-esteem. There may be physiological factors that come in here too—such as menstruation or the effects of seasons (seasonal affective disorder). You may want to use the method of scaling, rating yourself on a scale of five, from least confident to most confident, at these different times. You could go back and see if you agree with yourself later.

The Bigger Picture

It is sometimes useful to consider the bigger picture—where you are in your life. Here are a couple of "bigger picture" activities. There are lots of different ways of doing these activities—but absolutely no brownie points for artistry (see pages 72, 75)!

> **Road map:** Draw a route map or a road map of your life from birth to the present. You may find that the territory was hard going at times (a windy, bendy road, or hills, or desert?). Sometimes it will have been very easy going and pleasant (what is this like?). You may find that there are intersections (roads that you chose not to travel)—are there still life choices that you could make at intersections? Where are you now? How did it change when you came into higher education? What is the landscape of the "now" like when you are a student? Where would you like the road to go to? Try doing the exercise with someone else and then you can take turns to discuss your maps. It is a good way to really get to know someone.

> **Picturing the people in your life:** Put a blob or a stick figure labelled "self" in the middle of a largish sheet of paper. Now, in whatever way you like, mark in the people in your life at appropriate social distances (I do not mean distance in the sense of where they live—but how close you are to them). You can do all sorts of things with this picture—you could think about where these people are in terms of distance and where you would like them to be. You could think about the kinds of relationships you have with them. How many of them are in authority over you or influence you? Are you happy with this? Are there two pictures—one to do with home and family and one to do with being at university? Is this all right?

Belief in Your Ability to Change—A Reminder of an Important Point

If you look back to Chapter 3 (page 22), you will find on the first page of the chapter the heading "Change." Under that heading I said that some people believe that they can change but that others feel that their nature is fixed. It is important, if you want to become more assertive, that you feel that you can change.

> **Think:** How do you feel about change now? Has your view of your ability to change changed? Do you feel that you have changed in doing the work of this book? Write a few notes on you and your ability to change.

Be More Relaxed

Being relaxed is about being calm in mind and body. These two tend to go together—can you imagine an apparently relaxed person telling you honestly that she is anxious beyond measure? Some people are more relaxed than others—some seem to thrive on tense situations. Others just slob about all the time and we might see them as wasting their lives.

> **Think:** Do you need to relax more? What helps you to be relaxed? What is your diagnosis of what you need to do in terms of relaxation?

Relaxation is a matter of learning as well as of practice. If you want to become more relaxed you may need to put time and effort into it. Others can tell when you are not relaxed and will respond to you in accordance with their observations. People who go around with shoulders hunched up and squared influence others to respond to them tensely. Sometimes it pays to pretend that you are relaxed. I noted the song in *The King and I* that is about whistling a happy tune and pretending to be all right when that is not how you feel at all (page 53)!

There are many methods of becoming more relaxed, including meditation, yoga, Tai Chi and other such activities, doing more exercise, reducing your caffeine intake (mostly coffee and soft drinks), reducing alcohol consumption, (which can generate anxiety), massage, having times when you switch off and laze, getting out of your current environment and going somewhere different on a regular basis, having a holiday.

You will find local relaxation classes (in the community, run privately or run by students), books, or websites that will support you in these activities.

Learn to be More Organized

Not being organized tends to lead to me making mistakes, being late for things, and missing dates in my diary. I feel out of control and that then reduces my self-esteem and my confidence. It also diminishes my ability to be assertive. I notice that I get less organized when the level of stress in my life rises beyond a certain level. Being organized means that you are more in control of things, such as the way you use time, the way you spend and save money, the way you look after your possessions, and the more general way in which you socialize with others. There is another issue about how prepared you are for things you have to do. This section is organized as a series of questions.

How Do You Organize Your Space and Your Possessions?

Are there contradictions here—for example, you have a very untidy desk but yet you know that you do your best work when things around you are tidy? Does this apply to your whole room? And does it matter? If you notice contradictions, you do not necessarily need to change everything. It is possible to develop personal rules that might mean, for example, that some surfaces are cleared every night, even if they get messy in the daytime. I often have clothes all over the bedroom during the day, but the room is cleared and tidy when I go to bed. It feels like a way of retaining control.

How Do You Organize Your Money?

Money is fundamental to the way we live. Our relationship with money has a lot to do with our attitudes to life and living, and our values, and it is often the case that people have to take on new relationships with money when they become students. Poor organisation of money can be a major source of stress. Are you happy with your money and the way you spend money (spending too easily or being too spendthrift)? Are you happy with the manner in which you save? Are there things that you need to do to improve the organisation of your life with respect to money? If you need advice around money, there is likely to be someone available to help you in the sstudent union. Get on top of money!

How Do You Organize Your Time?

When students come to university from non-traditional backgrounds (in other words as mature students or not from traditional educational backgrounds), one of the is biggest challenges can be time management. This may be the management of their personal lives as opposed to study time, or it can be the management of the timing of assignments, revision, and study. It is easy to assume that they just need to get better at organising their time, but my view is that they are often incredibly good at organizing time, but just have too much to do in the time that they have. In addition, it can often be the case in a modular system that you will be asked to submit several pieces of work at the same time in a semester. If this is the case, you may have good reason to talk to tutors about it. Individually they may not realize that this has happened.

If you have a problem with organizing your time, consider the following:

- Whose fault is it that you have this problem? Who has to solve it?
- Do you have any negative self-statements that rule this? They can be changed (see techniques, page 150).

- Are there ways in which you could organize your time better? You could try making a note of three things you could do. These could involve short-term planning (get and use a diary) and longer-term planning (get or make a wallchart).

Are You Sufficiently Prepared for the Tasks in your Life?

I have added this topic here, under being organized, because it involves time. To be prepared, you have to look ahead and plan. Seminars and tutorials can come to be much more interesting and engaging if you have prepared for them in advance. Many people avoid engagement in seminars because they have not prepared. When one day, for some reason, they are prepared, they are amazed at how much more enjoyable the session is.

Are You Happy with the Organisation of Your Social Contacts?

Social life does not often come under "organisation," but it follows on from the organisation of time. In some periods of my life I have spent a lot of time with people whose company has not been particularly rewarding or entertaining. I have probably done it because it might have seemed better than being alone—I was afraid of loneliness. Think about where you spend your time in relation to the value of that time and reorganize it accordingly. Remember that spending time alone can come to be very rewarding and important, even if this does not seem to be the case at first.

Being With Others and How You Come Over to Others

Low self-esteem and confidence can show up most when we are in the company of others. This section on being with others, and the next on how you appear to others, are important in this respect. All that I have said about the display of assertive behavior (Chapter 4) is relevant to this. So I am just going to prompt your thinking about a few things.

Some tips about being with others:

- When people with low confidence or self-esteem talk with others they often tend to talk only about themselves. A key factor in engaging with others is to show interest in the others—to ask about their lives and their situations. Getting used to pushing the focus of a conversation onto the other person is an important skill of conversation. It takes practice. Learning to show interest in another person in conversation is also a technique that helps those who are very shy.
- Showing interest in another person is also demonstrated by leaning slightly towards them (but of course respecting personal space) and in particular showing that you are listening. You can do that by good eye

contact, giving your attention to the other person and asking relevant and open questions that enable the other person to keep talking.

- You need to think about the kinds of questions that you ask. Open questions are best when you are trying to start a conversation and keep it flowing. Open questions are those that do not have a "yes", "no" or other one-word answer. They force a person to respond in more words.
- Even if you are not going to say much in a group, make sure that your presence is noticed—do something that says "I am here and want to be counted, even though I think that I am going to observe from the outside."
- Feeling that you look and sound confident will help you to be confident even if you do not feel confident. Think, for a moment, of how people look when they are engaged with others and think about how they look when they are isolated. What is their stance, their facial expression, in what direction is their gaze? Make this observation into a set of small rules for yourself when you are not feeling part of a group.
- When do you feel at your strongest—what are you wearing? Go out and buy some clothing that supports you in looking and feeling strong.
- Spend a bit of time in front of a mirror looking at your body and how you express it. Find a way of standing that says "I am confident."

Davies (2003) has produced a very useful and attractive little book about becoming more confident.

Bring New Things into Your Life

Another way in which you can develop your confidence or self-esteem is to open your life to something new. That may be a new pastime, new friends, a new interest, or something new that you go out to. Doing this may mean that you face risks and challenges. That, as I have said before, is part of learning to be assertive.

> **Think:** Write a list of things that have been interests during different stages of your life. This list should include those interests that were generated and then faded or were rejected—so include the ballet classes that you loved then hated as a child! Underline those interests that might still have some mileage in them for the present.

> **Could dos:** List the interests that you could possibly see yourself taking up in the current context. There are probably more opportunities now than there ever will be again. So which are you going to pursue?

What Are You Waiting For?

If you find yourself making excuses, do something about the saboteur that is getting in your way. There are plenty of methods for dealing with these obstructive thoughts (page 151). As Dickson (1982) says, what are you waiting for? Here are some excuses that you might want to make:

> "I cannot manage to get there every week."
> "I wash my hair on a Tuesday."
> "I don't know anyone else who goes to that."
> "I might not like it."
> "I would feel funny going there on my own."
> And so on.

Maybe Touch on the Spiritual?

For me, "spiritual" is not religious; for you it might be. Sometimes particular books have inspired me in a spiritual way, and enabled me to view life with a new perspective. These books are special to me. They bring a sense of excitement and aliveness. Some of them I have in duplicate because I want to lend them or give them to others. Some of my special books are: *The Prophet* (Gibran, 1926), *The Road Less Travelled* (Peck, 1985), *Solitude* (Storr, 1988), and *Gift from the Sea* (Lindberg, 1978). What are yours?

What has been helpful or stimulating for you? It could be a book or poetry, a website, or music. Get it off the shelf and wander in its pages.

Or find something that is uplifting. Maybe you will want to take a walk to the bookshop and find a book that stirs you in some way, that changes the way you see things. . . .

Managing the Negatives and the Setbacks

This section is relevant here in this chapter, but also it is designed to introduce the notions of fear and failure, which is much of the subject matter of the next chapter. Setbacks and failures, or not meeting expectations, are part of the processes of achievement and success. If you do not experience the feelings of disappointment, you would not experience the joy at success. Remember that if negativity and bad feelings get too much, there will be support services available at your institutions.

Poor performance or failure on a task: Remember, it is the task with which you have a problem, not you that is the problem. Beware the language that attributes failure to a person when it should be focused on the task.

Think about whether feelings of guilt are useful or not: Look again at what I have said about guilt on page 81. I have included a range of techniques in this chapter for dealing with non-useful guilt feelings.

Focus on "now": When you feel anxious, it is often because you are worrying about what might happen in the future. We can never know what is going to happen in the future, so not infrequently such anticipatory worry is a waste of your present time. Try to focus on living in each moment, "the now." Plan for the time ahead, but do not waste too much effort worrying about what may not even happen. A book that expounds this, the philosophy of living in the "now" is *The Power of Now* by Erkhart Tolle (2001).

Depression

We all get depressed from time to time. I would like to give you a view of depression that has worked for me as a counselor. Depression occurs when you know that something in you needs to change or is outgrown, and you are not yet willing to do anything about it. In this way, some depression is associated with the growth of a person (Peck, 1985: 70). When I have felt depressed, there are often things around that I have not wanted to acknowledge at the time.

And. . . . Learn to be More Assertive

I said that we would come full circle. Being more assertive will support your self-esteem and build your confidence and, correspondingly, developing self-esteem and confidence will support the development of assertiveness.

Activities and Journal Exercises

As I said at the introduction to this chapter, this whole chapter is full of exercises and activities for your use in your journal so I am not this time adding them separately. Do practice the activities. You do not need to wait until you have an issue on which you feel you need to work. It will be easy to find subject matter for the activities. How about trying one now!

The Journals of Christina and Tom

Christina's Journal

Thurs March 24th

Last week of the course . . . it has been interesting. I did not know there was so much to behavior, all those glances and slight body movements that affect the way we act with each other. It was funny saying goodbye to the group at the end—because we have been doing all these sort of close things, we have got to know each other really well. I was a bit sad really.

We talked about some weird things today. Phil says that they work but he could not always tell us how. They are all about getting a bit of control on your mind and stress and emotion, and all the sorts of things that get in the way of communicating. Some of the techniques we actually did. I have added one into my journal because it might be good to look at again. It was bizarre doing it. It was called "Dialogues". I had a dialogue with Steve, my little brother (age 15) because I was feeling so irritated when he was around me when I went home at Easter.

Dialogue with Steve

Me: "Hello Steve, I want to talk with you about how irritated you make me feel when you are around." (Actually as I write that down it makes me realize that I am doing what I accused Mum of doing to me last week when I was writing about her and me on holiday several years ago (March 18th). I have said "You make me irritated." But that is wrong—the irritation is mine. As Dee would say, I made myself irritated).

Me again: "OK, Steve, I want to talk about how irritated I feel when you are around."

Steve: "What do you want Chrissie? Make it quick—I'm off to Jon's."

Me: "OK Steve—I want to talk about why I get irritated."

Steve: "Nothing to do with me. Seems like everything is peaceful and then you're home and it all changes. Mum's flapping around as if you are some sort of honoured guest, even Dad said a few things at dinner last night—personally I get out of it as quick as I can."

Me: "So everything is disrupted when I get home is it? Are you a bit envious of me getting that treatment from Mum and of me being away from home as well? Mum and Dad's behavior gets you feeling irritated and you want to get out too?"

Steve: "A bit—now can I go? They're waiting. . . ."

Me: "Please Steve, I want to sort this out. I don't like the feelings in me about you. It's like if I speak to you, you are tetchy and you don't want to hear me. It makes me feel sad. We used to be quite good together." (Not sure about that!)

Steve: "Well it's different now isn't it. Well I suppose I feel a bit sad too. I'm fed up with Mum treating me as her little boy when I'm not. I need space and they don't give it to me—and then seeing you escaping and being treated as grown up. . . ."

Me: "Well it's not always like that Steve—often I'm the little girl in frilly dresses—but yes, it has got easier, and it's good to be away at uni with a different life. I remember what it's like—I had hard times with them too, not understanding that I was needing different things. I was only thinking about that disastrous holiday in France we had a few years ago. God, I hated that. Steve, I do think I understand a bit more where you are coming from and maybe I do not need to feel so irritated when you are around if I remember that."

Funnily enough, Steve texted me tonight and then we spoke on the phone. He very rarely speaks to me, though Mum always says "Would you like to speak to your brother while we are on the phone?" He wanted to ask me a question about his school biology. It was odd, because I did manage to speak to him without feeling irritable. I felt much more open and comfortable with him. Maybe me being open helped him too. It was as if we had really had that conversation that I wrote on paper.

Tom's Journal

Thurs March 24th

Last day of the course today—I'll miss those who have been on this course. I still like Christina but Donna's the right choice. I did ask her out and am seeing her on Friday evening—yes!! But that is not to say that Gem's gone away completely. I think I have asked Donna out so quickly really because I want to wipe the thoughts of Gemma out. This week we did some exercises on the course about managing things in our minds—which all seemed very relevant to the problem that I've got. I still keep thinking about Gemma. Well we did go out for 5 months—longest ever by a long way for me. Anyway there was this exercise called "Thought stopping" and I thought I'd give it a go, though I can't see how it could work. So when Gem comes into my mind, I have to say "Go away" to the thought or something stronger than that and I have to push her away mentally. Well at first nothing happened—in fact I was so conscious of it that she was there more than before, but then it was as if I was gaining power over the thoughts and they were kind of melting away when I said the words and then I did notice, sort of in reverse, that I was not thinking of her so much.

Sat March 26th

I am still using the thought stopping exercise and feel much more comfortable with myself and thoughts of Gem. She no longer bugs me. When I saw her in the distance, the heart pounded a bit, but it was manageable.

And there's something else—Phil and Dee went on quite a bit about "what are you waiting for?" They went round the room asking each of us to identify something that we were waiting for—that we were making excuses about. When it came to me I said I was waiting to get a new laptop because mine is old and crashes and doesn't get wireless internet. Phil said—"Don't just tell me what is wrong with your current one, tell me why you are waiting before you get a new one." I said I supposed it was the money. (That was a lie. Mum promised me one for Christmas.) I don't think that

Phil was convinced. If I am honest, it is the hassle of trying to decide what to get, and what is a reasonable deal, and what software I need, and all that. So anyway, when I came back here, I e-mailed Mum and said I was going to get a new laptop and I got onto the Internet in the library and did some research. I think I have found one and am ordering it when the money comes through from Mum. And it was so much easier than I thought. Yes, that was good. Why was I waiting?

I want to keep on with this journal. I think it has helped me to think about some things. I will try to write in it every other day so I will put some dates in below.

Mon March 28th

I was going to write about assertiveness today but no time. . . .

Wed March 30th

No time . . . write tomorrow . . .

Fri April 1st

. . . .

10
Coping Assertively with Fear, Failure, and Disappointment

Introduction

This chapter is about dealing assertively with fear, failure, and disappointment in the contexts of higher education. Another way of saying the same thing is that it is about surviving in your educational world. This is not a chapter just for those who are about to drop out, but for anyone who has had an assignment back on which the mark is less than you had expected or hoped for—and if you have not experienced that then it may well be that your expectations are too low! I do, however, deal also with some aspects of more serious failure situations.

There are four sections to this chapter. The first concerns fear, failure, and disappointment in fairly general terms, including a reminder that you have a human right sometimes to make errors and to fail. The second section focuses on assertiveness in situations of failure and disappointment but I deal with what I call "local" failure first (e.g. failing to get the grades expected for an assignment) and then in another subsection I deal with "large-scale failures" in which it seems that everything is falling apart—such as where you have accommodation problems, not enough friends, and your academic work is deteriorating in quality. The third section focuses on assertive approaches to specific emotional experiences—such as competitiveness and jealousy and, more specifically, difficulties with study anxiety, academic fear, and (serious) procrastination.

Fear, Failure, and Disappointment: Some General Points

The first thing I want to say is—if the going gets really bad, seek help—and seek help early enough. Things can be sorted out easier in their early stages. You may need academic and/or emotional help. Go and see your tutor or seek out the support or counselling services available to you. Higher education is not always good at dealing with situations of failure, but it is very much in an institution's interest to help you to sort things out and continue on your course. It is an act of assertiveness to recognize that you need help and to seek it.

The next thing to say is that fear, failure, and disappointment are not all bad, though they may seem dreadful at the time. Most of us can look back at horrible experiences and know that we did come through, the bad feeling is resolved, and we could sometimes say that we ultimately benefited. I, who was unjustifiably proud of my academic ability on a Master's program, had to resubmit a Master's thesis once, and watched my colleagues get their degrees while I was rewriting. However, I realized that there were appalling mistakes in the first attempt which I should have picked up (though a caring supervisor should also have picked them up . . .). I did get the degree, so all was well.

In connection with failure not being all bad, as I have been contemplating the writing of this chapter, I have heard Rabbi Lionel Blue speaking on a UK radio program. He was talking about the fear of failure among a group of university students with whom he had been in conversation. He said that they should not be frightened by "a bit of failure" because failure is a common experience among all writers, artists, and public figures. Being a student is about having time to learn from experience. He said that "real" education is more than how you do in test situations, and that what is important is being honest to ourselves about failures and that "the beginning of wisdom" is about making good use of failure in order to grow (Blue, 2007).

Here is a story of failure. It is not an unusual one.

> Toby is an architecture student on a Master's program. In seminars, some of what he says seems to be illogical and does not make sense. Others challenge him and he sometimes justifies what he says, but tutors have some doubts about his real ability. He ploughs on and continues to seem "on the edge". His dissertation is excellent and very original. Subsequently Toby becomes a highly creative and well respcted architect.

This takes me to another point. You may wish to look again at the chapter on rights (Chapter 6). I restate three rights here because they are all relevant.

- You can make a mistake, though you would expect to take responsibility for it.
- You can change your mind.
- As a human being, you have a right sometimes to fail at endeavours; you will sometimes fail at endeavours.

Part of being assertive is recognizing that you change your mind, make mistakes, and fail too as part of being a growing human.

> Think of three times when you experienced failure or disappointment with a mark, grade, or with the comments made on work. What were the things that you said to yourself at the time? How do you see the situation now?

Remember that when you experience failure in your education, it is not *you* who is a failure—but that an ascribed standard or your own expectations has not been met on a task or on a set of tasks on this occasion. It is possible that they were not even the right set of tasks or standards for you to have engaged with. Many students who leave university before completing their programs feel as if they have failed but subsequently recognize that they made the wrong choice of program. That is not failure, but learning. Incidentally, it is also well-established that those same students are very often back in higher education within a couple of years.

Failure is, of course, relative to what you expect. If your aspiration and self-confidence is low, then failure on a task might be unsurprising and perhaps not too disappointing. You can sometimes even take satisfaction from proving that your low expectations were appropriate. However, recovery and later improved performance may then be more difficult because the energy and motivation are not likely to be there. For those with high expectations of themselves, failure might be an examination mark that is not top of the class. The sense of failure can still be devastating. When I was twelve I came second in a sprint race at the local guide sports. Arrogantly, I had felt "above" the standard of the sports, and not to win was devastating. I was quite desperate for while.

Here is another scenario of failure:

Selwyn is a medical student. In his program, a "progress test" is used. In this form of test all students in their first three years of their program do the same test. The test measures progress and this is indicated in a progressive increase in score from a very low score in the first test towards nearly a full score after the three years of study. Selwyn is in his first year and at school always had very high marks. He is deeply upset when he gets a very low mark on this test, even though has been told (several times) the principles of the test. He can only see his poor performance as negative failure. He has some learning to do to cope with the new patterns.

It will not surprise you to realize that an individual's perceptions of failure is related to their childhood experiences of failure. How would you regard your childhood experiences of failure and how do they relate to any failures that you have experienced in higher education?

There is an important point to be made from what I have just said here. I have come across the opinion among tutors that some students early on in their programs actually aim to do less well than they could in their studies. I can think of two possible reasons for this:

- If the students get a poor mark they quietly know that they have the capacity to do better next time.

- Those who achieve can sometimes be socially less acceptable to their peers. Therefore the avoidance of overt success is socially helpful. This is sad but often true.

Do question what is going on with yourself if you find yourself saying "There you are, I told you I was going to fail!"

Can you think of a time when you deliberately did less well on a task for one of the reasons above—or other reasons that I have not given? How did you feel about this then, and how do you feel now about it?

Think of situations in which one person has been particularly successful (in any pursuit). How do the people around her react? Is there something about the group and the manner in which the successful person "carries" her success that affects the way in which people behave towards her?

Being assertive around the issues of fear, failure, and disappointment is often a matter of being self-aware and conscious of the choices that you are making, and the reasons that underlie those choices. The choices to which I refer can be choices of how you perform relative to your potential as well as the choice of program. Remember that you may sometimes decide that although you have made the wrong choice, you will tolerate your wrong decision and stay the course. That is being assertive too.

These are, of course, all wise words when at a distance from failure or disappointment, but when serious failure stares you in the face, it seems to take over your entire world. This is the way our emotional reactions work.

Being Assertive About "Local" Academic Failure and Disappointment

I have coined the term "local" to distinguish small-scale failure from the large-scale forms of failure. In local failure, I would include the experiences of not meeting with your own or others' expectations in assignment work or in a placement crit, or not getting into a sports team, or not winning a match that seems certain and so on. This in contrast to situations where it seems that "everything falls apart"—large-scale failures.

Being assertive about failure is about being constructive, recovering, and moving on satisfactorily—because, as I have said, we all fail sometimes. It is helpful to pull apart the notion of "failure" in order to think more effectively about it. From what I have written above, we could say that failure is both:

- An event (usually you have not done well in something—in relative terms) and its consequences.

- An emotional experience in which your confidence and self-esteem is lowered and you feel disappointed.

Jac normally gets good grades for her geography assignments and this matters to her. However, her choice of modules last semester meant that she had three substantial pieces of work to get in on the same day and the quality of one of them has suffered. She is devastated with the bare pass and the feedback comments from her normally complimentary tutor. It is the end of the next semester, with more work to hand in. She now has a presentation to do and she has not gone about preparation for it in her usual relaxed manner, and when it comes to the actual event, she is tense and reads her paper, never looking up, and stalls on the questions that are asked.

The "failure" affects both the mechanics of the subsequent event, and the emotional aspects of it. In anything that we would actually bother to call a "failure," both of these are likely to be present but sometimes the emotion dominates (as in my sprint race—when the event was insignificant) and sometimes the event dominates because it is so significant in its immediate consequences for your life.

> Think of two situations of failure that you have experienced, one in which the emotion was the more dominant and one in which the event itself and its consequences dominated.

So it can be helpful to think of there being two parts to consider when you act assertively to manage with personal failure—the emotion and the event. These two parts are not completely separable. In dealing with the event, for example facing up to taking resits, or resubmitting an assignment, you will usually deal in some part with the emotional element, and dealing with the emotional element helps you to manage issues around the event better. I will say more about this later in the section.

We also need to think about how failure is defined in higher education. It is often defined by the existence of assessment procedures. If there were no assessment procedures, then some students, who are learning on the course perfectly satisfactorily, would not experience failure because it is the very fact that they face an overt assessment procedure that is a problem for them, either because of the emotional consequences or because of the mechanics of the procedure (or both). If this latter point is true for you, then you may find it a good idea to pay some deliberate attention to the assessment procedure itself. Are you just giving your assessors what you vaguely think is appropriate, or have you researched the learning outcomes that you have to achieve and the associated assessment criteria? I did poorly in my first degree in Zoology because I did not pay attention to what was required in assessments. Students who tend to succeed are those who have "sussed out" the system of assessment (Wareham, 2002: 91). These may not be the brightest students. Unfortunately there is often a conflict in higher education between the desire that students should be creative and diverse in their responses to learning, and the forms of assessment that tie the system down. Beware of this conflict of values, and the information that you need about assessment procedures, and make up your mind how to play it to in order to meet the level of achievement you hope to attain.

Some more general advice in times of failure is to do what you need to do to feel strong, confident, and assertive ("I Whistle a Happy Tune", page 53). You might want to look again at what constitutes acting assertively (pages 23–24). Chapter 9 covers many ways of dealing with uncomfortable emotions and thoughts that might accompany forms of failure and disappointment. I particularly want to mention one of the ways in which some people can help themselves to feel stronger and more confident around failure, and that is to organize their time and their lives better. Failure is often associated with disorganisation in personal or academic life. Getting your tasks and your use of time sorted out is a way of sorting out your life. Sometimes it is good to tidy up your environment as a start to tidying up your life.

Another piece of generalized advice is that you should get things in perspective. When you are right on top of an uncomfortable event, it is hard to see it in relation to the rest of your life. It seems to dominate everything and you keep coming back to it. This will be the way it is for a few days—because, as I have said, this is simply how the mechanics of our emotions work (Damasio, 2000). However, as you draw away from hugely disappointing events, they usually do begin to sink into a reasonable place in your scale of important things in life. The trouble is that they will not do this when they are at their most painful and disruptive—this is the way emotions are—but keep in your mind that they will fade.

Books that may be of further help to you in providing more detailed advice are Phil Race's books *How to Study* (2003), and *How to Win as a Final Year Student* (2000) and Kate Van Haeften's book *Making the Most of University* (2003).

Go through this section and make a list of the ways you can help yourself through small-scale failures. Add two suggestions of your own.

When Everything Falls Apart . . . Assertiveness and Large-scale Failure

Another way of putting this is "when you are overwhelmed." The section is about the sorts of failures that can result in a student leaving higher education. There is no cutoff point between local and large-scale failures because the latter usually comprise many local failures—too many to manage and the problems seem to be conspiring to work against you. Often there is one local failure that is "the last straw," but you know things have been building up.

I want to describe what I think is a helpful and constructive view of this kind of failure, where a number of things seem to happen at the same time. It gives you a tool to use in your life when the chips are down. It is based on the work of Eugene Heimler (1967, 1975). Heimler was a Hungarian Jew who spent time in concentration camps in World War II. His experience there, and when later he worked with long-term unemployed people, led him to suggest that, as individuals, our ability to "survive" in society (or in this case, the higher education environment) is based on getting a balance between the satisfactions in our lives. He grouped sources of satisfaction under the following areas:

- Work (in this case you can see it as academic work and/or other work).
- Finances.
- Friendships.
- Family relationships.
- Personal relationships.

(Heimler, 1975)

Heimler called one of his books *Survival in Society* (1975). He suggested that to "survive" in one's environment, there is a need for an overall sense of satisfaction from all of these areas. So if, for example, a person is having difficulty in the work side of her life (e.g. having to retake a module and with difficulties with grades elsewhere as well), she will probably survive the experience if the other elements of her life are satisfactory. Supposing, however, that she worries also about her level of debt growing faster than she expected (finance), and she feels she has no friends (friendships) then her ability to survive and cope with the work problems (the retake) is likely to be seriously diminished. In other words, you might manage to survive one dip in satisfaction in your life if the others are in a good state, but if several dip, then survival becomes more difficult. It is about balances in these areas of satisfaction.

As a counselor, I found this philosophy and the practices implied by Heimler's work to be helpful. It provides a strategy for dealing with large-scale failure by taking an overview and deciding what can best be addressed to build up a person's ability to cope with other less easily managed areas. The student in the example above might initially focus on finding ways to make more friends to aid the satisfaction from friendships—basically building satisfactions and resilience in order to cope with other areas of life (e.g. work) that are more difficult to tackle. If you find these areas interesting, you might like to look at

Redman (nd) on the Internet. Redman has developed a scale that you can measure yourself by online. It is influenced by Heimler's work.

> Think of a time when you were at your lowest. Think about the areas of your life as in Heimler's scheme. Try rating them on a scale of 1–5 ("the pits" to good, satisfying, and satisfactory). How would you rate these areas of your life now?

Assertiveness and the Potentially Disabling Traits of Jealousy and Competitiveness

Jealousy and competitiveness go together to some extent, though one can certainly exist without the other. They can both hurt us and lead us to destructive actions. You could say that jealousy is passive and acts destructively in an inward direction, while competitiveness is active but can lead you to act destructively against others. Jealousy is not helpful to you or anyone, while being competitive is probably helpful to some extent in the academic progress of many people. I will explore that further once we have looked at jealousy. The orientation I take to both of these is that, when they cause you a problem, they can be tackled by taking an assertive stance, often towards yourself.

> Think of a time when you were jealous. If you could have admitted your jealousy to those of whom you were jealous, what would you have told them? The prompts below may help.
>
> "I am jealous of you because. . . ."
> "At the present time when I am jealous, I feel. . . ." (How did you feel?)

Jealousy is one of those traits that we tend to lay at the feet of others ("You make me feel jealous . . ."), though others sometimes perpetrate acts that provoke jealousy (if your boyfriend goes off with your best friend, for example). A first stage in dealing with jealousy is to own it. It is your own feeling, generated by you in response to something else. You had a conscious or subconscious choice to respond to the event jealously or not. Jealousy is a fallibility of being a human being and it does not help to feel guilty about feeling jealous, but it is a good idea to get on top of it and not let it drive the way you behave. The problem becomes compounded—as is the case with many forms of anxiety—because you start to feel anxious about experiencing the uncomfortable feelings of jealousy itself.

Fenny is jealous of Olga. They are on the same module and it seems that Olga is bright and attractive, and to cap it all she does well in her assignments.

Jervine was going out with Alberto. She always felt that he flirted with Sunita, her quieter and more retiring housemate, too much for her comfort. Now Sunita and Alberto are going out together. Jervine feels painfully jealous of Sunita. She cannot understand why Alberto could favour Sunita.

If you think about times when you have felt jealous, you will probably find that you have been most vulnerable to jealousy when your self-esteem has been at its lowest. In other words, the experience of jealousy is a lot about the way you are—and the event is the stimulus to dip you into your own sense of inadequacy. Dealing with feelings of jealousy, like other feelings, takes effort and the effort starts with an honest look at the depths of the situation. Try these questions.

- What would you like to say to those of whom you are jealous?
- What are the messages? What is it that really stirs your feelings? Try to get inside the matter. If you were Jervine, you might find that it is not just that Alberto favoured Sunita, but that you feel that your pride was hurt by his rejection of you. Your pride is hurt because at present you are feeling vulnerable and at a low ebb.

Once you have got to grips with identifying some of the issues that seem to be around any jealousies, make them as specific as you can, go back to Chapter 9, and use some of the techniques there—write dialogues (page 145), spring clean your feelings (page 147), and work with those uneasy thoughts. I would be surprised if you do not find an easing of the painful stabs of jealousy, if you work at it. Then look at strengthening your own life. Look back at the section above about Heimler's work (page 169) and do the little exercise I have suggested about rating the satisfactions in your life, thinking then about which could do with some attention—and do something about it!

Competitiveness, as I said, is related to jealousy but they are not the same. Competitiveness may be beneficial within a range of intensity. Without any competitiveness, some people do not function well. It is interesting to notice that when elements of a course are unassessed, there is often the question from individuals—well how did I do in relation to others in the class? However, many do not do their best and are not happy in highly competitive environments.

Think of a time when you were competitive and a time when you were not competitive. What was different in the way in which you performed and in the way you felt?

Again, think about what it is that you are competitive about. It may be about the self-satisfaction of doing better than someone else, or it may be the fact he or she who does better, gets the praise and acclaim of others. Which of these is most important? Ask yourself whether being the winner in this instance would be as meaningful if no one else in the world knew. Competition can also be a way of playing out an underlying conflict. How do you feel about the other person? Are there negative feelings there at all—are you trying to find reasons why you need to win this competition? In a sense, the competition in sport is ritualized conflict. Again, go back to Chapter 9 and think about some of the exercises to do with resolving difficulties with others. Some will be useful for resolving those senses of competitiveness. You might want to use the exercises on imagery. Would you like to feel that both of you involved in the competition could be even and equal? Could you see and feel yourself in imagery shaking hands or having a hug and letting go of the non-useful aspects of competition?

Feelings of intense competitiveness can be disabling and take over one's life. It is often the case then that self-esteem is low and there is a sense of vulnerability. Look at the Heimler material (page 169), as I have suggested for jealousy, and see if you have some thinking to do there.

Being Assertive about Specific Forms of Study Anxiety, Academic Fear, and Procrastination

There are forms of fear and anxiety that relate to specific areas of academic work. While the source of most of my material related to "writer's block," since writing is central to most academic activity, what I write applies to many situations in which able students have difficulty with study. This applies to undergraduate assignments of all types, postgraduate dissertations and theses, and to the research writing of teaching staff and other researchers.

The notion of "writer's block" tends to conjure up pictures of an author, with three-quarters of a book written, unable to lift a finger to the keyboard to type another word—utterly blocked, wandering around the room distraught with frustration. It is not helpful to see writer's block in that specific manner. Hall (1994) helpfully organizes the notion of it in three elements—which apply, as I say, to any area of study (and from now on I will use the term "study blocks"):

- Those who cannot get down to work (others have used the word "procrastinators" for this group). They may be daunted by the task set—perhaps because of an unfortunate previous experience.
- Those who may have done preparatory work—reading, thinking and notes—but cannot settle down to the final piece.
- Those who get started writing, but have difficulty in the completion, drafting, and polishing stages.

There are many ways of alleviating study blocks. I am simply going to give you a range of suggestions. Remember that to be assertive when you feel blocked, fearful, or anxious about study, is to take action. The first stage is (obviously) to acknowledge that you have a problem and to see if you can understand the nature of the problem. The second is, if it is bad enough, to seek help (at the study support service, for example), or to do something yourself that may alleviate the problem. A list of suggestions is below. I will order the suggestions as much as possible in Hall's sequence, above (i.e. starting with procrastination). Many of the suggestions will act at any of the stages Hall lists, though the way you use them may be different.

- Think about what you are waiting for (pages 157–8).
- Check you own negative statements. What are you telling yourself about this piece of work? Are you saying to yourself "I can't do this," "It is too hard for me," "I am not good enough," "I will not be able to meet the standard, so why try?" and so on. Make some positive self-statements (pages 150–1).
- Give yourself some advice about study (page 145).
- What is the purpose of the work you are about to do? It may be worth summarizing it in your own words, and this may lead you into it in a different way. Sometimes study blocks occur for me when I have drifted off course and away from the purpose of the writing.
- Try working somewhere else or at some other time. A change of environment can be very helpful. Try the library if you normally work at home, downstairs if you normally work upstairs. . . . Try morning instead of late night. Many people work best in the morning. Try music on or off (depending on what you normally do). Classical music, especially baroque music, is said to help the brain.
- Recognize and question your own myths. Do you say to yourself that you have to write on a laptop and not the university computer—or that you have to work under pressure when deadlines are a day or two away? Being assertive is a matter of knowing that you can change things.
- Be a bit more organized, thinking ahead for several days before you have to put anything down on paper. A notebook or the voice recorder on your MP3 player is useful for capturing ideas. You then have a head start when you do sit down to do the work.
- Try being more organized in your pattern of work. For example, decide to make notes about the structure of your work for an hour, have a coffee, then pull the notes together—and so on for another hour (or whatever). Keep work and non-work times separate.
- Physical exercise also helps the brain. Go to the gym or for a run before you work and do some stretching at times while you work.

- If you are having difficulty because, for example, the only writing you have done for years is a shopping list and you now have to write an essay, seek help; look at model essays or look at study skills books.
- Recognize the sub-tasks that you have to deal with in the current assignment and think about what you need to do within each, and how long it will take, and make a plan, bearing in mind the deadline (allowing a bit of leeway and that things may take more time than you expect).
- When you are finding it difficult to start writing, it will become easier once you have started. By that I mean that when you get some material down, you will probably know more about what to write next on the basis of what you have already written, and so it is something of a self-perpetuating system.
- At any stage in your work recognize that you could do study work or not do study work—it is a choice that you have made. Think about the gains and losses of working or not working and then make the decision, knowing it is based on good reasoning (based on Hall, 1994: 12).
- Try having a dialogue (pages 145–6) with your ideas about the subject matter for the writing.
- Work out systems for how you study—so you know how you take notes from books or articles, and so that you know how you develop the structure of any work you do. This may take some experimentation.
- If you need to do some reading and notetaking in preparation for the work there may be difficulty in deciding at which stage to break off from the reading and to start to write. I usually find that I start writing when I have some reading still to do, even if I return to more reading. The sense of being ready to start comes with a sense of frustration and figityness about the reading.
- Write a list of your procrastinating behaviors so that you are more aware of them!
- When you stop (to go to lectures to bed, etc.), think about the point at which you stop in relation to getting started again—do not stop in the middle of some complex ideas.
- When you stop work for a while, write a note for yourself (I usually do this in italics or in colour) about what you are going to do when you start again. It makes it a lot easier to start again.
- If you cannot get started again after a break, go to the beginning of the work (or a suitable place nearer where you are) and start to do some editing and redrafting, and then carry on writing when you reach the point at which you had stopped. This is an important strategy for me.

- Recognize that some days are good days for working or writing and some are less good. On the less good days, the writing does not flow. On the bad days, keep going, and rely on the editing and drafting processes to sort the style later. The material that you write may not be as bad as you think, despite the greater effort that it takes.
- Have a dialogue with the piece of work that you cannot get on with (pages 145–6).
- Think back again to the purpose this work is designed to fulfil—or think about the criteria that it needs to meet. Write this down in your own words, even if you have started the work. Are you still on course?
- Before you return to your desk after a break, do some imagery work—of you sitting and working, with the ideas flowing easily onto the page/screen (pages 149–50).
- Talk through your ideas with someone who is not involved in this work. Tell them what you have to say about the work and where you are going with it.
- If you know what is getting in the way of your working, deal with it: have a mental spring clean (page 147).
- If you feel blocked because you think that you cannot risk not meeting the standards or, more likely, your standards, be realistic about what it is that you are actually expected to do. Your tutors want you to pass.

Then there is some more general advice:

- Relax, go and have some fun as well as working, get enough sleep (when I cannot get down to writing, it is often because I am tired).
- Trust that you will be able to do the work—it will happen even if you cannot imagine how it will happen at present.
- Remember that writing and study in higher education is a demanding skill. Few people, especially in the UK, are actually taught to write. Meet the challenge.

There are many sites on writer's block and other academic fear on the Internet. I found the material from The Writing Centre at the University of North Carolina (UNC) is good (The Writing Centre, UNC, nd). Hall (1994) is a useful paper-based source on writer's block.

I round off this section with a selection of items from "The Procrastinator's Code":

I must be perfect;
Everything I do should go easily and without effort;
It's safer to do nothing than to take a risk and fail;
If it's not right, it's not worth doing at all;
I must avoid being challenged;
If I succeed, someone will get hurt;

If I do well this time, I must always do well;
There is a right answer and I'll wait until I find it.

From National University of Ireland,
Galway, student services website (nd)

This procrastinator's code is, of course, a lot to do with negative self-statements (see above and pages 150–1).

> Reading the procrastinator's code above, which are the three items that are closest to the way in which you might, at times, talk to yourself?
>
> Again, with reference to the code, what would you put in a non-procrastinator's code? Such a code is published on the same site, but it is much better made up by you as an individual using your own personal experience.

Specific Fears of Math and Science

In this chapter on fear and failure, I want to say a few words about a specific problem that is very common, and that is a fear of math and the sciences. I will, in this section, do no more than raise your awareness of this problem because it is common. Math anxiety or fear is described as:

> a strong emotional sensation of anxiety, panic or fear that people feel when they think about or apply their ability to understand mathematics. Sufferers from math anxiety frequently believe that they are incapable of doing activities or taking classes that involve math skills. In fact some people with math anxiety have developed such a fear that it has become a phobia.
>
> (Morrison, 2006)

Anxiety about math is disabling—it means that millions of students avoid taking modules or classes that include math and the fear often extends also to sciences (presumably because of the likelihood of math content). The fear seems also to be much more common in females than males. There are many reasons why math might cause such an emotional reaction in people. Some reasons are that it is exact, it has often been badly taught, and is thought to be boring. In addition, at junior levels it is a matter of learning what you are told to learn. Math theory, which might be interesting, is too complex at that stage. The fear may also have something to do with the fact that math is usually right or wrong. Being wrong is failure and, as I have implied above, educational institutions tend to trade on success and achievement. Being wrong can reduce self-confidence, and reduced self-confidence brings on more anxiety and more likelihood of a sense of "I cannot do this," and more wrong answers. I add this section because the first way of doing something about an issue like this is being aware of it—and how common it is. Only then can you wield your capacities for assertiveness and do something about it.

Activities and Journal Exercises

What is Meaningful to You here?

There is only one real exercise that relates directly to this section because the section will not be relevant to everyone who reads it—though it may be very relevant to some. I would like you to look through the chapter and think about what parts are meaningful to you. You might write a short statement about each part that relates to you. At the bottom of each statement, think of three things that will be your strategy for assertively doing something about the problem or issue.

This is the end of the book if you are a student reading it for yourself. If you are still keeping up a journal there is a very important task now, and that is to read through the journal that you have written and reflect on what you have learnt, perhaps how you have changed and how you will do things differently. This secondary reflection is very valuable. If you want to go one step further, make a note of aspects of assertiveness that you still want to work on.

Part III

Leading Courses in Academic Assertiveness

11

A Chapter for Course Facilitators

Introduction

This chapter is completely different from the others. It is a chapter about how to run a course on academic assertiveness. Towards the end of the chapter, however, there is a synopsis of the content of the book. This may be of value to the student reader as a reminder of ideas or as a means of accessing more detail in the earlier parts of the book.

In this chapter, I have tried to put in the range of information that I, as a course leader, would want to think about in planning a course on academic assertiveness for students. Unlike other chapters, I will list the contents of this chapter with page references—again for easy reference.

A few words about short courses (pages 182–3).

Students and their needs for academic assertiveness (pages 183–5).
The range of students for whom a course in academic assertiveness might be arranged and a note of those for whom such a course might be particularly important.

A set of sample learning outcomes for an academic assertiveness course (page 185).

Contexts for academic assertiveness in higher education (pages 185–9).
Contexts in which academic assertiveness can be useful and in which a course might therefore be run.

Ways of presenting academic assertiveness material on a course (page 189).
Presentation of the material.

Ways of presenting a course on academic assertiveness (pages 189–94).
Means and media through which the whole course could be presented.

Assessment issues (if they should be relevant) **(pages 194–5).**

Synopsis of possible content for a short course/summary of content of this book (pages 195–9).
A synopsis of the content of a full academic assertiveness course.

Selecting material for academic assertiveness courses (page 198).
Ways of selecting content for a shorter course—what is the most important content to include?

In this chapter there will be various references to the role of this book. A set of suggestions for use of the book are included in Chapter 1 (page 5).

A Few Words About Short Courses

I am not going to deal with the principles of running short courses in any detail, but will pick out a few important points. The points generally concern short courses that assume a face-to-face mode, but they can be extrapolated to fit other forms of course presentation. I have written at length on these and other issues in the management of and learning from short courses (Moon, 2001).

Length and frequency of sessions is to be decided according to your local circumstances. It is always worth running more than one session in a course so that participants can do some activities in between sessions. They can also thereby have an opportunity to reflect on what they have learnt and to share it with others at the second session. In terms of the length of courses, I have made some suggestions as to what are the key features of academic assertiveness that should be included in a very short course.

In terms of the locations for running courses, you need space. Trying to run role play in insufficient space is very difficult, because role play is meant to match real life and life takes place in spaces like cafes, seminar rooms, libraries, and so on. Role playing will be distorted if used in unnaturally small spaces. In addition to space, you might want to think about the atmosphere and seating in the room. You preferably need to set up a room informally rather than seating in rows or, worse, behind desks. Desks or seating in rows gets in the way of communication and discussion. Easily moveable chairs will usually help and it is often good practice to get participants to get used to the idea of moving around early on.

Short courses are short—of course. This means that the time needs to be well organized, well structured, well spent, and generally relevant. One way of using time well when a course lasts for more than a day is to set activities to be done between sessions. There are many examples of such activities in this book.

I have used the term "course leader" for the person running the course in this book. It acknowledges that no one can *make* another become assertive by a teaching or training process. It is a matter of the one person encouraging and supporting learning in these areas. "Facilitator" could therefore be a preferable term but it would feel alien in higher education. The course leader could be anyone who is ahead, in terms of knowledge and understanding of academic assertiveness, of those with whom she works. She might not be much ahead, and she could be a student herself. In some self-help courses, the role of course leader is passed round from session to session. The leader then might be the person who sets content or guides the group through the material for that session.

An issue that will be important to consider in small group courses on academic assertiveness is how to build trust in the group so that participants feel free to share their own experiences. Many so-called trust exercises in books on training generate fear and embarrassment.

A course leader may want to think about the development of some ground rules. What ground rules are chosen will depend on the type of course that is being run, numbers involved, and so on. A useful ground rule concerns the giving of attention to those who want to describe a personal experience, but setting limits on this. A leader may need to regulate the time spent on any one individual's experiences as it can happen that some individuals want to take up the whole session. Another ground rule might relate to whether students are allowed to avoid participation in role play.

It is also worth thinking about the beginnings and endings of courses. As a participant on courses, and leading them, I have often thought that there are many myths about beginnings—such as "we must have a warm-up activity." "Warm ups" can often be "turn-offs"! Time is wasted while people are forced into social situations in which they are uncomfortable (Moon, 2001). You need an introduction of some sort, a way of getting participants to introduce themselves, and you need a way of ensuring participants are willing to talk with each other (even in a lecture theatre with 100 students), but these can be related to academic assertiveness and do not need to involve irrelevant activities such as tossing a coloured fluffy ball around.

At the end of courses, there may be value in encouraging participants to give contact details to one or several others, and thereby to maintain contact for support or the sharing and discussion of difficult situations—and to maintain the momentum of learning to be academically assertive.

Students and Their Needs for Academic Assertiveness

Any student—indeed any person—can find a course in academic assertiveness useful. Writing this book has been a reminder to me of techniques and principles and I have handled some situations more effectively as a result of my current writing and thinking. In the context of academic assertiveness, it is useful to think of groups of students in higher education who might have particular needs for the principles and practices. I am not suggesting necessarily that these groups need to be on separate courses, though this could be the case. The list will be useful to those who run courses for mixed groups as subject matter for the development of new scenarios. Any participant would do well to understand the difficulties and challenges that confront others. I list some ideas below.

- **New students who are school leavers.** For most of these students academia is a scary new world with new expectations and conventions. They can feel "at the bottom of the pile" when at school they had reached the top. Understanding the hierarchy and the titles of Doctor, Professor, Dean, or Head of Department is daunting. In addition, many such students have just left home to begin to live communally for the first time, and at induction there is a vast quantity of new information to absorb and rapidly to act on. It is a very stressful time.

- **Mature students.** Mature students are likely to have some of the same problems as school leavers, with comprehension about the hierarchy and their place in it, especially when they have had responsible professional positions themselves. The status of "being a student" can be challenging to a mature person. Some mature students will be shifting from an environment in which their main writing activity has been shopping lists, to one in which an academic essay is soon required. Mature students are often challenged by the management of time when they have families, and may be working part- or even full-time in addition to their new program.

- **Nontraditional students.** The issues for nontraditional students can overlap those of mature students. However, there is often the implication that such a student comes from a family that does not have experiences or histories of engagement with higher or professional education. There may not be, for example, prior habits of reading books or of seeking reference materials. A further issue is that the situation of "being a student" can seriously alienate an individual from her peers at home.

- **Overseas students.** "Overseas" is a big category. Assertiveness, particularly in an academic context, is a western culture (Durkin, 2004) and in some cultures, particularly those of Southeast Asia, the principles behind it are alien. While education in Western academic culture implies an expectation that learners will early on question their teachers and engage in critical thinking (Moon, 2008), in other cultures the teacher may be seen as the expert who is a source of knowledge to be learned and applied. Students from such cultures can therefore feel estranged from the activities of critical thinking and challenging discussion in seminars. Added to this, students from overseas are likely to be meeting many new experiences in being away from home, working in a language that is not native, eating unfamiliar food and so on.

- **Single gender groups of students.** Assertiveness training was originally an activity that was primarily the preserve of feminists and those helping women to attain a greater status in society. There are still gender issues, both for women and men.

- **Disabled and dyslexic students.** Such students have personal challenges in different areas of their lives in addition to those that any other students face. They can be subject to degrading stereotypes or overlooked, or they may need to ask for particular facilities or support.

- **Students who struggle with their work.** Inevitably some students fail academically, for various reasons. It is often, as I have said in the last chapter, that they are not happy with their choice of subjects. Struggling academically may mean failure, with consequent decisions to be made—or it may mean that the student has to regroup her thinking and accept the challenges of retakes and the extra work that is implied.

- **Students who struggle to cope with being at university.** For a variety of reasons some students find the process of being a student or being at university more than they can cope with. This may be because some other event has pushed them beyond their ability to cope and again there may be some serious decisions to make about their futures.

Staff need to understand the challenges the student is facing. For this reason they would find the content of an academic assertiveness course useful. The subject matter of academic assertiveness as described in this book is of relevance to anyone whose work involves interactions with others. It is simple to extrapolate from the student-related examples in this text.

A Set of Sample Learning Outcomes for an Academic Assertiveness Course

If academic assertiveness is included within the structure of an academic program, then it is likely to need to be described as learning outcomes which would be assessed. These learning outcomes might be useful for students on an academic assertiveness course in the early stages of a program.

When the sessions on academic assertiveness are completed, it is anticipated that the learner will be able to:

- in a brief form, relate the major principles of assertiveness (which could be listed) to academic situations that s/he has met.
- describe three situations in which she can illustrate the use of the principles she has learned to a positive effect. The situations could be imaginary.
- discuss given case studies or scenarios with respect to principles of assertiveness.
- put forward her point of view in a seminar situation with reasonable clarity and confidence.
- make valid observations about more and less effective behaviors or "voice" in seminar or discussion sessions where the object is for participants to learn from each other. The observations may apply to self and/or to others. (The discussion session may be real, recorded, or virtual).

It would not be difficult to modify these to fit other situations.

Contexts for Academic Assertiveness in Higher Education

There are many different contexts for running courses or using the content of academic assertiveness in higher education.

Personal development planning (PDP)

In the UK in recent times, universities have been charged with the responsibility for providing some form of personal development work with their students (QAA, 2001). This is variously called personal development profiling or planning (PDP). It largely started for undergraduate students, but this kind of program has spread into professional education contexts (such as for university teachers themselves or in professional situations) and it has many different forms. It can be run alongside modules, in association with a tutoring system, in modules, embedded in programs, and so on. It involves a wide range of possible development themes, but is generally intended to increase the personal capacities of students as potential members of the workforce. The principles and practices of academic assertiveness fit very appropriately within the broad PDP context.

Student success courses

Student success courses have recently been developing in higher education across the United States. Their content and the variety of ways in which they are presented broadly match the UK initiatives in personal development planning.

Professional development and professional education

There are many professions in which some knowledge and capacity for assertiveness is a part of the management requirements of the professional role. It applies to any situation in which there is a matter of dealing with people. Examples are in health and medical professions, business managers, personal relations, human resource management, and other business courses, those in education, law, and social work—and many more.

Work with groups of students who have specific needs

I have mentioned several groups of students who may benefit from courses on academic assertiveness. Academic assertiveness could, for example, be part of the induction process, though it is probably better run once students have settled a little and have recognized some of the challenges that they will face. Such groups may be students newly arrived from overseas, dyslexic, or disabled students.

Work in the context of counselling and student support services

When students have difficulties with the academic side of being at university it is likely that they will also struggle with self-confidence and self-esteem. A course in academic assertiveness generally raises self-confidence and can be a useful adjunct to study skills or other academic support work. As I have said above, there are other students who have problems with the emotional side of student life and likewise they can benefit from this material alongside any counselling or other support offered.

New teachers and others who need to understand the challenges that students face

Those who work with students in educational situations need to understand more than just student disciplines or jobs. Because the focus is on the education of the student, they need to understand the experiences that students face, and how they can be helped to manage. The most superbly informative lecture on physics will be lost on a student who is anxious about an accommodation crisis. This applies in particular to new teachers, but also to librarians, demonstrators, teaching assistants, counselors, student union staff, administrators, and so on.

Careers contexts

Much of the original rationale for personal development work in higher education was to support students at the stage of their transition to careers. In this situation, individuals cannot remain buried in the mass of students, but need to assert themselves both to acquire a job and then to maintain it. The principles of assertiveness are the same in an academic context or in work, even if the material in examples will differ.

Single gender groups (gays and other single sex groups)

There may be substantial issues for gays in higher education. Single sex sessions on the development of assertiveness can enable identities to be established and provide important support for students who have personal challenges to face.

Student development programs in student unions/organizations

One of the situations in which assertiveness courses have been run in higher education has been in the student union. Assertiveness courses have often been set up specifically for those students who are going to take roles in the union or who are to be student representatives in the review of their programs. In some cases the courses have subsequently been offered to wider groups of students. There is an advantage in running academic assertiveness in the context of the union in that students are sometimes more likely to attend if it is seen as "not part of the academic program" and thus away from the eyes of those who assess them.

Postgraduate students and postgraduate researchers

Academic assertiveness is not just useful for undergraduates. There are substantial challenges to being a postgraduate student in handling the new relationships, making sure that the supervision processes work, managing presentations in seminars, and in particular managing the viva and the teaching and tutoring sessions that many postgraduate students conduct, as well as the issues inherent in student day-to-day life.

As part of general induction for all students; student mentors

I have made the case throughout the book that academic assertiveness has an important role in academic work as well as in more general areas of the student experience. Some work on academic assertiveness could play a part in induction—but preferably not in the first week or two. I see induction as a long, drawn-out process and not as a box to be ticked off as soon as classes start. Academic assertiveness might be offered as a course to students halfway through their first year, when many of the problems that beset first years are actually emerging. It could be offered by more advanced students who themselves have successfully attended a course for facilitators.

Students who are going into service learning or work experiences

The confidence of such students can benefit from some work on assertiveness—for example, focusing on self-presentation. Similarly, work experience or service learning situations are excellent situations in which to learn to be more assertive with the support of courses or of this book alone.

Academic assertiveness as a basis for the development of critical thinkers

Academic assertiveness is central to being a good critical thinker, because critical thinking requires people to take a stand and to be willing and able to defend themselves and their points of view. Material on academic assertiveness therefore has a role in any courses that develop critical thinking (Moon, 2008) or study skills (though I do not see this as essentially a "study skills" book).

Those who are going to lead academic assertiveness

The other group who may need to do some work on academic assertiveness is those who are going to lead such courses with others. This could be staff, students, student union staff, librarians, and the many mentioned above.

Staff development

On the basis of this book, I have run courses in academic assertiveness for staff in higher education. I have found that, although the intention has been to run a course about helping students to become more assertive, the discussions have shifted between issues for students and issues for staff themselves with students.

Ways of Presenting Academic Assertiveness Material on a Course

In this section I will be looking at the ways in which the material on an academic assertiveness course may be presented. Courses can involve a number of forms of presentation and will benefit from variety, so it is a matter of judging what is the best approach. At the least, there is likely to be some combination of presentation and discussion between participants. Sometimes the form of presentation will be determined by issues external to the course, such as whether the participants are present physically or at a distance, or the numbers present, or whether or not they know each other or are, in effect, strangers. I give this material as a set of ideas with some words of explanation. The intention is that it should stimulate flexibility in running a course on academic assertiveness. I start, however, by considering a few general principles that underpin the choice of methods.

First, most research on learning indicates that learners should be engaged and involved, and possibly active in order to be maximally effective in learning—though whether we mean that their brains should be active, or their whole bodies should be active, is an issue rarely explored in the literature of learning (Moon, 2004). However, it is desirable to do more than simply talk to the group, tell, or lecture. The more the participants are involved, the better.

Second, nearly any way of presenting material can encourage passive behavior or active behavior on the part of the participants. The general atmosphere should be energetic, vibrant, and upbeat.

Third, good assertiveness courses involve, to a reasonable extent, consideration of the issues and experiences suggested by the participants themselves. This keeps the course relevant and of interest to the particular group. From experience of running courses, I suggest that you will need many more (preplanned) examples up your sleeve in the earlier sessions than later, when more participants' experiences will be available. So a strong suggestion is that you have a list of relevant illustrations of the points you are going to make. There are, of course, plenty in this book.

Presentation of Principles

Academic assertiveness involves the presentation of principles. You cannot always rely on a discussion format, particularly at the beginning of a course. Outlining the principles does not need to take long, however, and it is possible to give a short presentation (see forms of this on pages 193–4) and then start to illustrate it with examples, letting your examples and those offered by participants draw out and extend the principles. Sometimes you will be able to work directly from examples. For example, if you are wanting to make the point about the importance of body language, just presenting pictures of people demonstrating different aspects of body language can serve to generate conversation or thinking. The pictures could be a series of slides or photos, video clips, paper drawings, or still role plays (actors or participants).

The presentations of principles could be:

- Face to face.
- Online in text.
- Aural (e.g. on a DVD).
- Via video.
- Directly from printed text.

Discussion

Much learning in an assertiveness course can happen in the course of discussion of examples of the principles, or the general observations and experiences of participants. From my own background as a facilitator of such courses, you need to manage discussion. Once participants relax and trust each other, some will tend to begin to dominate, and make it difficult for those who are less comfortable in the group to talk. This is, of course, an eventuality that is directly relevant to the material of the course. You may be able to use the opportunity to deal with it as a learning point about academic assertiveness by process talk (page 110). However, it is probably best to mention in the beginning of a course that it is important to let everyone have a fair chance to talk and explore their own examples and scenarios. I have suggested that it can be mentioned as a ground rule.

Role Play

Role play is a way of illustrating the points you are making on a course and "bringing them to life." Though every participant can learn from role play, the idea of actually taking a role often generates fear ("I cannot act"). It is important to say to participants that it is not about acting skills—indeed, they can get in the way. I usually say that one can learn more from role plays that do not "work" than those that do. If you are going to use role play, it is often a good policy to introduce some minor role plays early in a course and make it part of the course. As trust grows in a group, there will be more willingness to get involved—but some participants will probably refuse, and that is their right. They will still learn from watching others. If you can make the point here without threatening the shyer students, you could remind them that facing up to challenge is part of learning to be assertive—but, of course, individuals interpret different demands at different levels of challenge. Role play can be started very simply. Many points can be made by simply asking participants to stand in particular positions in relation to another in a particular setting, or to just say a few already discussed phrases.

Role play may involve the course leader, any of the participating students or perhaps some specific volunteers from among participants who are used to performance (e.g. drama students). Ideally, with a small group, it is far better to get all participants involved because involvement is good learning about assertiveness principles and the practice of facing a challenge as well. With larger groups this is more difficult and you may want to use "actors," who may have the advantage of being able to take the role play a bit further than those less used to the technique.

You will find it valuable to have thought in advance about the settings for role plays. I would have a list from which to draw. Settings in which there is a customer expecting some service are useful for making more general points about what it is to be assertive, and rights. For example, I might use the coffee bar in which cold coffee has been served, "sticky issues" in library or bank settings, accommodation or housing agent's office, conversations with a landlord, seminar or supervision situations or situations in which one student is distracted by others (e.g. in the shared house or library). This book can provide plenty of material as the basis for further inspiration. You should, as I have said above, use some examples provided by the participants. If a participant suggests a scenario for role play, it can be useful to get her both to direct others and to play herself in the same scene. Often you will find it useful to run the same scene several times in order to explore different possibilities for assertive and nonassertive behaviors and reactions to that behavior. Alternatively you could bring in different twists to the event and see how it affects responses.

There are many different activities around the use of role play:

- Use it to illustrate a point and to support the learning of assertive behavior.
- Use it and discuss it, run it again, change elements in it, etc.
- Record it and run it through again so that those with roles can see themselves and their behaviors.
- Get all participants to write notes at the time and share the notes afterwards. The notes might contain feedback on ways in which a particular person behaved in role (e.g. in practicing new techniques).
- Comments on role play may be from the course leader, or from the whole group with the course leader commenting last.
- And so on.

As a matter of course, during a role play, I would have pen and paper in front of me so that I can make notes to jog my memory.

In courses where the material is printed or recorded in advance, prerecorded role play clips or short recordings of voice can be used to generate discussion in a group online or it can illustrate a point (e.g. in a course on DVD).

Use of Exercises in Assertiveness Courses

There are many different exercises in this book and this section overlaps with both that on role play and that on using learning journals (Moon, 2006). Some exercises can involve talk and some require writing and recording. Most of the exercises in this book are for individuals because this is the nature of the book. However, there are many others that can be done as a group. Exercises have the purpose of developing awareness of assertiveness in at least three ways—first by focusing attention on behavior, posture, appearances, gestures, and the other features of assertive (or otherwise) behavior in principle or by observing others. Second they work towards the development of self-awareness because the greater consciousness of oneself is a means towards changing one's behaviors. Third, they involve the practicing of techniques (for example, negative assertion, negative enquiry, fogging, giving and receiving compliments, criticising and giving feedback, and so on).

Exercises that involve the practicing of techniques can be done either through small role plays that focus on providing an opportunity for the technique to be played out. For practicing, the full group of participants is likely to be split into subgroups of three or four, all of whom are involved in each role play, taking turns at the different roles. Alternatively, the exercise can be done on paper/screen using, for example, a dialogue technique as described in Chapter 9, pages 145–6.

The Use of Learning Journals

I like the use of learning journals because I consider that the reflection that can be involved in keeping a journal enhances the process of learning in a number of different ways (Moon, 2004). In this book, I have both used, and suggested the use of, learning journals (Moon, 2006) in two different ways. First I have suggested that learners set up and use learning journals as a direct support for their learning to become more assertive. In this way they produce a record of the process of becoming more assertive both through their sensemaking of the principles and in recording of observations and personal practical matters. Second, the learning journal is a convenient space for working exercises. I have also used fictitious learning journals to provide examples of behavior.

Observing the Behavior of Others

Once learners have some idea of what assertive behavior is, they can enhance their learning from the world around them—in terms of assertiveness, the world is like a huge laboratory. It is hard to avoid noticing the unsuccessful transaction in a shop where one person is put-down, or situations of feedback given badly, or good and constructive criticism, or the use of empathy or self-disclosure to facilitate conversation, and so on. Learners can use their observations to support their learning and as examples to bring back into a group for discussion, role play or a "but . . . what if

. . ." treatment. Often there are aspects of the course leader's or the participants' behavior that tends to facilitate or to obstruct learning in the group. Groups themselves and the way in which they work or otherwise, can be the subject of discussion through the application of process comments (page 110).

The Development of and Learning from Fictitious Scenarios

This book is full of fictitious examples of material for learning academic assertiveness. There is, I consider, nearly as much to learn from fiction as from real experience (Moon, 2006). Sources of fiction that you might consider tapping to support running a course are:

- Television, film, DVD, video entertainment material.
- Literature, story (e.g. myth and folk tale).
- Developed case study material.
- Scenarios developed during a course by participants.
- Song lyrics, poetry, etc.

Ways of Presenting a Course on Academic Assertiveness

In this section I want to consider the means (and media) through which a course could be presented within any of the contexts mentioned above. Again I will present these in a listed format for easy use. There is some overlapping between the various forms. A variable that will determine which format proves best is the number of participants involved. On the whole, traditional assertiveness courses have been run face-to-face with a small number of individuals who would be expected to participate on a regular basis, bringing in their own examples of situations. However, there are other ways. The methods employed for presentation of the course will determine how the course is designed (see below).

- A course could be run with students as an induction to academic practices.
- Run the course face-to-face as a short course within the context of a module with a small group of participants. The module might be related to PDP, careers, study skills, or other topics mentioned in the section on contexts above. With large groups of students, the principles can be given and illustrated (with examples presented on video, as oral stories, or as sound clips, for example).
- A short academic assertiveness course could be run for tutorial groups, outside the modular system. The students could be asked to work on the chapters of this book and discuss the material in the tutorials.
- A course could be run with a large group of students based on this book, with principles given and some reading and activities from the book set to support and illustrate the principles.
- The principles of academic assertiveness could be embedded in other modules. Embedding material might seem to be an ideal, but it means

usually that the topic loses is prominence. Assertiveness usually needs to be actively practiced and related to a person's life. Embedding it may not achieve this.

- A course in academic assertiveness could be developed online (based, for example, on the content and activities in this book). It is then available to many students. They can contribute their own examples and get involved in discussion of experiences.
- Course material can be presented on CD. I have on cassette tape a very helpful assertiveness course that was presented as a series of talks to business people. A CD could be part of an induction pack for students.
- A course could be developed in DVD/video format.
- Self-help groups of students could study the chapters of the book in a prearranged manner and in their groups, support each other, and discuss issues and experiences.
- Students could be encouraged to purchase a book on assertiveness and to engage in the activities suggested. Some assessment of the learning would ensure that the reading and thinking is done.

I said above that I have also run academic assertiveness courses for staff in higher education, in the context of staff development. This is another way to increase the chance that students are presented with some principles of academic assertiveness. In the first few such courses I noticed that we have tended to shift around in the nature of the content when it came to discussions. I have commented on this in the courses and those present have wanted to continue in this way. It is worth, though, considering the potential focuses for staff development courses. They are:

- Academic assertiveness as a concept in higher education.
- The content of a potential academic assertiveness course for students.
- How to run a course in academic assertiveness for students.
- The principles of assertiveness applied to the job of teaching and working in the higher education environment.

Assessment Issues (if They Should be Relevant)

It may be that you are in a situation that will require academic assertiveness to be assessed in some way. Assessment focuses the minds of students and it is likely that it will promote more learning. However, what it is that participants learn may be compromised by a process of assessment. You do not, for example, want an outcome to be the ability to write down and describe a list of academic assertiveness techniques. In higher education, the assessment would need to be related to learning outcomes that you set up (see sample set of learning outcomes above, (page 185). Here are some ideas for assessment. These ideas are not related to the learning outcomes above. The first one is not often going to be viable in a higher education setting:

- Create a set scenario and assess students' display of academic assertiveness capabilities in the role play (having discussed criteria for the nature and quality of action that you expect to see).
- Directly assess a learning journal that has accompanied a course (having again talked about the criteria for purpose of the journal, issues of length and content, etc.).
- Ask students to write an account of what they have learnt about academic assertiveness, illustrated by examples of how it has helped them as students or in their studies.
- Provide a scenario of a difficult situation and ask students to consider the various roles taken by those involved and how the situation could develop or be resolved.
- For those in professional education or development, an assessment task could be a discussion of the role of assertiveness learning in their work situations.
- You might ask for an account such as why the practical knowledge of assertiveness is important in teaching/management/nursing, etc.
- Students might be asked to produce a short course on the development of capacities of assertiveness among school students, for new first year students or student nurses.
- Ask students to film assertive or nonassertive behavior, etc.

Synopsis of Possible Content for a Course/Summary of Content of This Book

In this section, I will be summarizing rather than following directly the subheadings in the chapters. The page number given will be where the topic begins and sometimes there will be overlaps in content.

Chapter 2: Coping with the Challenges of Advanced Education

- What academic assertiveness is (page 10).
- What can be learnt from working on academic assertiveness (page 11).
- The downside of learning to be assertive (page 12).
- How to learn from this book on academic assertiveness (page 15).
- Academic situations that can be challenging (page 18).

Chapter 3: Deciding to Cope Better with the Challenges of Student Life: Fight, Flight or Being Assertive!

- About deciding to change towards being more assertive—the idea of changing (page 22).
- A definition of academic assertiveness and the list of behaviors that are included under the term (page 23).

- Being assertive described in everyday language (page 23).
- Some principles associated with being assertive (page 24).
- Some common misinterpretations of what being assertive means (page 26).
- Behaviors that are not assertive—non assertion, aggression and manipulation (page 27).
- Nonassertive behavior (page 27).
- Aggressive behavior (page 29).
- Manipulative behavior (page 30).

Chapter 4: Beyond the Words: the Display of Behavior

- Components of the display of behavior (page 37).
- The outside behavior—speech and voice (page 38).
- The outside behavior—body language (page 42).
- Relevant behavior to do with the whole person—including personal space and relative height (page 46).
- Behavior and the way in which we think (page 49).
- A summary of ways in which we display assertive behavior (page 54).

Chapter 5: The Effects of Experience: the Origins of Assertive Behavior and the Effects of Context

- The influences of personal history on assertiveness (page 60).
- The effects of the context on assertiveness (page 62).
- Academic work as a particular kind of context (page 65).
- Emotion as a context for assertiveness (page 65).
- Barriers and triggers to an individual's assertiveness (page 69).

Chapter 6: As a Human, You Have Rights and Responsibilities. . . .

- What is meant by "rights" and "responsibilities" (page 77)?
- A list of rights (page 78).
- Some important issues about rights—responsibilities and recognizing that others have rights too; choosing not to uphold your rights, etc. (page 79).
- Each of the rights is examined in relation to academic assertiveness— listed under general rights, and rights that can have special significance in academic environments (page 82).
- Rights—some further thoughts (page 95).

Chapter 7: Managing More Assertively—Tools and Techniques

(The techniques introduced in this chapter are also summarized in the glossary—page 200).

- Verbal techniques and some principles (page 99).

  - Broken record (page 100).
  - The principle of persistence (page 100).
  - The principle of graduated response (page 102).
  - Criticism and put-down (page 104).
  - Negative assertion (page 104).
  - Negative inquiry (page 105).
  - Fogging (page 106).
  - Self-disclosure (page 107).
  - Signposting statements, clarifying, and summarising (page 108).
  - Making empathetic statements (page 109).
  - Deliberate use of a name (page 110).
  - Shifting into talk about the process (page 110).

Chapter 8: Managing Difficult Situations

- A reminder about basic assertive communication.

  - The difficult situations (page 117).
  - Saying "no" and other forms of declining (page 118).
  - Coping with persistent questioning (page 120).
  - Seeking a workable compromise (page 121).
  - The giving or receiving of compliments (page 122).
  - Giving and receiving constructive feedback or criticism (page 126).
  - Angry situations (page 131).
  - Expressing anger (page 133).
  - Being at the receiving end of anger (page 135).
  - Coping with a range of "wind-up" situations (page 137).

Chapter 9: Managing Thought, Emotion, and Self-confidence

- Techniques and activities for the management of thoughts and emotions (page 143).

  - Give yourself advice (page 145).
  - Dialogue methods (page 145).
  - Thought stopping (page 146).
  - Mental spring cleaning (page 147).
  - Burying discomforts (page 148).

Chapter 10: Coping Assertively with Fear, Failure, and Disappointment

Selecting Material for Academic Assertiveness Courses

In the reality of the mass higher education system and the over-filled timetables, it is unlikely that you will be running this course in its full detail. This short section will provide some suggestions as to how to select material for a shorter course—mainly based on what I think is important and where, from experience, the greatest gains are to be made. The important areas are:

- Providing a clear view of what assertiveness is, in particular using the contrast between assertiveness, nonassertion, aggression, and manipulation.
- Ensuring that assertiveness is not seen as finding ways to get what you want by aggressive means; nor is it seen as associated only with feminism.
- Demonstrating why it is useful to learn to be assertive in the academic context and noting aspects of student life in which greater assertiveness can bring greater success. This could be done through a collection of scenarios.

- Raising awareness of how assertiveness, nonassertion, and aggression are displayed verbally and in nonverbal behavior. It is worth including a little on the effects of dress, the environment, etc.
- Briefly discussing how we come to have an assertive or other approach because of our histories and as an individual reaction to the circumstances of any particular interaction.
- Providing a list of human rights and responsibilities. The discussion about this can be expanded or contracted as necessary. In my experience, this is a powerful element of a course.
- It is useful to do some work on the tools and techniques of assertiveness, particularly those that deal with unwarranted or unreasonable criticism (negative assertion, negative inquiry, and fogging). These could be integrated into the discussion of how to manage difficult situations. The most important situations are those that concern saying no (though this can be dealt with in talking about rights), about criticism, and the giving and receiving of compliments. The latter is important because it helps reserved students to find a way of engaging with others. The techniques could be given in print.
- The management of mind techniques and activities are important because they deal with matters that can inhibit much social interaction, but can be given as a printed list to be practiced away from the course.

Appendix I
Summary of Definitions, Words, and Techniques for Quick Reference

Academic Assertiveness: a definition and elaboration of the term (pages 23–4)

Academic assertiveness is a set of emotional and psychological orientations and behaviors that enables a learner appropriately to manage the challenges to the self in the course of learning and their experiences in formal education.

Academic assertiveness includes the following areas of behavior in the contexts of academic work and in the general experience of being a learner. The list is in no particular order and there are overlaps:

- The finding of an appropriate "voice" or form of expression through which to engage in critical thinking or debate.
- The willingness to challenge, to disagree, and to seek or accept a challenge.
- The ability to cope with the reality or the likelihood of not being "right" sometimes, making an error or failing; effective recovery from these situations.
- The willingness to change one's mind if necessary; the openness to feedback on one's performance (academic or otherwise).
- Willingness to listen and take account of the viewpoint of others, awareness that others can make mistakes and reasonable tolerance of their failings.
- Autonomy—a willingness to be proactive; to make and justify independent judgments and to act on them.
- An appropriate level of academic self-esteem.

Aggressive Behavior: an elaboration of the term (page 15)

Aggression in assertiveness training is usually described as "going for what one wants without taking account of the needs or rights of others." It is associated with not listening to, or taking account of the needs of, others; using put-downs or sarcasm to enhance one's own status at the cost of others, or using direct violence or threat.

Broken record and the principle of persistence (page 100)

Persistence means that if you feel you are in the right in a situation, you persist in your communications towards the rightful state, negotiation, or acceptable compromise. Broken record is a technique that concerns persistence. It involves working out what it is that you need to say and staying with that line, using more or less the same set of words regardless of what the other says and regardless of how the other tries to knock you off course. The aim of broken record is either to achieve the right that you believe yourself to have, or to reach a point of negotiation.

Criticism—justified and unjustified (page 23)

In terms of assertiveness, it is important to distinguish between justified (valid) criticism and unjustified criticism that is not valid, or is exaggerated. These forms of communication may be intermixed, but they should be treated differently by the receiver in assertive communication.

"Crumple buttons" (Dickson, 1982)—definition of a term (page 137)

This is a useful term that describes topics, patterns of talk, or criticism that typically or regularly engender a negative response in a person (upset, irritation, embarrassment, etc.). The term would tend to be used in a situation where one person manipulates another by taking advantage of her knowledge of the other's "crumple buttons."

Deliberate use of a name—a technique (page 110)

Use of a name can emphasise a statement or draw attention to something important or sometimes signal a change of emotional atmosphere.

Empathetic statements—a technique (page 109)

For a person to show genuine empathy is to demonstrate understanding of the position of another person's situation by way of some form of statement. The process can ease and facilitate communication but it can be used to soften up another before criticism is made (justified or unjustified) or as part of a strategy of manipulation.

Fogging—a technique (page 106)

Fogging is used when a person is being criticized and where the level or the content of criticism is unjustified and possibly manipulative. Fogging is a simple technique of agreeing to elements of the criticism that are actually true and thereby separating them out from those that are not true. It frustrates the power of the criticizer.

Graduated Response—a principle (page 103)

The principle of graduated response is that in a confrontation you should graduate your message, starting calmly and gently at first and raising the pressure as is required. Do not wade in with all guns blazing!

"Hooked Into"—definition of a term (page 107)

This term is helpful jargon! It usually means that one party in an interaction is distracted from what she intended to say (her intended "track") through the content of what another is saying. This may or may not be a deliberate tactic (or provocation) on the part of the other.

Manipulative behavior—an elaboration of the term (page 22)

Manipulative behavior is an effort to achieve goals in a covert manner that does not take account of the rights of others. It is often described as a kind of aggressive behavior on the grounds that it is a matter of going for what the person wants, regardless of the needs or rights of others. However, some of the characteristics of a manipulative person are apparently those of non-assertion such as not being direct, not expressing herself, and not being open. In this respect it could be called dishonest or disrespectful behavior.

Negative assertion—a technique (page 104)

Negative assertion is largely relevant to situations in which one person is being criticized and it deals with justified and valid criticism. It involves the simple acknowledgement of the truth in what is being said or implied.

Negative inquiry—a technique (page 105)

Negative inquiry is a technique that is used in situations of criticism and put-down and it is relevant to both justified and unjustified criticism. In using this technique, the person who is being criticized does not initially accept or reject the criticism, but asks for more information about it. This can calm a situation and allow the person who is criticized to decide how to manage the content of the criticism.

Nonassertive behavior—an elaboration of the term (page 22)

States of nonassertion are typified by tentativeness, indecisiveness, and passivity. Nonassertive people do not tend to deal with situations directly but they hope that what they want will materialize. The behavior may be described as "people pleasing" and it is often associated with low self-esteem, low levels of confidence, and "victim mentality" (Dickson, 1982).

Process talk—a technique (page 110)

Process talk acknowledges the difference between the content of a conversation and the processes involved in the conversation (what is going on behind the words). The technique involves making a deliberate shift from the content to talking about the process. It may be accompanied by nonverbal shifts in posture or in verbal pace or pattern. It is a powerful technique in many situations of criticism or confrontation.

Put-Down—a definition (page 103)

A situation of put-down is where one person attempts to demean or reduce the psychological state of another by verbal or nonverbal means. Often the communication is indirect and covert (hence manipulative).

Self-disclosure—a technique (page 107)

Self-disclosure is a powerful technique in many forms of social communication. It involves one party being open and saying something about how she feels, or providing a personal philosophy, or explaining how she is thinking or how she sees things. The effect is often to facilitate the communication.

Signposting statements, clarifying and summarising—techniques (page 108)

This is a matter of sharing a view of what should be discussed in a communication, or clarifying points already discussed, or summarising what has been communicated. The person taking the active role in these techniques usually assumes some power in the interaction through her action.

Workable compromise—a definition (page 121)

A workable compromise is a viable solution with which both or all parties in a communication feel comfortable. Reaching a workable compromise would usually be contrasted with situations in which one party "wins" or comes out on top in some way.

References

Alberti, R. and Emmons, M. (1983) *Your Perfect Right*, 4th edition, St Louis, Ca, Impact Publishers.
Back, K. and Back, K. (1982) *Assertiveness at Work*, London, McGraw-Hill.
Belenky, M., Clinchy, B., Goldberg, R. and Tarule, J. (1986) *Women's Ways of Knowing: The Development of Self, Voices, and Mind*, New York, Basic Books.
Berne, E. (1966) *Games People Play*, London, Andre Deutsch.
Blue, L. (2007) 'Thought for the Day,' February 12, 2007. http://www.bbc.co.uk/religion/programmes/thought/documents/t20070212.shtml.
Damasio, A. (2000) *The Feeling of What Happens*, London, Virago.
Davies, P. (2003) *Increasing Confidence*, London, Doring Kindersley.
Dickson, A. (1982) *A Woman in Your Own Right*, London, Quartet.
Durkin, K. (2004) "Adapting to Western Norms of Argumentation and Debate: The Critical Learning Journey of East Asian Students." Thesis submitted for PhD, Bournemouth University.
Dweck, C. (2000) *Self Theories – Their Role in Motivation, Personality and Development*, New York, The Psychology Press.
Dweck, C. (1999) 'Summary of Self Theories.' http://www.calstatela.edu/faculty/jshindl/cm/Summary%20of%20Self%20Theories.htm. Accessed September 2007.
Gibran, K. (1926) *The Prophet*, (1972 edition) London, Heinemann.
Gillen, T. (1992) *Assertiveness for Managers*, Aldershot, Gower.
Hall, C. (1994) *Getting Down to Writing: A Student's Guide to Overcoming Writer's Block*, Centre for Research into Human Communication and Learning, Cambridge, Peter Francis Publishers.
Heimler, E. (1967) *Mental Illness and Social Work*, Harmondsworth, Penguin.
Heimler, E. (1975) *Survival in Society*, Hoboken, NJ, John Wiley.
Joseph, J. (nd) Warning. crystal-forest.com/wheniamoldishallwearpurpple.html. Accessed July 2008.
Lenett, R. and Crane, B. (1986) *It's OK to Say No!* London, Thorsons.
Lindberg, A. M. (1978) *Gift from the Sea*, New York, Pantheon.
Lindenfield, G. (1987) *Assert Yourself*, Wellingborough, Northamptonshire, Thorsons.
Moon, J. (2001) *Short Courses and Workshops: Improving the Impact of Learning and Professional Development*, London, Routledge Falmer.
Moon, J. (2002) *The Module and Programme Development Handbook*, London, Routledge Falmer.
Moon, J. (2004) *A Handbook of Reflective and Experiential Learning*, London, Routledge Falmer.
Moon, J. (2006) *Learning Journals: A Handbook for Reflective Practice and Professional Development*, London, Routledge.
Moon, J. (2008) *Critical Thinking: An Exploration of Theory and Practice*, London, Routledge.
Moon, J. (2009) *Make Groups Work* (*in preparation*), ESCalate, www.ESCalate.ac.uk.
Morrison, P. (2006) 'Fear of math.' http://www.able2know.com/forums/about80631.html. Accessed November 2007.
National University of Ireland, Galway, Student Services Study skills (nd) 'Study Skills – Procrastination.' http://www.nuigalway.ie/student_services/study_skills/procrastination.html. Accessed November 2007.
Perls, F. (1969) "The Gestalt Prayer," in *Gestalt Therapy Verbatim*, Moab, Real People Press. http//:en.wikipedia.org.wiki.Gestalt_prayer. Accessed November 2007.
Peck, M. (1985) *The Road Less Travelled*, London, Rider.

QAA (Quality Assurance Agency (2001) *Progress Files in Higher Education.* http//:www.qaa.ac.uk/ academicinfrastructure/progressfiles/default.asp. Accessed November 2007.

Race, P. (2000) *How to Win as a Final Year Student,* Buckingham, Open University Press.

Race, P, (2003) *How to Study,* Oxford, Blackwell.

Redman, W. (nd) "Checking your emotional health." http://www.lifesherpa.com/mind-body/ 2003–04-redman-checking.htm. Accessed September 2007.

Rees, S. and Graham, R. (1991) *Assertion Training: How to be Who You Really Are,* London, Routledge.

Sheehy, R. and Horan, J. (2004) 'Effects of stress inoculation training for 1st year law students,' *International Journal of Management,* 11 (1) 44 – 55 – or http://vcc.asu.edu/vcc-pdf/d-rs-ijsm. pdf. Accessed September 2007.

Smith, M. (1975) *When I Say No I Feel Guilty,* New York, Bantam.

Storr, A. (1988) *Solitude,* London, Flamingo.

Stubbs, D. (1985) *Assertiveness at Work,* London, Gower.

Tolle, E. (2001) *The Power of Now,* Novato, CA, New World Library.

Van Haeften, K. (2003) *Making the Most of University,* Richmond, Surrey, Trotman.

Wareham, T. (2002) 'Failing Teachers, Failing Students,' in M. Peelo and T. Wareham, *Failing Students in Higher Education,* The Society for Research in Higher Education, and Open University Press, Buckingham, pages 87–112.

Writing Center, University of North Carolina (nd) Various articles about writing, including writer's block and procrastination. http://www.unc.edu/depts/wcweb. Accessed September 2007.

Index